PSYCHEDELIC REFUGEE

"It is ripe time for acknowledging the contributions of the female lineage of early psychonauts to the psychedelic countercultural currents. David F. Phillips has restored Rosemary Leary's authentic voice with great respect, diligence, and care so that it can tell us her own larger-than-life story of courage, adventures, and feminine values."

MARIA PAPASPYROU, MSc, COEDITOR OF
PSYCHEDELIC MYSTERIES OF THE FEMININE

"Rosemary Woodruff Leary lived a mythical life—not merely present at many of the defining moments in 60s and 70s psychedelic counterculture but helping to create them—and we are lucky enough to get to travel through these times and spaces with her in this lovingly reworked memoir. Rosemary's unerring commitment to knowing herself deeply—without taking herself too seriously—makes her a wonderful guide through these pages. I felt I had made a new friend by their close. Her principled commitment to living freely—yet never at the cost of sacrificing the freedom of others—inspires."

CHARLOTTE WALSH, AUTHOR, LECTURER,
ATTORNEY, AND DRUG POLICY ADVOCATE

"Rosemary Woodruff Leary was one of the world's great psychedelic pioneers. She worked throughout her life to educate people about the psychedelic experience and was instrumental in helping to orchestrate the cultural revolution of the Sixties. She did this at the expense of her personal freedom, which was compromised for a significant portion of her life. In a world where men often overshadow the accomplishments of women, Rosemary stands out as one of the most important psychedelic revolutionaries of our time—a brave and articulate heroine of highest integrity, sensitivity, and beaming intelligence. Interacting with many of the most influential cultural innovators of her time, she was not only at the center of all the action during the countercultural revolution of the 1960s—helping to orchestrate much of it behind the scenes—she was also an extraordinary writer, brilliantly recording her insightful observations. As a result, this book is at once an invaluable historical document and, although heartbreaking at times, a beautiful work of literature, a page-turning romance adventure story, and a spiritual inspiration. David F. Phillips did an extraordinary job at piecing this book together from numerous sources and reconstructing the memoir as Rosemary had intended it to be. Most highly recommended!"

DAVID JAY BROWN, AUTHOR OF *DREAMING WIDE AWAKE*
AND *THE NEW SCIENCE OF PSYCHEDELICS*

"*Psychedelic Refugee* covers Rosemary's intimate life with the charismatic Timothy Leary, her public life as a performer in his psychedelic roadshows, their harrowing arrests for marijuana and LSD, and her secret life as a primary player in his prison escape. She also tells the story of her years with Leary on the run in Algeria and Switzerland and her 23 years in hiding from the wrath of the American government for the act of freeing him from an unjust sentence. The Learys' associations with the Castalia Foundation, the League for Spiritual Discovery, the Brotherhood of Eternal Love, the Weather Underground, and the international Black Panther Party are described in the author's riveting firsthand account. This is the compelling untold story of an exceptional woman who was a pioneer of the psychedelic generation."

MICHAEL HOROWITZ, COEDITOR OF *MOKSHA: ALDOUS HUXLEY'S
CLASSIC WRITINGS ON PSYCHEDELICS AND THE VISIONARY EXPERIENCE*
AND *SISTERS OF THE EXTREME: WOMEN WRITING
ON THE DRUG EXPERIENCE*

PSYCHEDELIC REFUGEE

THE LEAGUE FOR SPIRITUAL DISCOVERY,
THE 1960s CULTURAL REVOLUTION,
AND 23 YEARS ON THE RUN

ROSEMARY WOODRUFF LEARY

EDITED BY DAVID F. PHILLIPS

Park Street Press
Rochester, Vermont

Park Street Press
One Park Street
Rochester, Vermont 05767
www.ParkStPress.com

Text stock is SFI certified

Park Street Press is a division of Inner Traditions International

Cataloging-in-Publication Data for this title is available from the Library of Congress

ISBN 978-1-64411-180-2 (print)
ISBN 978-1-64411-181-9 (ebook)

Printed and bound in the United States by Lake Book Manufacturing, Inc.
The text stock is SFI certified. The Sustainable Forestry Initiative® program
promotes sustainable forest management.

10 9 8 7 6 5 4 3 2 1

Text design by Priscilla Baker and layout by Debbie Glogover
This book was typeset in Garamond Premier Pro with Calibri, Gotham
Condensed, and Gill Sans MT Pro used as display typefaces

Chapter 12, copyright © 1997 by Robert Greenfield, reprinted here in slightly
edited form with his kind permission. The portrait of Rosemary on page v, by
an unknown photographer, is reproduced with the permission of her estate. The
portrait of Rosemary, copyright © 1998 by Robert Altman, is reproduced on
page 275 with his kind permission; it was displayed with powerful effect at her
memorial service in 2002. The map of the Millbrook estate on page 26 is by
Art Kleps and was the copyrighted cover art for his book *Millbrook: A Narrative
of the Early Years of American Psychedelianism* (1975). It is reproduced here from
the cover of the 2005 edition, without the cover copy, with the kind permission of
Daphne Kleps and the Original Kleptonian Neo-American Church. The sprig of
rosemary by Nata Altonhess, used as an ornament on the title page and elsewhere,
is reproduced under license from Vectorstock.com. Pages scanned from the
Rosemary Woodruff Leary Papers and from the New York Public Library website
are reproduced with the library's kind permission.

Rise up, ye women that are at ease;
hear my voice, ye careless daughters;
give ear unto my speech.

Isaiah 32:9

Rosemary Woodruff Leary
1935–2002

Contents

Rosemary Woodruff Leary, Psychedelic Pioneer

MARTINA HOFFMANN

with Friends of Rosemary Woodruff Leary

One of the great female Psychedelic Pioneers, Rosemary Woodruff Leary, died on February 7, 2002, at her home in Aptos, California. She was sixty-six years old. Born in St. Louis, Missouri, on April 26, 1935, into a conservative Baptist environment, "Ro," as she was known to her friends, began her psychedelic journey long before her relationship with Dr. Timothy Leary. In the fifties, as one of the early seekers who prefigured America's emerging counterculture, she escaped to New York City at a tender age, where she became part of the city's most progressive music (jazz), art, and literary (Beat) circles and experimented with psilocybin mushrooms and peyote. From here the course of events brought her to eventually become the "accomplice" of "the most dangerous man in America."

The sheer number of psychedelic luminaries present at her memorial, held on April 20 (2002) in Santa Cruz, gave testimony to the fundamental role she played during the psychedelic revolution and beyond. Among them were Ralph Metzner, Frank Barron, Peggy Hitchcock, Robert Anton Wilson, Michael and Cindy Horowitz, Chet Helms, and many others, including Ram Dass, who was at her hospital bed.

In the nineteen fifties and early nineteen sixties era, because of the pervasive sexism, which obscured women's intellectual contributions, women rebels were viewed mostly as being muses to their male counterparts. Rosemary Leary soon transcended this role by becoming Timothy Leary's partner in creating the setting, which shaped LSD experimentation in its formative years. As he described in *Flashbacks*:

> Rosemary and I shared the work too. I was finishing the work of psychedelic poetry based on the Tao Te Ching. Rosemary edited the manuscript. She joined . . . me in preparing the slide shows and tapes we used in our weekend workshops in various cities around the East Coast. We tried to stimulate LSD experiences with sounds, strobes, and slides, as Ralph, Michael, and I alternated murmured narration and Yogi instructions, while Rosemary whispered philosophic poetry, hour upon hour, recapitulating the evolution of the species, taking our astounding participants up the chakras of their bodies. (*Flashbacks*, pp. 232–33)

Her greatest contribution to the psychedelic movement was surely her consistent refusal to cooperate with federal authorities. She received thirty days of solitary confinement for not testifying against Leary after G. Gordon Liddy busted Millbrook in 1966. Then she proceeded to orchestrate Leary's escape from prison in 1970 with the aid of the Weather Underground and planned for their subsequent escape to Algeria. Most critically, that same year she refused an offer of amnesty from the FBI in exchange for providing names of others who had committed illegal acts in the name of freedom of consciousness. This selfless show of bravery was to define the course of her life.

In her own words:

> After escaping from Algeria, and suffering through yet another arrest and release in Switzerland, I left Leary, searching for a country that would allow me to find some peace and sanity. What followed were years of adventure and fear in some very far-flung places.

I lived underground as a fugitive for twenty-four years in Europe and the Americas, long after Leary was captured again and eventually released from the U.S. prison system.

Because of Rosemary Leary, many founding members of the psychedelic movement lived out their lives in freedom rather than in jail cells. She paid a high price for the freedom of others: not until 1995 could she say, "I have regained my freedom, and I am free again to write." But she paid this price willingly because of what psychedelics had taught her: that there are truths more fundamental and significant than the laws of men intoxicated with power.

MARTINA HOFFMANN is a world-renowned painter and sculptor and a central figure in contemporary Visionary art. Hoffmann's work can be found in numerous books, magazines, and other publications, including Stanislav Grof's *Modern Consciousness Research and the Understanding of Art* and as a featured artist in the book *Women of Visionary Art*. She keeps a home and studio in both the United States and France.

Rescuing Rosemary's Memoir

How This Book Came to Be

DAVID F. PHILLIPS

For a bird of the air shall carry the voice,
and that which hath wings shall tell the matter.

ECCLESIASTES 10:20

Rosemary Woodruff Leary was thirty-five when I first met her in the summer of 1970 in the San Francisco office of attorney Michael Kennedy, where I was working as a law clerk helping represent her famous husband Timothy. She offered me a swig of cherry juice from her own bottle. But that fall I went back East to finish law school, and that same fall she left for Algeria, and I did not see her again until 1983. By that time, having long since turned on, tuned in, and dropped out, I had moved to my family's former summer house in the small town of Truro, Massachusetts, the last town before the tip of Cape Cod. Rosemary was then living in Provincetown, at the very tip, still a fugitive, and some friends who knew of my long-ago association with Timothy introduced us. We became good friends almost at once after this second introduction and remained very close until Rosemary died

Rosemary Woodruff Leary and David F. Phillips, circa 2000

almost twenty years later, in 2002. She lived for some years as a welcome guest in my house in Truro, and again later in my house in San Francisco. I was fortunate to have been able to help in the effort in 1994 that worked her free from the threat of prosecution.

Early in our friendship Rosemary showed me some chapters of the memoir she was writing. I now know that she had been working on this memoir during the time, after she separated from Timothy in 1971, when she wandered the world as a fugitive with John Schewel, from Switzerland to Afghanistan to Colombia to Costa Rica to her eventual return to the United States in 1976. The need to be able to pack up and leave on a moment's notice had made it impractical to carry a typewriter with her, but once back in America she was able to use one at a library on Cape Cod, and the book you are now reading began to take a more definite shape.

Very unfortunately, though, Rosemary was not able to work on her book in a patient and orderly fashion until she had a complete first draft. She was chronically, desperately short of money and needed to publish individual chapters, if she could, to bring in some payment and to use the developing chapters as samples for publishers and agents so she could get an advance. She did publish a few excerpts here and there, but she was never able to secure a contract for the finished book.[1]

Also she made a practice of showing draft chapters to people whose opinion she respected, asking for comments. I was one of those people, and some of my comments on her draft chapters, and the comments of many others too, survive among her papers at the New York Public Library. It would have been much better for her and the book if she had finished a complete draft and *then* had *one* skilled and uninvolved editor work with her to refine it. But the widespread farming out of individual chapters to separate reviewers resulted in lots of well-meaning but inconsistent criticism and conflicting edits. Some people wanted more of Timothy in her book; others wanted less. Some wanted closer attention to the chronological details of what happened when others wanted more focus on her emotional state and inner feelings. Some, editing her work like a news article or an academic biography, tried to make her diction more orthodox, perhaps not knowing how deeply Rosemary had read in twentieth-century experimental writing (including James Joyce, Virginia Woolf, Jack Kerouac, William Burroughs, and especially John Dos Passos, whose newsreel-based devices of interpolated headlines and scraps of dialogue Rosemary used freely).

There were two regrettable results of all this. First, irreconcilable drafts multiplied until her text became largely unmanageable. And second, I think the accumulated and sometimes inconsistent criticism led her first to doubt her skill and her own voice and finally to get bored with a project that never got appreciably closer to completion. Too many drafts, too many suggestions, too much discouragement—finally there were too many cooks, and it spoiled the broth for her. Eventually she

---

1. Published excerpts include those from *WOMR-FM Airwaves Magazine* (Provincetown, Mass., September 1988), in *High Times* magazine (July 1996), in Cindy Palmer and Michael Horowitz, *Shaman Women, Mainline Lady: Women's Writing on the Drug Experience* (New York: William Morrow, 1982), and from Robert Forte, ed., *Timothy Leary: Outside Looking In* (Rochester, Vt.: Park Street Press, 1999).

more or less abandoned the project, both because it had grown unwieldy and because, after decades had passed, she was getting tired of dwelling on her past adventures. So the book was never finished, and when she died in 2002, at the age of sixty-six, it remained a collection of disconnected drafts.

When Rosemary died, her brother, Gary Woodruff, inherited all her papers, and also her intellectual property rights.[2] In 2016 Denis Berry, who had arranged for Timothy's vast archives to be placed in the New York Public Library (NYPL), introduced me to Thomas Lannon, the curator of this collection at NYPL's Archives and Manuscripts Division. He said that NYPL would welcome Rosemary's papers there, and if Gary agreed they would establish a separate archive for them, distinct from Timothy's. Gary did agree, and just about all her surviving papers were shipped to the NYPL in sturdy sealed plastic crates.[3] You can consult them there today—I reproduce the library's finding list in appendix D.

At the time of the transfer, the most completely assembled version of Rosemary's memoir was a thick comb-bound book of photocopies of draft chapters, made at different times. It included one draft each for chapters 1 through 6 and 9 and 10. Some of these drafts showed heavy editing; there were also some fragments of other chapters. We called this book the Blue Binder.

John Schewel, Rosemary's companion for a lot of the time when she composed her memoir, was able to supply me with digital files of a different set of draft chapters, including basic texts for chapters 7 and 8, not included in the Blue Binder. But this draft, too, was not complete or in publishable form. With Gary's encouragement, and John's, I went to NYPL in April 2017 to see what other material was available. The Rosemary Woodruff Leary Papers (RWLP) then consisted of twenty

---

2. Some years later he gave half his interest in her archive and IP rights to his daughter, Rosemary's niece Kate Woodruff Felton.

3. Some of her papers were already in other public collections, including the Timothy Leary Papers at NYPL, the Michael Horowitz Collection on Timothy Leary (also at NYPL), Stanford University Special Collections.

boxes (there are some more now), filled with carefully labeled and numbered files. Of these, four boxes were marked as containing material relating to *The Magician's Daughter,* as the memoir was then informally known from the title of the first chapter. Rosemary had named it that when she sent parts of it to agents, hoping for an advance, but in other places she called it *Holding Together,* named after the eighth chapter of the I Ching.[4] The material had been separated out into these boxes, first by Gary and then by library staff, in the expectation that I would be coming to work on them.

There was quite a lot of material from the memoir in the RWLP archive at the library. I found different versions of most of the chapters, sometimes many versions, sometimes fragmentary, and sometimes seemingly complete. I found handwritten drafts and scraps of notes, and isolated pages without any sign I could then recognize about where they were to go. I powered my way through the four boxes, not stopping to read or analyze very closely, but just separating out what I wanted the library to scan for me. If I was in any doubt, I ordered scans. I also had the library copy some electronic material they had salvaged from Rosemary's computer, which Gary had saved, and some other materials too. In the end I ordered about six hundred pages scanned, including some electronic files.

My next step was to read the Blue Binder again, and when I did, it became evident to me that the well-meaning edits and suggested "corrections" were interfering with the directness and authenticity of the narrative. I knew Rosemary's voice as well as almost anyone living, and the corrected manuscript did not sound right. It was like looking at Rosemary through a dirty window; the bubbles had been taken out of the champagne. These edits (including many of my own) might have been helpful for Rosemary's short-term objective to get the memoir published while she was alive to work on it (although not helpful enough to actually get that done). But they did not serve the new objective, which was to assemble as much of the original as possible, in a coherent form and in her own style and language.

---

4. See the I Ching, chapter 8, note 1.

So I decided it would be best to start with a text as close to Rosemary's original work as could be managed, *ignoring all the changes,* and see if I could get between covers the book she had so much wanted to see published. Gary Woodruff, Kate Woodruff Felton, John Schewel, and Denis Berry agreed with this plan of approach. I began by having the Blue Binder typed up (so I could work with it on the computer), leaving out *all* the handwritten editorial changes and restoring the original typescript. Master word processor Will James accomplished this, carefully identifying places where the original was illegible beneath the corrections, and I then checked them against the Blue Binder itself. Will did the same thing again on hundreds of pages of library scans. Removing all the edits, some of which Rosemary had made herself, was drastic but necessary, I felt, in the same way it is necessary to remove the paint from a table before refinishing it. It is not done to harm the table, but to let its true wood be seen.

Then I started in editing the cores of chapters 1 through 10 as gently as I could, beginning with the Blue Binder for chapters 1 through 6 and 9 and 10 and with John's text for chapters 7 and 8. Chapter 11 existed only in fragments, and there was no trace of any chapter beyond those, despite synopses and outlines and chapter lists by Rosemary ranging from fourteen up to twenty-two chapters (I discuss these chapter plans, and reproduce some of the synopses, in appendix A).[5] Rosemary also prepared two detailed time lines covering events in her life from 1965 to 1974. I found them in one of the boxes, and they are so interesting and useful that I have combined them to publish here as appendix B.

I edited these core chapter texts very lightly indeed, correcting spelling and capitalization but only occasionally correcting punctuation, and adjusting word order only where absolutely needed to preserve sense. In particular, I preserved Rosemary's habit of connecting independent clauses with commas instead of using semicolons or separating them

---

5. Rosemary placed chapter synopses at the head of most drafts of her chapters, but they came from previously prepared synopses and usually did not reflect what was actually in the chapter drafts themselves. Especially as I have reproduced several versions of the chapter synopses in appendix A, I felt justified in omitting them from the text.

into new sentences. This sounded more like Rosemary, and I let myself be guided by the sound of her voice in my head.

Once I had a basic text for the ten existing chapters, I then went through every other version of each chapter I could find and compared it *word for word* with the basic text, toggling back and forth from one screen to another. This meant I had to read these chapters so many times I was often able to recognize variations in the text just by reading. Sometimes (not always) they were quite heavily marked up—Document 1 on page xxv is one example of many that could have been chosen.

Where the material was almost the same, I made judgments based on what sounded better and what sounded more authentically like Rosemary, authenticity trumping betterness where I had to choose. I made all changes in a contrasting font, using Calibri instead of Times Roman because it was different enough to be distinctive but not so different as to be distracting. Where two readings both seemed reasonably authentic, I followed a practice sometimes used in translating ancient texts and kept one in the main body of the work and the other in a footnote so the reader could make a choice. Probably in such cases both versions were Rosemary's own. If I were actually working with Rosemary to edit this manuscript in the usual way, I might have recommended that she adopt or alter one reading and discard the other. As this is no longer possible, I give both wherever they differ materially. Providing alternate readings allows a closer and more intimate view into Rosemary's thought process than a single definitive text would have done, and anyway there isn't a single definitive text.

In many places I found whole sections of narrative not in my basic text at all, and my general practice was to add to the basic text, again in Calibri, whatever additional material seemed to belong to Rosemary's narrative and add value to the chapter. The result was that by the end of this process most of the chapters were considerably longer than any single previous draft had been, and the story included just about all of Rosemary's accounts that have survived (or at least that I could find). Rosemary included many of her letters to her family in her draft chapters, and these I have not changed at all.

I reproduce a sample page as Document 2, on page xxvi, to show what those interim pages looked like. In the finished version, except where varying readings are offered in the footnotes, I have put all the Calibri into Times Roman so the seams are hidden. In a sense, though, it was arbitrary what went into Calibri. Material was added to a chapter because it happened not to have been in the version I started with, but the version I started with (usually but not always the Blue Binder) was actually no more canonical than any other. Where Rosemary used pseudonyms—Harry for Ralph Metzner, for example, or Gil Baines for Bill Haines—I have removed them and restored the correct names, identifying the first such substitution for each name in a footnote.

I also added a number of footnotes explaining who people were that Rosemary mentioned but did not identify. Aficionados of the Leariad and psychedelic history may know, for example, who Michael Hollingshead was, but that's not everyone, and I hope Rosemary's story will have a wide enough audience that these identifications may be useful. I feel comfortable doing this, as in one of her book proposals Rosemary herself said that "footnotes and notes will be used to clarify obscure historical events and persons."[6] I have also used footnotes to identify unattributed quotations, fix the exact dates of events where that was possible, briefly explore certain factual issues where needed to clarify the sense or correct a misremembering, define obscure or foreign words or words in dated slang, and for other purposes. I hope they are not too intrusive—they have helped me keep my own voice almost completely out of the main text. They are intended to be helpful, but if the footnotes get in your way, *just ignore them.*

As I worked my way through the scanned pages, I found lists of chapters under completely different titles, with annotations saying that pages of many of these had been prepared.[7] At that point, since I had

---

6. In a letter she even says, "There will have to be a lot of footnotes explaining who everybody was or is." Letter to Diana Jordan, October 27, 1997. In a postscript to a 1973 letter to her mother, reproduced below on page 287, she said she intended to have a whole chapter of notes.

7. I reproduce one of these as Document 5 in appendix A, on page 291.

returned to California, I asked my nephew Noah Phillips to go back to the RWLP and check the other boxes to see if any trace of these differently marked chapters could be found there. He combed through the remaining boxes and did find some useful material (for example, the comments of publishers and agents who reviewed portions of the memoir Rosemary sent them), but no other narrative that did not substantially duplicate what was in the four principal boxes.

I adopted three rules early in the editorial process—they were necessary to make the task manageable. First, there were folders of notes and scraps of clippings, and some drafts and outlines in longhand. These were not only difficult to read with any confidence, they would have been very difficult to transcribe and almost impossible to organize and compare with existing typescripts. I decided as a threshold matter that whatever was not typed, Rosemary had not considered finished enough even to circulate for comment. So (with a few exceptions) I did not use or incorporate any of that material. It is still there in the RWLP for others to explore, but it was not possible to include it here.

Second, I did not try to recreate missing material or absent chapters. I limited my effort to preparing an edition of *what there actually was*. A lot that we would have liked to hear about—including almost everything after she and Timothy separated in 1971—is not here. Toward the end the narrative is fragmented. I have published fragments as fragments and left blank spaces blank—it was all I could do with what I had.

Third, I was not writing a biography of Rosemary, although one is needed, and ample materials are available at the RWLP and elsewhere for this work to be done. It *should* be done while witnesses to Rosemary's life still remain and remember. But this book is not that—it is only an attempt to rescue as much of her memoir as she completed and make it accessible to all in a usable form. As her preface, which follows, makes clear, she wanted to tell her story and wanted her own voice to be heard amid the clamor of louder (mostly male) voices. She was for a time at the center of events of great cultural significance, and she was a personality worth remembering for her own sake. This book is an attempt to preserve Rosemary's story and her voice and her memory.[8]

Since narrative of the surviving chapters stopped in 1972, before the years of wandering and return, the book as originally conceived was rather unbalanced, like a bird with only one wing. But very fortunately, in 1997 the author Robert Greenfield interviewed Rosemary for his book *Timothy Leary: A Biography* (New York: Houghton Mifflin Harcourt, 2006). He sent her a copy of his notes for her to review, and she kept it.[9] It covers the years the memoir does not, and being in Rosemary's own voice fits perfectly into this work. I am very grateful to Robert Greenfield for allowing me to include it as a final chapter. Thanks also to the photographer Robert Altman for permission to reproduce his portrait of Rosemary that closes that chapter.

Ultimately the choices I made in editing this text are my responsibility—someone had to make the choices. I am grateful that Rosemary's brother Gary Woodruff, her niece Kate Woodruff Felton, and her companion in exile John Schewel trusted me with this responsibility. I have done the best I could with it. They all agreed to my suggestion for the reworked title. I have reconstructed the preface, published here under her name, from various versions she wrote to accompany manuscripts sent to agents and publishers. The original plan for the book included an introduction by Laura Huxley, but if it was ever written I have not found it, and she died in 2007. The chapter titles (except for chapter 12) are all Rosemary's—appendix A shows some of the changes the chapter titles went through before she settled on these. The epigraphs to the chapters and the general epigraph on page 40, are all Rosemary's.

I want to express my gratitude to Thomas Lannon, Assistant Director for Manuscripts, Archives and Rare Books at the New York Public

---

8. For those who would like to hear Rosemary's actual speaking voice, a brief video clip of her being interviewed, probably in the late 1990s, can be seen online at tinyurl.com/roseclip.

9. She made a few corrections, which I have incorporated, but she accepted almost all of Greenfield's text as accurate.

Library, and the staff of the NYPL Archives and Manuscripts Division, both for making my work at the library (and also my nephew's) as easy and efficient as possible and for their service in operating and maintaining this priceless and irreplaceable resource. Additional thanks to the staff at Inner Traditions: the acquisitions editor, Jon Graham; project editor Mindy Branstetter; editor in chief Jeanie Levitan; production editor Eliza Homick; sales and marketing representative Ashley Kolesnik; editorial assistant Patricia Rydle; copy editor Elizabeth Wilson; and to my agent Kristin Moeller, and Bill Gladstone, of Waterside Productions, and to Michael Horowitz (again) for making the necessary introductions. Special thanks to Stephen F. Breimer for his generous guidance in placing the manuscript.

Thanks also (again) to Robert Greenfield, not only for his contribution of a final chapter but also for his deeply researched *Timothy Leary: A Biography,* which I found immensely valuable for understanding the chaotic kaleidoscope of events in Rosemary's life when she was part of the Leariad. Thanks to Michael Horowitz for his *Annotated Bibliography of Timothy Leary* (Hamden, Conn.: Archon Books, 1988), which helped me identify the threads of Timothy's writings that Rosemary included in many places in her book, and for other help generously given. Thanks to the late Art Kleps for his boisterously entertaining and idiosyncratic memoir *Millbrook: A Narrative of the Early Years of American Psychedelianism,* 3rd ed. (Austin, Tex.: Original Kleptonian Neo-American Church, 2005), which made a lot of that period and its personalities clearer to me; and thanks to his daughter Daphne Kleps and the Original Kleptonian Neo-American Church for permission to reproduce from it the map of the Millbrook estate that appears on page 26. Thanks again to Will James, this time for his microscopically precise copy editing. And deep thanks to two departed friends, without whom neither my long friendship with Rosemary, nor this edition of her book, would ever have happened: Michael Kennedy, who introduced us for the first time in San Francisco in 1970, and Judy Given, who introduced us for the second time in Provincetown in 1983.

I would also like to thank (in alphabetical order) Annette Barbasch,

Denis Berry, Alex Best, Katherine Forer, Eleanora Kennedy, Adam Phillips, Noah Phillips, Andrew Jay Schwartzman, Gerald Stiebel, and (as always) the San Francisco Public Library for their contributions to this project. Honor, praise, and gratitude to Sri Lord Ganesha, blessed be He, the great god of India, Patron of Literature and Learning, Who for this as for all my books has been my Inspiration and Scribe.

SAN FRANCISCO
MAY 2019

mar.ry/'mar.e/vb 1 a : to join as husband and wife according to
law or custom 2 : to unite in close and usu. permanent relation

The main
house, ~~It~~ was overrun with cowboys and Indians., A new movie
was being made, a 'psyychedelic western.' Day-glo painted teepes
were sprouting up on the grounds, the house was full with a
camera crew from the city. Tim would play a benevolent sherrif,
he posed for publicity pictures wearing a cowboy hat and silver
star, joked with reporters that he would be a peace maker as
opposed to the Sherrif of Dutchess County, who was again, denouncing
the 'public menace' of ~~Dr./Timothy/Leary's/residency/in/the/state.~~
The Leagues camp in the woods. ~~had/been/several/visitations/from/~~
~~Several representatives~~ from the Public Health and Safety Office. visited, They
said they were, interested in our latrines.

There wasn't a part in the movie for me, though I felt like
having been
a lonesome cowgirl, ~~living/had/lived~~ at Millbrook for two years
'administrative assistant'
as mistress-housekeeper-~~companion-office-manager-but~~ wife was
what I longed to be, ~~...~~

We quarreled, I went to California. ~~Home again,~~ I waited for
the phone to ring, when it didn't I called him ~~...~~
~~...~~ He'd be out in a month, he said, ~~...~~ the movie was a failure,
the producers were quarreling, the comune ~~of~~ players from the
city had reported to the local hospital for penicillan and the

Document I: Sample page with longhand edits

Document 2: Sample page, transcribed, with editorial revisions in Calibri font (footnotes omitted)

Roadman spoke of the purpose of the gathering. Two children were sick, their mother and father were sponsoring the meeting. They spoke briefly, welcoming us and our desire to pray with them. We smoked the cigarettes and Fireman collected the remains, placing them on the altar. Roadman poured peyote tea; it was handed around the circle. He explained his way for the ceremony and the sun-wise path we would follow when passing the prayer drum, eagle fan, sage, staff, and rattle. Sun-wise all the instruments would go.

An old woman seemed to be complaining of our presence. Roadman talked quietly to her and she seemed to agree. A young couple across from us smiled their amusement; we exchanged smiles. They were Native American, beautiful, young, and obviously experienced peyote takers. Two small, bundled children were curled behind their mother next to Drummer. We had not yet drunk the tea.

We were eight from Los Angeles. Long-haired Anglos in cowboy boots with turquoise beads purchased that afternoon in the pawnshops of Gallup. Red-eyed men had leaned tipsily against the lampposts. Police in county cars patrolled the streets, keeping a watchful eye on every Navaho man reeling tipsily from doorway to lamppost. Now, deep in the reservation, we sat in the hogan with the peyote church members, short-haired, hard-working people in sober clothes, neatly pressed jeans and plaid jackets.

Roadman prayed while Drummer played. We drank the tea. It was not bitter. Roadman spoke again in English. He prayed for sons lost in the wars, for those who drank whiskey, for those who did not know the Road, or who'd lost it, following the white man's way, forgetting their fathers. He prayed for those in jail, arrested for bringing peyote home, for understanding and good will between all people, for the sick children here with us, for all children, for all beings. His prayer ended.

Drummer spoke while Roadman drummed. The peyote buttons from the altar were passed around the circle. They were much less bitter than I expected. Drummer spoke with his drums, the air hummed, the sound was oceanic. Cedarman placed sage on the fire, then passed the prayer instruments in our direction. One of the group attempted to sing but truth stopped him. Left hand, right hand, we handed sage, staff, fan, and rattle, those with songs sang them. The young couple had many songs. The drum went round again. The peyote came: it was sweet, it was sweet. All prayed, sang aloud. I wept not unhappily.

In the middle of the night, Fireman spoke in his native tongue; I understood him. The fire flamed with his words, they were strong and full of courage.

Water Lady opened the door and passed the water gourd. We tasted water for the first time in many hours, then left the hogan. Everything outside in the still dark night was changed.

PSYCHEDELIC
REFUGEE

Fugitive in Exile

ROSEMARY WOODRUFF LEARY

When you strike off on your own, leave some trace of your passage which will guide you coming back, one stone set on another, some grass weighted by a stick. But if you come to an impasse or a dangerous spot, remember that the trail you have left could lead people coming after you into trouble. So go back along your trail and obliterate any traces that you have left. This applies to anyone who wishes to leave some mark of his passage in the world. Even without wanting to, you always leave a few traces. Be ready to answer to your fellow men for the trail you leave behind you.

RENÉ DAUMAL, *MOUNT ANALOGUE*

fugitive *1. n. someone fleeing from punishment, danger, pursuit, authority, etc.*
2. adj. in flight, running away; liable to change, not durable, a fugitive color; (of literary compositions) scattered, occasional, ephemeral.

The history of a life does not always end with the final passing of that life. The memorabilia linger for a time; a great disorder of unpaid bills, half-legible letters, and mysterious writings often remain for others to clear away.

It was with that heap of paper in mind that I looked into my old leather trunk, full of photos and the chapters of an almost forgotten memoir I had begun to write long ago, by kerosene lamp and candle-light in Asian hotels, unheated European farmhouses, and a South American jungle hut. I was trying then to understand the process that had led me into exile and my life as a fugitive from my homeland.

I was a fugitive from my past and from authority. For over twenty-four years, ever since I put on a wig and borrowed a dead child's identity, I had pretended to be someone other than my mother's child.[1] That I was successful at this for so long was not due to any special skill or ability on my part, but rather to the growing indifference of the law, and how well my disguise came to fit. But the law was always there and the past kept me someone else. With time I became the person I pretended to be, with weight as a costume, and age as makeup. Ms. Everybody.

As a fugitive, the realities of the past intersected the present, with the continual threat of capture and prison. At the time, I often thought how sweet it would sound to hear someone call me by my real name. Now that I am free I can finally tell my story.

Books have been a passion of mine since childhood, and my personal adventures were inspired by all that I read. Nancy Drew proved to me that girls could be smart.[2] Jo March taught me that girls could

---

1. Rosemary is referring to the false passport she used for her flight to Algeria, described in chapter 8. As that flight took place in September 1970, we can date this passage to 1994, the year she was able to emerge from fugitivity, or 1995 at the latest.

2. The Nancy Drew Mystery Stories was a series of novels for girls, featuring a clever and resourceful girl detective. They were girls' counterparts of the Hardy Boys stories for boys, issued by the same publisher. They first appeared in 1930, and like the Hardy Boys books were all issued under a single pseudonym (Carolyn Keene for Nancy Drew) despite having many different authors. The series continued into the twenty-first century.

be noble, true, and write our way into life.[3] From *Forever Amber*, which I read as a child by flashlight under the bedcovers after everyone else had gone to bed, I learned that bad girls had affairs, yet continued searching for true love.[4] Much later, with Aldous Huxley's *The Genius and the Goddess*[5] I learned that it was possible to find one's way home to Olympus "by the road of sensuality." From Alexandra David-Néel and Madam Blavatsky I learned that travel in search of a spiritual truth was ennobling and difficult.[6] Orage taught me that love could have no boundaries and Gurdjieff that tricksters were fascinating.[7]

At the same time I discovered that once the journey had begun there was no turning back. One can rarely go home again, but I learned that being on the road wasn't such a bad place to be.

In 1952, I left St. Louis at seventeen as an air force officer's wife bound for an isolated desert base in Washington State. During the 1950s, while the McCarthy hearings were frightening Americans about Communism, I was living in New York City.[8] I did walk-on parts live on television, I was an interior decorator, beatnik stewardess,

---

3. Josephine "Jo" March was one of the sisters in Louisa May Alcott's *Little Women* (1869) and two sequels.

4. Kathleen Winsor's 1944 historical novel, set in seventeenth-century England, became a scandalous success due to its frank sensuality and forthright treatment of a woman using sex for social advancement.

5. A novel of sex and ideas (1955).

6. Alexandra David-Néel (1868–1969), a Buddhist and pioneer Western traveler to Tibet, and Helena Blavatsky (1831–1891), Russian founder of the Theosophical society, were highly influential popularizers of what came to be known in Europe and America as "Eastern religions."

7. George Ivanovich Gurdjieff (died 1949) was a spiritual teacher of surpassing eccentricity. His works and system of self-development, called The Fourth Way, are known mainly through the writings of others, of whom Alfred Richard Orage (1873–1934) was one of the most important.

8. Senator Joseph McCarthy (1908–1957) was a demagogue whose often baseless accusations about supposed Communists in government and elsewhere in American society set the tone for widespread hysteria. The Senate hearing about supposed subversion in the United States Army was a national sensation when televised in 1954 and led to the decline of his influence.

and had countless other personalities. I married a jazz musician, and every night I would wait for my husband in one of the jazz clubs to finish his gig. Then we would go up to Harlem for breakfast in one of the after-hour clubs.

In 1964 I met two former Harvard professors who were experimenting with LSD.[9] When American culture was in the midst of a rapid and radical cultural metamorphosis, I was married to the controversial and charismatic spokesperson for the psychedelic movement, Dr. Timothy Leary.

As a result of this marriage and my rebellious spirit, I found myself in the center of the whirling action and witnessed much of the revolutionary cultural transformation. I became a stepmother, seminar instructor, chatelaine of a sixty-four-room mansion, League for Spiritual Discovery guide, and light show artist in the psychedelic theater of the nineteen sixties. In this memoir I have tried to describe what happened, how it felt to be there.[10]

At the celebrated Millbrook estate in upstate New York, Timothy and I explored the positive potential of psychedelic sacraments, and played host to an endless stream of influential and talented artists, scientists, writers, musicians, and spiritual teachers.[11] Millbrook was an early example of the New Age communities and human potential

---

9. Timothy Leary, of course, and Ralph Metzner. Timothy Leary (1920–1996), psychologist, philosopher, and popularizer of LSD, needs no introduction to readers of this memoir—Rosemary's turbulent pair-bond with him lasted from 1965 to 1971. Ralph Metzner (1936–2019) was a psychotherapist and professor of psychology at the California Institute of Integral Studies. He was a colleague of Timothy's at Harvard, and co-author (with Leary and Alpert) of *The Psychedelic Experience* (1963). Rosemary speaks of her liaison with him on page 120 below.

10. In another version Rosemary adds "and what I believe the lasting effects of this revolution have been." I have not included this because she does not treat this subject anywhere in the surviving manuscript.

11. In the original versions, Rosemary lists a number of famous and influential people she encountered in the course of her involvement with Leary and his circle, and whom in her book proposals she promised to write about. I have not included them because she did not end up writing in any detail about most of those people, at least in the parts of the manuscript that have survived.

movements, and LSD was a shamanic gateway into expanded realities of creativity, spirituality, and ecstasy.

It was a time of enchantment; there were moments of radiant grace. But the party ended when we were busted during a midnight raid, led by Watergate mastermind G. Gordon Liddy, who jailed me for a month for contempt of court.[12] A marijuana charge later sent Timothy to prison; I helped him escape with the assistance of the Weather Underground, and we fled to Algeria together.

Ironically, after leaving America, we ended up captives again, held this time by Eldridge Cleaver and the Black Panther Party in Algeria. After escaping from Algeria too, and after another arrest in Switzerland, I left Tim, searching for a country that would allow me to find peace and sanity again. What followed were years of adventure and fear in some very far-flung places.

I became a fugitive on four continents, and a refugee. I lived underground as a fugitive in Europe and the Americas long after Timothy was captured again and eventually released from the prison system. After having had no contact for over twenty years, he and I reconnected once again at the end of his life and I was, as he wanted me to be, witness to his death.

Recently I have regained my freedom, and now I can tell my story. With the law finally appeased, and the optimism that has become my survival trait, and time running out, I have written this book to document what I experienced.[13] *The Magician's Daughter* is a memoir of chaotic times. I have attempted to make it a comic and provocative look at the spirit of the times.

---

12. It was actually the judge who jailed Rosemary for refusing to testify to a grand jury. Liddy was an assistant district attorney in Dutchess County, New York, at the time of the Millbrook raid. He later worked for Nixon's White House and 1972 reelection campaign and was the chief of the "Plumbers" who committed the Watergate burglary in 1972. In 1973 he was himself sentenced to prison for conspiracy, burglary, and wiretapping in the Watergate affair.

13. In another version she says, "I hope to leave a record of my adventures."

ALTERNATE ENDING

It was a time of enchantment. There were moments of radiant grace, knowing that we were all in this beauty together—the beauty of this earth.[14] Suspecting sacrifice as a wrong idea, we knew the unity transcending generations. We were Indians, cowboys, settlers, with tepee fires and tribal ways, seeking doors to Eden. We were city guerrillas, urban warriors, priestesses, pirates, prophets, utopian visionaries, mystical anarchists, revolutionaries, and outlaws. We were yogis and shaktis. And there was the down side too: the wars went on, and there were children following "smiling men with bad reputations."[15]

We wanted to be armed with wit, militant with intelligence, realizing the vision of the harmony of all things. We wanted to be able to define ourselves in terms of the above—the eternal human.

The book, which seemed never finished, never-ending, began when I was in exile. Now it is being completed when I am finally home again, with the hope of leaving my past in good order for those who care to know it—for history, for lessons learned, for journeys taken.[16]

ROSEMARY WOODRUFF LEARY

---

14. "We're all in this beauty together" is a line from Frank Herbert's *Dune Messiah* (1970).

15. This is the closing line of Leary's *Psychedelic Prayers* (Millbrook, 1966), a poetic rendition of the *Tao Te Ching* of Lao-tse. The work ends: "The lesson of the Tao is more likely to be found among—" followed by a list of twenty categories (for example, "men who look at sunsets / men who walk in the woods / beautiful women"), with this as the twenty-first and final category. The full text of *Psychedelic Prayers* is archived online at perma.cc/8pa6-hmx6.

Psychedelic Prayers is item A5 in Michael Horowitz's *Annotated Bibliography of Timothy Leary* (Hamden, Conn.: Archon Books, 1988), 29. This bibliography is archived online at tinyurl.com/learibib; further citations will be in this form: Horowitz A5.

16. This paragraph was written to accompany a completed manuscript that Rosemary never did complete. Only now, many years after she died, has it become in some sense true with this volume.

ONE

The Magician's Daughter

Learn therefore, O Sisters
to distinguish the Eternal Human
That walks about among the stones of fire in bliss & woe
Alternate, from these States or Worlds in which the Spirit travels
This is the only means to forgiveness of Enemies.

WILLIAM BLAKE, *JERUSALEM*

The adverse aspect between the planets Venus and Neptune is very serious and unfortunate, affecting the whole of the emotional life, these two planets representing personal and universal love respectively; and the conflict between the two means that you need to purify your love nature from the selfish element, seeking to make that which is personal universal. There is a dangerous side to this aspect, and that is the tendency it brings to fall completely under the sway of the senses. You yourself will know if there is any fear of this in your own case, but if so you should battle against it with all the strength of your nature, for when evil, the effect of Neptune is most insidious. Avoid all narcotic drugs as you would the plague.

ALAN LEO, *THE KEY TO YOUR OWN NATIVITY*[1]

---

1. Alan Leo (1860–1917), *The Key to Your Own Nativity* (London, 1910). Leo was an English astrologer and Theosophist whose influence helped refocus astrology more on character and tendency than on specific concrete predictions.

My father plucked pennies from my ears, dealt cards to choose and remember, placed back in the deck they'd appear next in my hair, four kings in a row beside them.[2] His finger was a wand to be watched carefully, it created invisibility. He is slender, elegant in tails with slick black hair, smiling at the costumed girl beside him. He holds a rifle, there's a hole in the Ace of Spades. The photograph calls him VICTOR THE MAGICIAN.

He was the last but one of ten, raised in southern Missouri. Tales of Indian blood, land grants, but he didn't really know or care, leaving to older sisters the heritage of dried-up farms and family pride, tribal ways, and close-knit kin.

My aunts were missionaries and I the little heathen, with Bible verse and Baptist hymns to save me from the devil sins of cards and dancing. They were relieved to have someone to save. I was counted among the saved one Sunday. The minister wore fishing boots, said a long prayer while he dunked me in the pool behind the pulpit. The choir sang "Washed in the Blood of the Lamb." A trick painting of Jesus hung on the wall, his eyes opening and closing to my questions. I wanted religion and a place to belong to, but Sweet Jesus set me free from Bible class and religious aunts.

Even at seven I knew there was something more than what everyone was telling me, and one bright day I got a glimpse. It was a shining moment, with an energy that hovered in the air, so strong and real. I suddenly realized that I was a part of everything. I was walking on a leafy street near my house, and everything was illuminated in gold. Time stopped. It was only a moment. I promised the presence that hovered near me in the air that I would remember. That night in my dreams I flew above lampposts and trees, though it was frightening to be so high.

---

2. In a letter to her father, dated January 28, 1973, Rosemary says she intended to begin her memoir with the words, "My father's hands never beat me, he plucked pennies from my nose." But no surviving version of chapter 1 has that text. I reproduce her letter on page 21 as an appendix to this chapter. See also her postscript in a letter to her mother on page 287.

There were summers full of mint, matching my growth against the corn, a seat on the gray swayback mare safe from the mean old rooster that pecked around the barn. Silky dust against bare feet, feather beds, gourd water cups, kerosene lamps, fresh warm milk, the smell of honeysuckle and clover, streams with cottonmouth snakes slithering from logs. Heat lightning and thunderstorms sent Mother under cover; I'd be out dancing, washing my hair under the summer's shower. One autumn a hog killing, chipped enamel basins full of blood, high-pitched squeals, thick smoke in the air.

The dry delicate touch of my blind uncle's hands, he said I was pretty. My city grandfather's long stained fingers turning the package of Camels to show me the hotel in the desert. The smell of my country grandfather's Sunday suit, mothballs and pipe tobacco. They all died the same year; I wore the same yellow dress to the funerals.

Lonely, rebellious, and inventive, I lived in my own world, for the rules of the other made no sense to me. I mythologized everything. I wanted things to be grander than they were in my own little neighborhood, in my little home. Living in St. Louis, a city that had long since turned its back on the River that for centuries had been part of its history, I loved the idea that there had perhaps been French fur trappers in my family. Names like *Maupin* led me to muse on handsome, burly Frenchmen making their way down the Mississippi, set on the world's greatest adventure.

Cold city winters; chapped, skinned knees; a tin lunch box with hot chocolate. Icy salted streets, snow ice cream with vanilla. Daddy left for work on the levee wearing mittens and two pairs of pants. Magic was a part-time thing, couldn't make a living. He'd only do his tricks for me, said his fingers had grown too clumsy. Saturday nights I was the performer down at the family tavern. The bar cleared of glasses and foam, I'd toe dance or do backbends.

—Fine little acrobat you've got there, ought to be in pictures. Have another beer?

—No thanks, daughter's got Sunday school, the wife's waiting.

—What about your daddy's still, that time you outran him?

—Little pitchers got big ears, nope, he's got a turkey farm down in French Village, doing fine, going on seventy.

Mother made costumes for my dolls to match the ones I wore in recitals and on the river boat with my tap dance group. They were usually red, white, and blue—our dances were done to military airs.

Coffee tins full of grease saved for the butcher, stomping on cans, collecting paper, war bonds, and "dirty Krauts."

—Our next door neighbor's German.

Hula skirts cut from the family funnies, dance recitals, the morale of the Boys Over There.

—Uncle Howie's fighting Nazis.[3]

Or so we thought until a coded letter arrived, with the old joke about Prince Albert tobacco and the word *Dad* underlined. It was figured out that he was in the Prince Albert Islands near Trinidad.[4] My father's job at the railroad yard was considered too important for him to be drafted.

ROOSEVELT DIES[5]

—Grandpa cursed him to it!

A neighborhood girl surrounded by aunts, uncles, and cousins in a four-family apartment. I was unaware of there being any wrong side of town.

I was a good Indian-ball player, fast and skinny until timid breasts appeared.[6] Nothing fit and everything was awful. My baby brother was born,[7] and I became a babysitter on permanent duty. My parents sent me to Kentucky to my father's youngest sister. She taught me to curtsey and make bouquets of flowers from paper doilies to present to her

---

3. Rosemary would probably have been at least eight at this time. Born in April 1935, she was not yet seven when the United States went to war with Germany in December 1941. American troops would not be "fighting Nazis" directly in any significant way for another year, until after the invasion of North Africa in November 1942.

4. This is obscure—there are no islands in the Caribbean or elsewhere with this name.

5. On April 12, 1945—Rosemary was almost ten.

6. Indian ball is a local Missouri form of baseball or softball, adapted to fewer players and/or a smaller field than usual.

7. Gary Woodruff, born on June 15, 1947.

friends when we went calling. I spent the summer as an only child reading Shakespeare and listening to *The Mikado* on tin-pierced records.[8] I
never wanted to go home again.

Then I was in love with the boy next door, his dog, the Catholic
Church, movies, radio serials like *Our Gal Sunday,* anything with heroines.

> Can this girl from a little mining town in the West find happiness
> as the wife of a wealthy and titled Englishman?[9]

I lied about my age to get my first job, popcorn girl, then cashier, at
the local movie house. I was tall and looked older than my age, thirteen.
The manager of the movie house called me *quail bait.* I didn't understand. The high school hero about to graduate asked me to the prom.
From then on I was going steady.

My grandmother moved in with us, and I lost my room. We moved
to the suburbs, I got the basement and a radio and some privacy.

Lawdy Miss Clawdy![10] Rhythm and blues on the late-night radio
taught me to dance not like a white girl should. *The Gospel Hour* at
midnight taught me what those old hymns should really sound like.

Then bored with proms, sorority meetings, cheerleading, who's
going to Korea. Out of school at fifteen, regretting it later, working.
Given a diamond ring, the pleasures he promised, under a tree by the
river, bitten by mosquitoes. Sixteen. Full of a long summer's waiting till
he finished pilot training and we could be married. Buying silver on
time, rapt in my dreams, writing him letters. Tired in the mornings

---

8. This reference is puzzling. There were recordings on pierced metal discs for music
boxes and similar devices, and aluminum disks for one-off nonprofessional recordings,
but by the onset of World War II American gramophone and phonograph records were
overwhelmingly of the spiral groove variety, on a vinyl or shellac surface.
9. *Our Gal Sunday,* a radio serial broadcast daily from 1937 to 1959, opened each show
with this question. I have slightly corrected Rosemary's recollection of the wording.
10. "Lawdy Miss Clawdy," by Lloyd Price, was a highly successful and very influential rhythm-and-blues song. Although at this point in the chapter Rosemary is not
yet fifteen, the recording by Price and pianist Fats Domino was actually released in
April 1952, when she was about seventeen.

walking to work past the whores in the doors of the old levee houses.

Married wearing pink,[11] a friend sang "Because You Promised Me," my hand shook for the ring. My father rose to steady me.[12] Honeymoon in Las Vegas where gambling claimed him. Slept most of the way to my new home, an air force base in the West.[13]

I was uncomfortable with the major's wife and officers' club dinners. Unwilling to learn bridge or patience. Beaten when I answered back, swore, or got angry. Plagued by desert winds and cowboys riding eastwards. Protective of my budding self, running back to St. Louis pregnant, seventeen. Four days on the train and I was home.

—I can't believe Brad would hit you, what did you do?

His lower blows unmade the baby.

Daddy is scared, holds my hands when the pains come faster. Black-habited nuns go round in squares, ether fills the air.

—You bad girl, what did you do, you're losing the baby.

—The baby died, she'll live to have another.

—I called the base. He said you'd made your bed. He found your wedding ring in the sugar bowl. Oh, Ro!

With my girlfriend in her daddy's Cadillac we'd cross the bridge to East St. Louis blues on weekends, roadhouses, nightclubs, anywhere there was music—better live than on the soul stations. Back at dawn, listening to gospel on the car radio, we'd lie to each other's mother.

My mother had cancer. My grandmother told me it was my fault because I was such a bad girl. I met a thin, glib tap dancer, the third of a famous dancing trio, followed him to the City.

CHINATOWN . . . WALL STREET . . . STATUE OF LIBERTY . . . AIR-CONDITIONED RIDE . . . UPTOWN . . . DOWNTOWN . . . GET YOUR TICKETS HERE[14]

---

11. Another version reads, "pink tulle and pearls."

12. Another version reads, "My father's hand held me still."

13. Another version reads, "the Pacific Northwest."

14. Headline-style inserts like this, interrupting a narrative, were a characteristic device of the novelist John Dos Passos (1896–1970), whose work Rosemary knew well.

Billboard Camel sailor blowing down on sidewalk preacher.[15]

—Beloved, believe not every spirit . . . there are many false prophets here among us.[16]

—Hello, surprise, you said you wanted me near. My family's moved to California and there's no more home to go to.

But he had a wife, kids, didn't want another.

—I'll call some hoofers I know, they might let you stay.

They did.

—Listen, I've got a john coming at midnight, you can take the dog to the hairdresser; it's open all night. I want him dyed shocking pink. How old are you, anyway?

PRIVATE ROOM EXCHANGED FOR EVE BABY-SIT WEST END AVE

—Good morning, Walruses Handbags. No, Mr. Rose is not in.

—Why don't you try modeling? You got the height.

—Pull in your cheeks, lift your chin, that's it.

—Two pastramis on rye toast . . .

—I can make you the best known face in New York.

. . . and an egg salad on whole wheat.

Dear Family,

New York is so exciting! I've taken a part-time job at a restaurant, I wear a cowboy hat and say Howdy! I'm doing a Toni commercial next week, I'm the Easy to Wave Girl.[17] Don't sneeze or you'll miss me. Write me at the Alperton House for Women.[18] No men allowed except for the ancient elevator operator.

LOVE

---

15. From 1941 to 1966 a famous billboard in Times Square, advertising Camel cigarettes, showed a dapper man (during the war a soldier or sailor) blowing out a smoke ring made of steam.

16. "Beloved, believe not every spirit, but try the spirits whether they are of God: because many false prophets are gone out into the world." 1 John 4:1.

17. The Toni Home Permanent was a home-use product offering women a "permanent wave" without going to a beauty parlor.

18. Perhaps a real place, but more likely the twenty-three-story Barbizon Hotel at 140 East Sixty-Third Street, a safe, cheap, and stylish residence for women only.

Later, with Mat Mathews, a jazz accordionist from Holland who'd learned to speak English in Harlem, I lived at a musicians' hotel off Broadway. We had breakfast from a paper cup and dinner at Charlie's Tavern.[19]

—Lady wanted me to go on the road.

—Hamp's whole band lined up to get vaccinated, everybody's sleeve rolled up.

—And Mingus threw the guy off the balcony.

—Bird won't play there anymore.[20]

—Ely, *Nevada,* where is that at?

It was a little mining town between Reno and Las Vegas.[21] Broke short-order cooks, hustlers, cowboys, miners, Indians, whores. Three civic leaders died in a plane crash. Their widows kept the bingo parlors, cribs, slot machines going. The bus station burned down—no way out. Justice of the peace married us. Two weeks with a funny hat trio playing to drunken potato farmers, and we had the airfare back to New York.

PERRY STREET WEST TWO & HALF KITCHEN FIREPLACE FURNISHED

—You paid your dues, man . . .

—I've got to meet some cats uptown, don't wait up.

Lonely, I met Charles, a different kind of musician. He smelled of pipe tobacco and ripe experience, the scent of my grandfather.

December 12, 1958

Dear Family,

It's snowing and the streets are white and quiet. I like this neighborhood. There is a Puerto Rican church next door; I hear all the old Baptist hymns in Spanish. There are pushcarts selling everything. I buy vegetables from

19. Mat Mathews (Mathieu Hubert Wijnandts Schwarts) (1924–2009); Charlie's Tavern, a jazz hangout in the center of the New York Jazz District, was on Seventh Avenue between Fifty-First and Fifty-Second Streets.

20. Jazz musicians Billie Holiday (singer), Lionel Hampton (vibraphone and piano), Charles Mingus (bass), and Charlie Parker (saxophone).

21. Actually Ely is in eastern Nevada, near the Utah state line.

an old woman called Apple Annie. She uses a baby carriage as her store. Charles is working on a new symphony; he has dedicated it to me. It is called Chief Crazy Horse. Our life is very simple. I bake bread and read everything from A to Z in the Tenth Street library. Mat is divorcing me so he can stay in the States.[22] *I know you don't approve, but please try to understand and don't worry.*

LOVE

—You boil them up and drink the juice. There's a nursery in Texas that will send them through the mail.

—And so I said to my mother, "I've just eaten some mushrooms," and she said, "what's the matter they're poisonous or something? You look green." I couldn't stop laughing.

—Everyone is on the blacklist, no one is working.

—Did you hear Art Tatum died?[23]

—Come on over, Kerouac will be there and Aram is bringing his movie.[24]

—I saw him look at you, do you think I'm blind?

January 30, 1959

Dear Family,

I've moved to the Chelsea Hotel.[25] *If Charles calls please don't tell him where I am. He is a fine man but perhaps there is just too much difference in our ages. I might come home for a while. Please write.*

LOVE

---

22. Gary Woodruff remembers Rosemary saying she was married to Mathews, but a Wikipedia article in 2018 (since vanished) showed Mathews married to other people during most of this time. It is unclear in any event why divorcing Rosemary would help him stay in the United States.

23. Art Tatum (1909–1956), one of the most important jazz pianists ever, died on November 5, 1956.

24. Jack Kerouac (1922–1969), novelist of the Beat Generation, best known for *On the Road* (1957), and Aram Avakian (1926–1987), film director and editor, whose work around this time included films about jazz.

25. At 222 West Twenty-Third Street. For many years a popular residence for artists and writers. It is still standing (2018) but is no longer a residential hotel.

I ran away again, this time from loving a married man. I put on a uniform and joined an airline.[26]

—Havana was really great as a layover. You have to work too hard now that it's a turnaround.

—Bring me another coffee will you, hon?

—Good morning. Welcome aboard Flight 111 to Havana, Cuba. PLEASE FASTEN YOUR SEAT BELTS AND OBSERVE THE NO-SMOKING SIGN WHEN IT APPEARS. BREAKFAST AND COMPLIMENTARY DAIQUIRIS WILL BE SERVED SHORTLY AFTER TAKEOFF. THANK YOU.

—Never mind what the captain says, bring me another drink.

—You know they call you the Beatnik Stew?

—She bumped me off that flight so she could fly with her boyfriend; they lost three engines over the Gulf. They never found the wreckage.

—I don't care if you've flown ninety hours and you've got the flu, you're scheduled on this one.

—Screw crew scheduling, call in sick.

—We went to Puerto Rico and all we did was take cocaine and read *Faust* to one another.

—Goethe or Marlowe?

—Brett says he's into Wittgenstein. He'll be teaching him next spring.

—Nica showed me how to use the I Ching.

—Ouspensky is far out, but you ought to read Orage.[27]

—Jerry brought back the entire bush! I think they just went out to the desert and pulled up the first likely looking plant.

—Two hundred dollars for a pound of this?

---

26. El Al Israel Airlines, as a stewardess.

27. Peter D. Ouspensky (1878–1947), in his posthumous book *In Search of the Miraculous* (1949), was the writer most responsible for spreading the ideas of the philosopher of consciousness G. I. Gurdjieff (1866/77?–1949). Alfred R. Orage (1873–1934) was a British writer and student of Gurdjieff's whose commentaries and translations contributed to the Gurdjieff movement.

—Maybe we can bake it, have you seen the *Alice B. Toklas Cook Book*?[28]

—Peggy Glanville-Hicks used the letter and they sang "I'm Sending You Some Majoun Candy." Charles told me that story years ago.[29]

March 10, 1961

Dear Family,

I really like working at El Al, especially when there is an Orthodox group leaving for Tel Aviv, everyone is crying and singing. I did a publicity poster. It says Willkomen in Zürich, they think I look Swiss. I've taken a lease on an old sailmaker's loft at the foot of Manhattan; there is so much space and light. I can see the Statue of Liberty and a glimpse of the ocean. Tugboats dock in front of the building; the cooks wave me aboard for a cup of coffee. In the early morning the street is full of seagulls, so strange to walk among knee-high birds. My few neighbors are artists. We meet at a fishermen's luncheonette called Mary's Rest. She looks like the duchess in Alice but feeds me double portions of everything. Perhaps I'll see you at Xmas.

LOVE

—Monk's at the Five Spot, Trane's at the Half Note, Miles is at the Vanguard. Who do you want to hear?[30]

—Amphetamine makes you crazy; I don't care if it gives you visions.

—Subways underground while missile crisis sent those who could to Mexico or overseas.[31] I spent all my salary on taxis.

---

28. Alice B. Toklas (1877–1967), companion of the poet Gertrude Stein, published the *Cook Book* in 1954. It was notorious for including a recipe for hashish fudge.
29. Peggy Glanville-Hicks (1912–1990) was an Australian composer and music critic. She worked for some years in America, but not during the time of this chapter. Majoun candy is a Moroccan specialty, mixing cannabis with spices, nuts, and dried fruit.
30. Jazz musicians Thelonious Monk (piano), John Coltrane (saxophone), and Miles Davis (trumpet). Who do you want to hear?
31. The Cuban Missile Crisis of October 1962.

—Harry Smith's movie is really incredible.[32]

—Did you see the version with Charlie Parker's music?

—He wants me to go on working so he can write a play.

—They sold the company to IBM.

—With Leary and Alpert at Harvard, Ginsberg went there, Huxley too.[33]

EAST NINTH STREET HI CEIL FIREPLACE THREE FLIGHTS GARDEN VIEW PRODUCTION ASST TV STUDIO ATTRACTIVE HARD WORKING CONGENIAL RESPONSIBLE PROPS, CASTING FOR COMMERCIALS

—Backward flip on a trampoline with a girdle on, she's got to be a champion.

—The noodles are supposed to *pour* out of the egg, not fall in a clump.

I was at lunch with fourteen ad executives talking about their soup commercial when Kennedy was killed.[34] Who would absorb the cost of the day's unfinished commercial: union or management? I was fired before it was resolved.

—No, I don't hear voices. I'm just depressed.

—Ira Cohen came back from Morocco with a whole briefcase full.[35]

—One more summer in New York and I'll die.

—LSD in a sugar cube? What does it do?

—It sounds beautiful, Kate, how long before you come down?

---

32. Harry Everett Smith (1923–1991) was an experimental filmmaker, musicologist, occultist, psychedelic pioneer, and a key figure in the Beat Generation.

33. Readers of this memoir will recognize Richard Alpert (later Ram Dass), Timothy's colleague at Harvard and at Millbrook. Allen Ginsberg (1926–1997) was one of the most important poets of the twentieth century, a psychedelic pioneer, an activist for peace, and a tireless voice for personal, artistic, sexual, and political freedom. Aldous Huxley (1894–1963) was a British novelist, satirist, and philosopher; his 1954 book *The Doors of Perception,* about a mescaline trip, provided a frame of reference for many of the first generation of the psychedelic movement.

34. On November 22, 1963. Aldous Huxley died the same day.

35. Ira Cohen (1935–2011), poet, publisher, and photographer, lived in Morocco from 1961 to 1965. He published *The Hashish Cookbook* (1966) after he returned to the United States.

ROSEMARY'S LETTER TO HER FATHER

Jan 28, 1973

Dear Daddy,

I believe that the book called The Magician's Daughter *will begin this way.*

"My father's hands never beat me but plucked pennies from my nose, dealt cards to choose and remember. Placed back in the deck, they'd appear next to my ear, four kings in a row beside them. His finger was a wand to be watched carefully, creating invisibility. He was slender, elegant in tails and slick black hair, smiling at the costumed girl beside him. He stands with a rifle, there's a hole in the Ace of Spades. He knew magic words but wouldn't tell them. No one could beat him at sleight of hand, he's learned from a master. People would come from miles around to watch him but he couldn't make a living at it, there was a depression. Handbills called him Victor, the Magician."

I hope you like it.

Happy Birthday

Love,

Ro

INTERLUDE

❦

Editor's Note: Rosemary's First Acid Trip

This recounting of Rosemary's first acid trip was found among other fragments in a file containing elements that became chapter 5. But it clearly belongs just after chapter 1, which ends with her discussing with Kate the idea of taking some acid on a sugar cube. The title "Generatrix" and the date are Rosemary's. In January 1965 Rosemary was 29.

Generatrix

January 1965

She divided the sugar cube.

I lay on the floor looking up, waiting to feel for the first time the effects of LSD. No taste, other than the sudden flow of saliva, sugar dissolving in my mouth.

Candles, incense, fire. Wait.

Skylight pulsing, white frame, dark night, a touch of red with every heartbeat. How my heart beats.

Absorbed by the patterns till intensity seems moronic.

Kate lay beside me, a gentle smile on her face. The fire, now dense, layer upon layer like paint applied in countless strokes.

Flames spiral close with indrawn breath. Exhale. They retreat a bit as do flowers, walls. It is not a pleasant sensation, exactly. The flowers look wise. The skylight is suddenly very distant in a vaulted chamber filled with overlapping times.[36]

I feel longer, my body extending, a serpent, stretching across the room. Carpet soft beneath me. I must see on the other side.

---

36. Perhaps overlapping *tiles* is meant. But *times* works too, on LSD. Two versions both say *times*.

A shrine. Before the candles, head bowed to the floor. I thrust up, find balance, look deep into the painted eyes. Her many hands wave flowers, skulls, bells, weapons. Her eyes upturned, crescent moon cradling the sun.

Armed and militant. Dancing upon the lovers, flailing the abyss.

Mother.

Kali.[37]

Generatrix.[38]

I want air.

We pass through the door out into the dawn; sparkling, crisp day, "Where to, ladies?" A taxi.

"To the end of the island."

A right turn onto a road straight and clear, a tunnel with blue sky above the not too distant sea.

We stopped before a dock stretching into the river. Far from the city sounds the distant shore, a dream of towers.

A glimpse of the Statue of Liberty. She. Seagulls wheeled above us. Laughing gulls tipped with black.

Golden wings tracing webs in the skylight of the sun. I go with them. High above the two shadows on the dock, flying. Kate calls. Clouds, cold sea breeze.

We are tired and hungry.

Under the span of the East River Drive, a van with a sign in the window.

PLEASE HELP KOREAN STUDENT MEDICAL STUDIES, BRING HEALTH AND SANITY TO THE WORLD. THANK YOU.

---

37. An important Hindu goddess, usually shown in black in terrifyingly threatening form, a destroyer, but also a preserver and protectress, the Divine Mother. Her many hands wave flowers, skulls, bells, weapons.

38. The word *generatrix* is the feminine of *generator,* cognate to the English words *progenitor* and *generation.* It denotes the active, creative energy often imagined as masculine in contrast to the so-called feminine, receptive energy. The I Ching, which Rosemary studied extensively, is saturated with this dichotomy. In geometry a generatrix is a point (or a curve or surface) that generates a new shape when moved in space.

Across the dark caverned street, a truck flash-filming whoever stops to read the printed sign.[39]

We hailed a cab, wanting oatmeal and hot coffee.

Sunday *Times* in the brightly lit restaurant.[40]

U.S. BOMBS NORTH VIETNAM RETALIATION FOR VIETCONG ATTACK AT U.S. INSTALLATIONS.

Spongy wastelands. With milk and honey, steamy swamps, molten rivers.[41] Dinosaurs in my porridge.

My stomach says I cannot eat yet.

"What's the matter, you in love? Why don't you eat your nice cereal?" Kate and I giggled until the waiter went away shaking his head.

---

39. Oddly, one version ends this sentence with a question mark.

40. Another version identifies this as "Ratner's," a famous Jewish delicatessen at 138 Delancey Street in Lower Manhattan. In chapter 4 Rosemary mentions another visit there.

41. "If the Lord delight in us, then he will bring us into this land, and give it us; a land which floweth with milk and honey." Numbers 14:8. This image appears twenty times in the Old Testament.

TWO

Illusions

*It is possible to "come to," to awake, to be liberated from
the prison of illusory perceptions and conflicting emotions.*

CASTALIA FOUNDATION
MILLBROOK, NEW YORK

SPRING 1965

LSD was still legal in New York in the summer of 1965. I didn't know
that then. I was busy with a band of acid gypsies. Travel-worn from
defying the laws of gravity and economics, they said they were magicians
and crashed amidst the antiques, drew crazy patterns on the prayer rug,
dripped candle wax across the sheets, played Dylan slowed down, more
mournful than he was at normal speed.

> *nobodies taut yew how to live out on the streets*
> *anow yer gonna half tu get usetuit!*[1]

I did, watching New York dissolve till it got boring.

They left, all but one, a musician, more wounded than the rest. I

---

1. This is Rosemary's phonetic transcription of Bob Dylan's snarly yowl in his 1965 song
"Like a Rolling Stone": "Nobody's ever taught you how to live out on the street / And
now you're gonna have to get used to it."

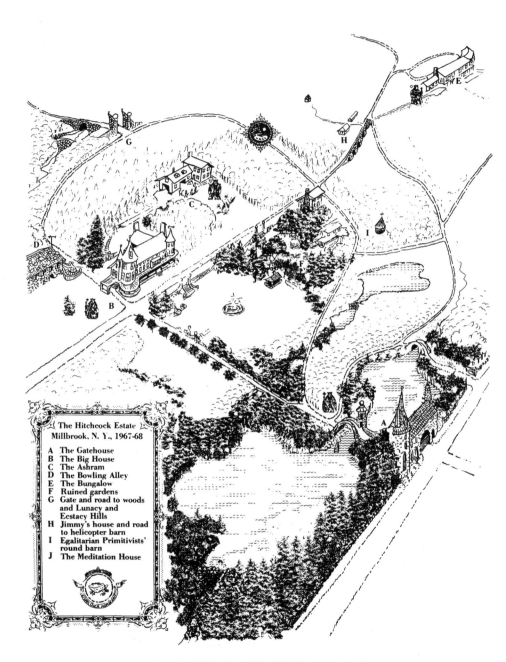

The Hitchcock Estate
Millbrook, N. Y., 1967-68

A The Gatehouse
B The Big House
C The Ashram
D The Bowling Alley
E The Bungalow
F Ruined gardens
G Gate and road to woods
  and Lunacy and
  Ecstacy Hills
H Jimmy's house and road
  to helicopter barn
I Egalitarian Primitivists'
  round barn
J The Meditation House

MAP OF MILLBROOK ESTATE, by Art Kleps
From the cover of his *Millbrook: A Narrative of the Early Years of American Psychedelianism*, 3rd ed. (2005). Reproduced with the kind permission of Daphne Kleps and the Original Kleptonian Neo-American Church (cover copy omitted).

liked his strong Indian face, remembering it from another lifetime, loving. Famed from another era, kept beautifully by an heiress, he gave up the music learned at Ben Webster's knee but stuck to the needle and an expensive need for health spas and psychoanalysis. He was the epitome of graceful dissipation. Appreciating jazz and elegance as I did, I loved him at first sight. A second meeting years later at Millbrook, the Hitchcock estate, confirmed the attraction; there, he claimed, LSD cured his addiction to more dangerous drugs.[2]

Early in the summer we met again. He came to live with me, bringing music and madness. Dark rhythms stirred his veins. It was a grace junk gave him. I could not follow.

I called my very best friend, crying, "Sugar tit won't cure that prick of angry consciousness . . . acid every day can't change him . . . knocks on the door . . . some junkie queen . . . she washed her feet in all my perfumes . . . his ring cut my . . . my jewelry in pawn . . . he'd rather stick a needle in his arm than love me . . . what to do?" Her cool voice assessed the damage.

"Well," she said, "Tim's in town, he'd like to see you. Why don't you go back to Millbrook with him?"

Tim fetched me in a borrowed Jeep. Running away from home—one black eye, patched jeans, a ripped sneaker—I was shy, being saved that way.

"What have you been doing all summer?"

"Dying by degrees of heat and madness."

"I have a theory about death, would you like to hear it? Ecstasy comes to everyone at that moment, dying is a merging with the life process. What do you think?"

"I don't know, I really don't believe that death is a way out. But lately I've found myself wishing this life would cease."

"So have I, many a time. Let's make an agreement, shall we?"

"What's that smell?" The car was full of smoke.

---

2. In some versions "he claimed" is not set off by commas, making it uncertain whether it was the claim or the cure (or both) that happened at Millbrook. I have been unable to identify the musician.

"Open your window. I forgot the muffler's broken, this was the only car working." The cool dark air banished the fumes, but the knocking grew louder.

"What did you say?" I had to shout.

"Let's go together."

"Where?"

"Everywhere. Why didn't you come to Millbrook when I asked you to?"

"I didn't need rescuing then."

When I'd met him at an art gallery opening in early June, I'd taken LSD alone earlier in the day. I was wonderfully happy, happy to be solitary, completely within myself, peaceful yet exhilarated. A sweet sensation. That evening Tim spoke of psychedelic art and the techniques of "audio-olfactory-visual alterations of consciousness." He was didactic, oracular, self-aggrandizing, and very amusing. Afterward we walked to the corner for a drink.

"You remind me of someone I once loved."

"Let's see." I took from my pocket the small pane of two-way mirror an artist had given me, held it up between us. "My hair and your smile. My nose and your eyes. What do you see?"

"Good match." He lit a cigarette.

"Perhaps." I lifted my glass to him.

He was exhilarating, like the first draft of pure oxygen after a trip in the dentist's chair. There was the sense of having shared a most profound experience with him in some unremembered time. But I had to decline his invitation to Millbrook that weekend. He was married to a beautiful, blonde, highly paid model.[3] And I'd found an eager musician.

Now escaping that fell love and a summer of sadness, I was on my way to Millbrook with Tim, rather than to California where I felt I ought to be. I wondered about the state of his marriage.

"How is your lady?"

"Which one?"

---

3. Nena von Schlebrügge. See note on page 71.

"You've more than one then?"

"Had, alas, those pleasures are now forbidden."

"Will I find them in the attic behind a secret door?"

"Actually she's with a Tibetan monk, of the second I rarely speak."[4]

"And the first?"

"She killed herself on my 35th birthday."[5]

"Poor soul, how, why?"

"Our car, a locked garage, carbon monoxide, I was asleep." Blue eyes smiled companionably.

"Now, what would you like?" he asked me.

"Sensual enjoyment and mental excitement."

"What else?" I looked at him, handsome profile, strong hands on the wheel. Keen, flame-colored eyes, a man once dark, now silver-haired and fair. "To love. You, I suppose."[6]

Last spring he'd smiled over my first gift, some woodruff-flavored May wine.[7] I thought he was kind. When we walked in the woods he showed me where he'd thrown his wedding ring into the pond, where a man had drowned. Last year's leaves were brown under the shallow waters. I thought he was lonely.

Full moon in Aquarius, August midnight.[8] We turned through the gates, across the bridge, under a tunnel of trees.[9] The windows of

---

4. The monk was Robert Thurman (born 1941), a very distinguished Tibetan Buddhist scholar and still at this writing (2019) a Columbia professor of Indo-Tibetan Buddhist Studies. Buddhist monks are not bound by lifelong vows; Nena von Schlebrügge married him in 1967. Timothy's second wife was Mary Della Cioppa—they were married briefly in the mid-1950s. (Robert Greenfield, *Timothy Leary: A Biography,* New York: Houghton Mifflin Harcourt, 2006, 88–97).

5. Marianne Busch Leary, mother of Timothy's children Susan and Jack. She died on October 22, 1955.

6. Other versions have, "To love you, I suppose." Not quite the same thing.

7. Woodruff, *Asperula odorata,* is a fragrant plant sometimes used to flavor food and wine. In another version Rosemary identifies this exchange as happening on her "third visit to Millbrook in the spring of 1965." Perhaps this would read better with a comma: her third visit to Millbrook, in the spring of 1965.

8. The moon was full on August 12–13, 1965.

9. This and other features of the Millbrook estate become clearer after consulting the map on page 26.

the large white house were lit with red and blue, a castle with towers surrounded by countless acres of woods, lakes, gardens, and ruins. All the elements of myth and fancy were here and the master of it all, in a courtly way, opened the door. He led me up to the tower room. With a slow smile he left, descending the narrow stairs.

I woke to a soft summer day, sucking sweet white hoya blossoms from the window vine, forgetting my vow of solitude, remembering last night's long, slow waves of his desire that came hurtling up the stairs. I had felt him all through the night, footsteps pounding the maze of corridors, bare feet echoing the final rounds. My dreams were of a restless man in scarlet robes in the chamber below. I wanted to know him if I could; he seemed wise.

It was a seminar weekend at Millbrook, Gurdjieff's techniques were the theme.[10] The house was full of guests signed on for two days of lectures, light shows, "theories of expanding awareness," the brochure said. There was also a television crew. I didn't want to be in the movie, self-conscious about how I would look with a black eye in a not-too-favorable documentary. In the afternoon Tim swiveled in the office chair, tossing metaphors to listeners at his feet.

"You lose your mind to use your head," he explained with a smile.

"How often do you coin such . . ." He stopped me with a look. How could I question him? I was the apprentice.

In the early evening, with two dogs walking near us, we paced the carriage drive through the overhanging maples to the gatehouse at the edge of the property. The medieval bell tower of the gatehouse was the residence of a wise mother of five, and an extraordinary musician—Flo and Maynard Ferguson.[11] I'd met them at Millbrook before and liked them immensely. Flo's humor and grace, and Maynard's good nature and deserved reputation as one of the few consistently successful band leaders, lent gaiety and glamour to the small community of Millbrook. We shared a bottle of wine and laughter with them and

---

10. Techniques for developing consciousness.

11. Maynard Ferguson (1928–2006) was a trumpeter and band leader; he, his wife Flo, and their children were early and longtime residents of Millbrook.

then decided, reluctantly, that we had to return to the main house for the evening lecture. We stopped when we came to the small watch tower on the bridge to look out over the stillness of the lake. We kissed, hesitant at first, then knowingly, a sweet kiss, a promise. I wouldn't go to California.

The southwest room was a theater for the guests on Saturday night. Michael Hollingshead fed slides to the projectors while Ralph Metzner played musical tapes.[12] Cross-legged on a rug before the baronial fireplace, Tim commanded the room's attention, directing guests and staff ranged around the walls. We all played parts. This was the plot: a spaceship, far from home, the oxygen was almost gone. With only five minutes to live, what would be the message home?

Some made jokes, a few confessed their sins. Most spoke of love and family, then it was time for Captain Tim. He cleared his throat. Then the fuses blew and the lights went out. The microphone was dead. Our five minutes of oxygen were up before Tim got to send his message home.

"We need some light here," he said testily. But everyone was too spaced to move.

I crossed the room and settled at his side. I had the sense of having made a perilous journey. Maynard and Flo made a welcoming gesture, arranging pillows so I could be near. I felt love and a desire to dedicate myself, also a bit of pride that I'd safely navigated the large room while feeling the effects of LSD in the wine.

"Did you bring a candle?"

"No, but here's a match."

Then there was light from outside, Michael Hollingshead, whose fitful sense of humor could only be described as weird, was in a kilt with a strobe light flashing while he did leaps and flings on the trampoline. A startling sight and a fitting end to the disrupted lecture.

---

12. Michael Hollingshead (1931–1984?) was an English researcher who worked with Leary and Metzner on some of the Harvard projects. He was an early propagator of LSD and introduced Timothy to it in 1961.

Gate of the soft mystery
Constantly enduring
Gate of the soft mystery.
Use her gently
And without the touch of pain.[13]

I was in bed before an open window and a midnight sky puzzling over Tim's alterations of Lao-tse when he came into the tower room. I pointed to his poems scattered over the bed.

"Why a 'touch of pain,' and what do you mean 'lose your mind?'"

"I'll tell you a story." He blew out the light. "Once there were three princes; their father, the king, sent them on a quest. To answer the riddle of what every woman wants would prove which prince was the best." His voice caressed me softly. I felt it slide across my skin; I felt it so intently, I almost missed the end.

". . . and this is what the witch replied: Complete submission is the answer to a woman's pride."

I wondered—his surrender to the moment seemed so much more complete than mine. But pleasure was promised by his hand, voice, mind.

We painted crossed triangles on the chimney, put a gilded Buddha in a niche, restored a glass ruby to a plaster lion's eye, then had our first LSD session together. He brought all his experience of lamas coughing deep in the Himalayas and a few other tapes. Dylan was the familiar friend he couldn't hear, though I sang in his ear *all I really want to dooo, is baby be friends with you* . . .[14]

The Hitchcock estate, set on 2,500 acres in the county of Dutchess, New York, had been created by a man named Dieterich, who was

---

13. From a "III–11: Gate of the Soft Mystery" in Leary's *Psychedelic Prayers*, 23. See note on page 8. The full text of *Psychedelic Prayers* is archived at perma.cc/8pa6-hmx6.

14. From Bob Dylan's 1964 song "All I Really Want to Do." Timothy was hard of hearing due to overexposure to artillery fire during military training in the army in 1944 (Robert Greenfield, *Timothy Leary: A Biography,* New York: Houghton Mifflin Harcourt, 2006, 63).

reportedly a Rosicrucian.[15] The main house was called Der Alte Haus,[16] a Swiss chalet with a gymnasium and a bowling alley, cellars below a vast fieldstone terrace, a hothouse, and gardens. Thirty-foot walls throughout the estate, a medieval fortress of a barn, a rustic woodsman's shack. A tennis house, rose arbors, a spruce grove.

A road with a canopy of maple trees led to the estate, beyond the medieval bell tower and gatehouse where Flo and Maynard reigned, across the bridge spanning the lake below the waterfall, toward the turreted wings and sixty-four rooms of the main house, with its copper roof and bronze lightning rods strung with Tibetan flags. Rolling meadows, dark forests, hidden streams, and a forgotten lake deep in the back acreage where loons cried at midnight and the swamp gases rose and danced.[17]

Millbrook is the name of the village. The main street began at the gate of the Dieterich estate—it had a library, post office, white steeples, granite buildings meant to last, a haberdashery with riding togs, a dinette silver-sleek in front of the only bus stop. The village population were the descendants of the stonemasons and workers Dieterich imported to build the walls and the castellated buildings. The Hitchcock Cattle Corporation leased the vast acreage for ninety-nine years—we thought we'd be there at least that long.[18] Millbrook meant the enchanted kingdom.

The village had a sparseness about it, as though it had been settled

---

15. Dutchess County is three counties north of New York City on the east shore of the Hudson River. Millbrook is about ninety miles north of Manhattan. Charles F. Dieterich (1836–1927), born in Germany, made a fortune in acetylene gas (once used for lighting and still used for welding), and was one of the founders of the Union Carbide Corporation. He originally called his estate Daheim (German for "at home"). The structures Rosemary describes were designed by the architect Addison Mizner in 1912. The Rosicrucians are spiritual aspirants of a mystical type—the main American branch (Ancient Mystical Order Rosae Crucis) was founded in 1915, on the pattern of earlier societies in Europe.

16. German for "the old house."

17. I have had to reconstruct this paragraph.

18. At this writing (2019), the Hitchcock Cattle Corporation still exists, based in Millbrook, New York, but it is not clear whether it is still in the cattle business.

and then preserved for the future. The houses were few, set back from the street, private, lacking the closeness of early settlements with additions through the centuries. No neon, even the dinette presented a modest exterior, a silver oblong of windows like a temporarily stranded Super Chief dining car.[19] The supermarket was tucked away out of sight around a corner—it wasn't actually a supermarket but rather an extended specialty shop. The S. S. Pierce gourmet section extended the length of the store,[20] venison and quail were sold in the meat department, it had out of season artichokes and strawberries. Charge accounts were allowed and we were never dunned for the bill.

The Hitchcocks and friends were in residence at the bungalow, a perfect F. Scott Fitzgerald manor house complete with tennis court, swimming pool, billiard room, palazzo entry with fountain, and a Scottish serving couple, Jack and Mary. Billy Hitchcock's twin brother, Tommy, and his wife, Susan, returned from their honeymoon; Peggy was with her soon-to-be ex-husband, a society doctor.[21] Van Wolf was there as always. So was "Champagne Charlie," Billy's good friend and lawyer, and Darlene.[22]

After a rather plain dinner elaborately served, we adjourned to the

---

19. The Super Chief was a luxurious train running scheduled service between Chicago and Los Angeles from 1937 to 1971. It was the flagship train of the Santa Fe Line (Atchison, Topeka and Santa Fe Railway).

20. S. S. Pierce was a Boston grocer known for serving a luxury trade.

21. The Hitchcocks were members of the Mellon banking family. Peggy was Margaret Mellon Hitchcock. Bill Haines said that "[s]he 'married the good doctor on the rebound when Tim latched on to Rosemary'" (Art Kleps, *Millbrook: A Narrative of the Early Years of American Psychedelianism*, Burlington, Vt.: Neo-American Church, 1975, 121). Shortly thereafter Peggy married Walter Bowart (1939–2007), founder in 1967 of the *East Village Other*, whom she met through Timothy.

22. Van Wolf was a friend of Peggy Hitchcock's who introduced her to Timothy (Robert Greenfield, *Timothy Leary: A Biography*, New York: Houghton Mifflin Harcourt, 2006, 169). Darlene deSedle was a fashion editor at *Mademoiselle* and had been present at Timothy's Millbrook wedding to Nena von Schlebrügge (Robert Greenfield, *Timothy Leary: A Biography*, New York: Houghton Mifflin Harcourt, 2006, 217, 223–24). "Champagne Charlie" Rumsey was an early advocate and propagator of LSD. He was one of Timothy's lawyers in the constitutional case arising from the Laredo arrest (see page 43). The nickname "Champagne Charlie" was not original to him, but goes back at least to a popular nineteenth-century English music hall song.

living room where eight crystal champagne glasses with bits of paper stuck to the bottom stood on a table behind the sofa. Billy dismissed Mary and Jack and their offer of after-dinner demitasse and told them they'd not be needed. Tommy filled the glasses from a decanter and after looking at the bits of paper on the glasses handed them round.

Aurora declined and wished us a good night. Lou, Peggy's husband, refused the glass—he hadn't quite decided to risk taking a trip.

"What is the dosage, Tommy?" I asked.

"It's an experiment, try to guess," he replied.

I sat close to Tim and we held hands till I felt his hand grow lax and cold in mine. I felt his presence leave. I looked to the others. Billy was very much the Lord and Master standing before the fireplace under the large oil painting of a distant ancestor. He'd just returned from grouse shooting in Scotland. How very different the pursuits of the rich, I thought. Darlene was languorous on the bearskin rug at Billy's feet before the fire. Charlie had a silly, schoolboy prankster's look. Peggy was vibrant, moving about the room adjusting the lights. The conversations the others were having seemed just out of reach.

Back at the big house we settled in front of the fire. It was peaceful for only a moment. Tambimuttu joined us, resplendent in his Ceylonese clothes. His brown wizened elfin face became vulturelike when he had too much to drink. He'd come to read his poems.

> *Oh my family*
> *Oh my family*
> *Thorny as a rose*
> *Tied up in a pose.*

It was one of his lighter works. His epic work, an iconography of Hindu deities, ran to thousands of pages.[23]

---

23. Meary James Thurairajah Tambimuttu (1915–1983) was a Tamil poet and publisher from Ceylon (now Sri Lanka). He did sometimes publish under the single name Tambimuttu. But Worldcat does not list any published work of Tambimuttu's fitting this description. Perhaps it was published, if at all, only in Tamil.

League members entered the room rather ceremoniously it seemed to my enhanced eye. Everyone seemed to be costumed in some variation of medieval court dress, and they bowed to Tim as they entered the room. There seemed to be a Steinberg cartoon miasma in the air balloon above our heads with a pencil drawing dialogue.[24] Tambi's was in Sanskrit, Tim's was in Celtic runes, Bhavani's in greeting-card English.

Tim was beaming, from the ineffectual wizard dismissed from the emperor's court he'd become a radiant king, happily accepting homage. Then we were alone again and playing our particular games suggested by a gesture, a posture, reading one another's minds, laughing telepathically. He became a movie star, a French noble, a war veteran.

The seminars finished, we went on the road with weekend workshops. A caravan of cars full of equipment, Don Snyder, Michael, Ralph, Tim, and me.[25] We took over hotel rooms or donated apartments, covered the walls with paisley Indian cloth, set up projectors and lights, conducted twenty or more people on daily tours through their nervous systems and ours. Eighty-year-old Vedantists, Reichians, Wiccans, Episcopalians, Amway salesmen, mystic housewives, wistful thinkers, a broad spectrum of occultists seeking epiphany.[26]

> The aim is to produce a psychedelic or ecstatic experience without using drugs. The methods involve an intense ten-hour inundation of programmed stimuli . . . sensory, emotional and intellectual, artistic, philosophical . . . which reproduce and induce the LSD experience.[27]

---

24. Saul Steinberg (1914–1999) was a cartoonist for the *New Yorker* magazine whose elaborate drawings often looked just like this.

25. Don Snyder (1934–2010) was an experimental photographer. His book *Aquarian Odyssey: A Photographic Trip into the Sixties* (1979) contained many photographs of Timothy and his circle at Millbrook.

26. Amway is an enormous pyramid-shaped multilevel marketing company. It is not clear whether Rosemary has actual Amway salesmen in mind or is just using the term as a shorthand for *square*.

27. From an original program "Psychedelic Sessions. Timothy Leary and Ralph Metzner. Fall and Winter 1965–66" (Horowitz L10). Quoted in Robert Forte, ed., *Timothy Leary: Outside Looking In* (1999), and in the 2016 catalogue of Leary ephemera published by bookseller Brian Cassidy (No. 11, p. 23), archived at perma.cc/v5uv-gxjf.

Ralph read relaxation rituals in measured monotone. Then Tim explained his theories of consciousness expansion—the need to "go out of your mind to use your head."

You have to pass beyond everything you have learned in order to become acquainted with the new areas of consciousness.[28]

I sat behind a projector, sliding high colors on the walls, listening to his voice gliding down long acid-red tunnels. Mesmerized, murmuring his poems with him.

Can you float through the universe of your body and not lose your way? Lose all, fusing?[29]

His voice was the thread I was attached to. Not the timbre but the tone of genial warmth and wealth of wit. The element of persuasiveness was faith amplified to public certainty of a chemically induced divinity and Irish charm gifted with the magic of the word. The word become flesh.[30]

Dear Mother,

I will write at length later. I wanted to send you a photograph and some literature concerning the foundation and assure you again of my happiness and good health. I am living on a beautiful estate with friends and I have never before enjoyed my life as much as I do now. Please write to me c/o Leary, Castalia Foundation, Millbrook, N.Y.

LOVE

---

28. From a Castalia Foundation brochure advertising workshops at Millbrook (Horowitz L10). Quoted in Jay Stevens, *Storming Heaven: LSD and the American Dream* (New York: Grove Press, 1987), 262.

29. The first line is from "V–1: The Eliminative Cakra," in Leary's *Psychedelic Prayers,* page 28. The second line is from "V–2: The Sex Cakra," *Psychedelic Prayers,* at page 30. A cakra, usually spelled *chakra* in English, is in the Indian conception of the body, one of the seven nodes of energy ranged along the spine from the coccyx to the crown of the head, each governing a different physical and spiritual aspect.

30. "And the Word was made flesh, and dwelt among us, and we beheld his glory . . . full of grace and truth." John 1:14.

The weekend workshops were finished by mid-December 1965. Michael Hollingshead left to turn on England, Ralph Metzner rented my apartment in the city, Richard Alpert went west with the Grateful Dead, Don went back to New York to teach. All other residents were banished. It was a curious dispersal of old friends—some had been with Tim since the Harvard experiments in 1961. Only one had a word of warning: *He'll use you as a sexual symbol.* I had no idea what was meant.

I thought Tim an unsung genius. In the months we were together I realized he perceived the world with the knowledge that psychology gave him and the unfettered imagination of an Irish hero, a combination that produced a fey charisma, a likable madness, an outrageous optimism. The magic of loving and being loved by such a man would keep me enthralled for many years. I could not imagine loving anyone else. Everyone was boring compared to him.[31]

He asked me to marry him. I said yes. But we would have to wait for his divorce. With his daughter Susan, we went to New York City to bring my furniture and belongings to Millbrook.

Ninth Street off Fifth Avenue in the Village had been my address for several years. The large room with high ceilings and fireplace had been a refuge and a solace. I never thought to leave it; my only ambition had been to acquire the apartment next door and have that rarity, a floor-through flat. Everything in it had memory and meaning and I was proud and comfortable in my own environment. I wondered if I'd be the same in the many-roomed mansion at Millbrook.

Tim and Susan were sitting on the window seat. He turned to Susan.

"Who does Rosemary remind you of?"

I stopped packing. For the first time it seemed Susan was really looking at me. Her manner in the few times she'd been home from boarding school had been distinctly disinterested, but not unfriendly.

---

31. Another version of this chapter characterizes this assessment as a summation of Rosemary's feelings after five months with Tim and places it at the end of the chapter. It seems to fit better here.

"Who?" Susan demanded.

"Marianne."

Susan's response was unexpected. Her face, usually on the verge of perfect beauty, had become a mask of dislike.

Mary Anne? Was that her mother's name? Tim's first wife who'd killed herself—Susan had been a child then. But there was a brief second marriage to someone named Mary.[32] Tim had said she was thoughtless about the children. Who was he saying I resembled?

The cool, marble bathroom was a retreat from unfriendly scrutiny. Tim entered and stood next to me before the mirror.

"Well, how would you like to spend eternity?"

"Not looking in a mirror, or being swatted on the rear by a book" (as he was doing to me then).

"It's not so bad, a little love tap now and then." He was holding Burton's *Hashish Tales* from *The Arabian Nights*.[33]

"Is that the tale then?"

"Sure, if you keep the pipe lit."

"I much prefer mythic humor to Gothic terror. Am I to be a houri or a wicked stepmother?"[34]

"Empress, you can count on me." He offered his arm. "For all eternity?"[35]

The large Alice in Wonderland mirror from every apartment and loft move in Manhattan was left with a neighbor, as it was too big for the small van. But books, records, speakers, antiques, a Persian rug, my clothes were packed and carried below.

Susan returned to school. We were three in the huge echoing house: Jack Leary, Tim's sixteen-year-old son, handsome as the prince of any

---

32. As noted, Timothy's first wife (Susan's mother) was Marianne Busch, and his second wife was Mary Della Cioppa.

33. "The Tale of the Hashish Eater" was one of the stories in the famous translation by the British explorer and orientalist Sir Richard Francis Burton (1821–1890). Burton's translation was actually called *The Book of a Thousand Nights and a Night* (1885).

34. Houris in Islamic imagination are the companions of the faithful in paradise.

35. The Empress is trump number three in the tarot, denoting biological, intellectual, and spiritual fertility.

fairy tale, and Timothy and I. I grew to love them in that brief, quiet time, a space between the wars, long walks through the estate with the dogs, starry, moony nights.

In our room on the third floor we would have dinner before a fire. After Jack left to do his homework, Tim talked and paced the room and I watched him—he was so graceful, so likable. When he reached a point, he would turn and grin at me with pleasure. He reshaped the world according to his momentary vision, which surrounded me like a bower, all flowers and laughing children.

More flattering still was the assumption that I shared his views, understood his aims, appreciated his wit. Instructing, bragging, flattering, and charming, what he said didn't seem important. What was important was the response he drew from me. I felt clever, graceful, chosen, and that I'd met my match. Besides, he needed me for the happiness no one else had or could ever give him—the possibility, he said, of perfect love.[36]

Then he would listen to my tales, his eyes never leaving my face. Embraces of the eye and mind encouraged me to humor, making light of marriages, miscarriages, and mishaps of all the years before him.[37]

Uptown, downtown, nightclubs, hard-hearted owners, the decline of jazz, society gigs, waiting for the union check, paying dues, blues, brief flush of success, California, Hollywood movies . . . New York again . . . ran away with a man twice my age, a composer of classical music. Silver-haired Southern madman, wrote symphonies all week, got drunk and lost on weekends.[38] He turned me on to peyote and real poverty on the Lower East Side before it was fashionable or even Puerto Rican, all orthodox Jews and Ukrainians . . . more jazz . . . Thank God I never got onto junk . . .

---

36. Another version has "we said" instead of "he said," which is not the same thing. Also, in other versions Rosemary says the "zenith of happiness" or the "gambit of happiness," neither of which matches the sense of the passage.

37. Another version adds a comma after "mishaps," which alters the sense.

38. Charles Mills.

When all the tales I cared to tell were told, the past was banished.[39] Our lovemaking had a new depth of meaning. He wanted me to have his child.[40] My mental hero, I loved him.

It snowed for days, covering the hills and trees, adding height to the pillars before the garden, a pristine blanket of renewal. We dreamed of sun, warm sand, clear waters, a Christmas trip. The travel folders called Yucatan, Mexico, a land of hemp and honey.[41] Jack, Susan, and someone Tim would select to help with the driving would go with us.

December 12, 1965
Millbrook

Dear Family,

A week from today, Tim, Susan, Jackie and I will start for Mexico, with a boy named Rene as a companion for the kids. We'll all take turns driving a new Ford station wagon. We plan to go to Merida, Yucatan, and find a quiet place to stay for a few months. We should be back in Millbrook by the end of March. The house will need a lot of work to get it ready for our summer seminars.

My life is serene. The country is beautiful at all times. I enjoy even the cold and rainy days.[42] I take long walks accompanied by large dogs named Fang and Obie. We walk all over the estate, they've shown me the deer graveyard full of antlers and where they go to catch rabbits. I know and love this land so well.

There are lots of visitors on weekends. We had thirty people here for Thanksgiving. I cooked two turkeys, a ham and a haunch of venison. During the week I try to get the house in order and read and walk with Tim. Susan is away at school and in all these rooms there are just Tim, Jackie, me and two dogs, four cats.

---

39. Other versions have, "Then all the tales I cared to tell were told."
40. Another version has, "We wanted to have a child," which is not the same thing.
41. "I am come down to deliver them out of the hand of the Egyptians, and to bring them up out of that land unto a good land and a large, unto a land flowing with milk and honey." Exodus 3:8.
42. Another version has "rainy nights."

I'm really excited about the trip to Mexico. I'll send you postcards along the way.

LOVE

It was a long, lazy drive to Nuevo Laredo in a car loaded with family vacation gear—sun hats, scuba tanks, and flippers. Escaping the cold, snow-covered hills of the estate and all the responsibilities of a huge house and heating bills, we took the Southern route through New Orleans, across the Louisiana swampland to the big open skies of Texas. Susan, just home from school, found her spot next to her dad in the back where Tim and I had planned to rest together on a paisley-covered mattress. So Jackie and I were in the front singing Dylan songs while he drove. He knew all the lyrics. In with my sewing basket among the embroidery thread was an egg-shaped silver box containing our cannabis. I rolled while Jackie drove.

Ain't gonna work on Maggie's faaarm no more . . .[43]

We crossed the U.S. border at Laredo into Mexico headed toward matrimonial hammocks, palm trees, and warm beaches. A bit of shame waited there.

"Señor Tim."

A familiar face and uniform greeted Tim on the Mexican side of the border. Strangely, it was the same police agent[44] who'd escorted him to the plane in Mexico City two years before when the Mexican government expelled Tim and his group, the International Federation for Internal Freedom. We were forbidden to enter, had to go back to the American side. Mexico City would be consulted; perhaps we could cross the next day if all was in order, the agent said. We walked the few yards to our luggage-crowded car. It was surrounded by Mexican police, idle, sunning themselves perhaps. I got in the back and hurriedly looked through our packed gear. Tim started the motor. I asked him to wait but he didn't hear.

---

43. From Bob Dylan's 1965 song "Maggie's Farm."
44. Another version reads "secret police operative."

I found what I was looking for and tried to open the window but it was blocked by clothes and books. I turned to Rene and asked him to open his window, but he was frozen in fear. We were a few hundred yards from American customs.

"Jackie, shake this out of the window." I handed the silver egg-shaped snuff box up to the front seat and searched the floor frantically for rolling papers and seeds. Tim asked if everything was all right, we were almost there. Again I told him to wait, but he didn't hear. Quietly, Susan said she'd hidden the silver egg.

Customs agents approached the car. "Do you have anything to declare?" Tim said we hadn't even left the country, but they'd seen us coming and going and knew we hadn't been anywhere. They looked through our luggage and food, found nothing illegal. Then we were stripped, searched; hair, ears, even ass. Even sixteen-year-old Jack and eighteen-year-old Susan.

Susan was last: charged with evasion of taxes, smuggling, transporting.[45] We were jailed in Laredo, Texas, for less than half a lid of very weak grass in Susan's clothes. There wasn't time for Jackie to throw it out the window, and Susan had taken it from him to hide.

"Laredo Jail, isn't there a song about this place?" Susan stopped her ballet exercises at the cell door.

This was the first time Susan and I had had a moment together since she got back from boarding school. Because of her unusual life with Tim, she had learned to mask her feelings in all sorts of odd situations. I didn't really know Susan. I thought we'd get to know each other on the beach in Yucatan, not in a jail cell in Laredo with metal cots. I stood at the barred window looking out. I couldn't remember the song.[46] I had only one association with the place.

"I almost married someone who was jailed here."

"Why was he here?" Susan asked.

---

45. The tax charge was for not paying the eccentrically spelled Marihuana Tax, whose constitutionality Timothy challenged in court and eventually won, see *Leary v. United States*, 395 U.S. 6 (1969).

46. Rosemary probably means "The Streets of Laredo," a traditional cowboy lament.

"He and a friend crossed with some grass in the trunk of a car. I hadn't wanted him to and told him it looked just like a false bottom, but he wouldn't listen. I had to raise the money to bail him out." Susan looked at me oddly.

"Kenneth was really a wonderful person. He introduced me to Kate and she turned me on. Through Kate and Allen I met Tim and here I am in jail in Laredo. Funny isn't it?"

But I was talking to myself. Susan was back at the cell door doing pliés.[47]

Bailed out, we arrived back at Millbrook on Christmas Day. We were not a happy family. Susan told Tim it was my fault, that my karma had put us in jail in Laredo. He did not disagree—nor finally, did I.[48]

January 20, 1966

Dear Mother,

I've put off writing till I could give you some news about what is happening in Texas. The government will not press charges against Jackie, me or the friend who was with us. They are going to indict Tim and Susan on charges of smuggling, transportation and evasion of tax payments. The lawyers believe Susan will be let off as a juvenile offender, but because of Tim's prominence they might wish to make an example of him. It is going to be a tough and interesting case as Tim plans to fight the charges on the unconstitutionality of laws governing possession and use of marijuana. It is well known, medically documented that marijuana is not a narcotic, does not turn people into dope fiends, doesn't lead to the use of heroin, is not toxic (unlike alcohol) but the government does not recognize this. This will be (I believe) the first time it will be fought in the federal courts.

The alternative is for Tim to make a deal with the government, plead guilty to the tax law and face a possible sentence of one to five years, be branded a felon and lose his civil rights. It is going to be a cruel fight—

---

47. A ballet movement: bending the knees with the body straight.
48. Another version reads "nor, finally, perhaps because of my early hard-shell Baptist upbringing, did I."

costly, time-consuming and awesome to be actually pitted against the laws of this country.

When I learned that I was not going to be tried I felt no relief. Tim's facing a prison sentence and Susan's situation weighs on my heart—she is just eighteen. She laughed when the Commissioner called Tim a bad father.[49] He has brought up Jackie and Susan to be loving and reasonable beings and he has had to do it all alone. I want to do everything I can to help them.

Meanwhile, Susan has gone back to school to confront her schoolmates, Jackie returned to Millbrook High and his daily torments there, Tim is busy with the defense fund in N.Y. I wake early, ice skate on the pond, cook three meals a day and give the house a lick and a promise, dreaming of how beautiful it would look if I had a hundred gallons of paint. Sometimes, late at night, in the kitchen, the waterpipes play at being ghosts of lost pleasure and weeping. Please write soon and let me know how you all are.

LOVE

The trial took place in February. I waited by the phone for word of the results. Tim called once to ask if he might say I'd given him the marijuana, as he would be charged with contempt of court if he refused to answer. I said yes—there was no question of implicating the friend whose gift was greatly exaggerated evidence in the trial.[50]

The next time the phone rang it was a newspaper reporter wanting to know how I felt about the sentence Dr. Leary had received. "Patently absurd," was my answer. Tim was sentenced to thirty years and a $40,000 fine. Susan, who had never smoked marijuana, was placed on probation. But also absurd was our part in this comedy of errors—taking grass *to Mexico.*

I thought I was responsible for the loss of a life free of courtrooms

---

49. United States Commissioners such as Tim and Susan appeared before have now been replaced by United States magistrate judges.
50. In another version of this chapter Rosemary wrote instead, "And there was a second call saying he had to name the friend whose gift was, greatly exaggerated, evidence in the trial."

and prisons and for the lessening of love between us all. The pain of the responsibility would keep me in thrall for many years.

No more quiet walks on moony nights. He was busy with lawyers, press conferences, marshalling an impressive array of people to head the Timothy Leary Defense Fund. He spent more time at the office of the Defense Fund than at Millbrook, and the weekends were taken up by lawyers and the curious. I tried to remember that he was doing what he had to do, fighting the government, answering his critics, testifying to his revelations and to his certainty that LSD was the tool mankind needed to be free.

FRAGMENT

> ❦
>
> **Editor's Note**
>
> There seems no place to put this in chapter 2 that does not break the narrative or repeat part of it, but it does not seem right to omit it either, so I add it here as a fragment.

When we were first arrested I knew that we had all shared in the structure of the event.[51] Tim, suggesting that we take some marijuana on the trip, asked me to ask a mutual friend to get some, then gave me the snuff box to put it in and expected me to carry it. Susan, sleeping through most of the trip with Tim in the back of the station wagon, had not smoked. But Jackie wanted to smoke, and I cleaned the grass and dropped some seeds. But they needn't have been found if Tim had realized that we could have spent the night in Nuevo Laredo.[52] Perhaps the phone at Millbrook was tapped—maybe "they" knew we'd be in

---

51. Another version has "matrix destiny" instead of structure.
52. It is unclear how they could have spent the night in Nuevo Laredo, as that is in Mexico, and they were refused entry into Mexico. Maybe Rosemary meant Laredo, Texas.

Laredo, and that's why the Mexican secret service agent was waiting for us across the border.[53] Rene was innocent, but he looked like a hippie with his beard and knapsack. He wasn't aware that I was trying to open the window. Then Tim drove back over the bridge—and Jackie let Susan hide the grass that I handed to him.

---

53. Not the United States Secret Service. Again Rosemary suggests that the Mexican official was a secret police agent. If so, he wasn't all that secret.

THREE

Scarlet Woman

One knows that madness is contagious but the mad are particularly dangerous when they are amiable and sympathetic. One enters little by little into their circle of ideas, one ends by understanding their exaggerations while partaking of their enthusiasms, one grows accustomed to their logic that has lost its way, one ends by finding that they are not as mad as one thought at first. Thence to believing that they alone are right there is but one step. One approves of them, one is as mad as they are.

ÉLIPHAS LÉVI, *THE KEY OF THE MYSTERIES*[1]

I am defending the right of every American citizen to lead the religious life of his own conviction, to worship, to experience, to commune with universal forces, to transcend his ego and dissolve the petty differences that divide men whom love should bind, to seek religious ecstasy, revelation and truth as men have done throughout the ages.

TIMOTHY LEARY,
TIMOTHY LEARY DEFENSE FUND BROCHURE[2]

---

1. Éliphas Lévi (Alphonse Louis Constant) (1810–1875) was a French socialist and writer on magic and occult subjects. His book *The Key to the Great Mysteries* (1861) was one of several in which he defined a magical system. Lévi believed that an elite of initiates had the responsibility for the emancipation of the masses, which they would be unable to accomplish by themselves. Rosemary is quoting from Aleister Crowley's translation, called *The Key of the Mysteries,* published posthumously in 1959.
2. Probably the leaflet is the one listed as L16 in Horowitz's bibliography.

We planted the garden early at Millbrook, reseeding heavenly blue morning glories around the fence. Plans for a summer school were in progress. Each weekend the house was full with visitors from the city. There were fifteen or more staff members, guests, and reporters this particular April night. Tim, Jack, and I were in the bedroom smoking mint leaves and DMT when we heard a loud noise at the front entrance. Jack went to investigate; he came flying back, slammed the door.

"There are a bunch of hunters, men with guns, down there."

The sound of heavy booted feet echoed through the house, up the stairs, closer to our room. Tim confronted the closed door with clenched fists. I shoved the glass pipe and vial under the covers. The beaded curtain between the dressing room and bedroom was pushed aside, ten men entered the room. I thought they looked rather crestfallen finding a peaceful family scene rather than the orgy they'd surely been anticipating. They led Tim and Jack downstairs. Told not to move, I stayed in bed, watched by a nervous young trooper holding a spotlight.

I asked if he could move the light, it bothered my eyes. He turned, I checked the covers with my toes, assumed a more dignified position when three men with clipboards and frowns entered the room. Hurriedly they turned out closets and drawers, then called in a photographer to record the mess. A leather-jacketed snooper poked fingers into creams and lotions, sniffed my cologne. A second looked under the bed. The third dropped old birth control pills into an envelope, licked the flap.

"You can get up now and go downstairs with the others."

The dining room was usually lit by candles. Floodlights gave it a detective-story atmosphere, illuminating the old wall tapestries to which we had added emerald birds and amber fields in Day-Glo paint. In the midst of this baronial atmosphere seldom touched by evil sat Sheriff Quinlan of Dutchess County, interrogating the guests. Standing next to him was G. Gordon Liddy, a local prosecutor formerly with the FBI.[3] He'd been the first into our room, with a gun in his hand. I recognized

---

3. Lawrence M. Quinlan (1915–2003) was sheriff of Dutchess County from 1960 to 1978. G. Gordon Liddy (born 1930) was a prosecutor on the Dutchess County

him from his clenched-face newspaper photographs. In the local newspapers after our arrest in Laredo, he'd vowed to "crack down hard on drugs." A major conspirator in this evening's event, he whispered into the sheriff's ear.

Tim demanded that the phone be reconnected so he could call a lawyer. A deputy said it was the phone company's problem, not his. A trooper kept a gun trained on the peace-loving Great Dane who was asleep next to Michael Bowen when his room was broken into.[4] A beery invader tried to make friends with the Ferguson children he'd frightened awake. Their babysitter, Susie Blue, kept a protective arm around the children and a wary eye on him.

Two crying, outraged women were led into the room by a police matron. Marya Mannes and Helen Putnam had planned to interview the residents of Castalia for a national magazine. (Mannes, known as a social critic, had been a prosecution witness in one of Lenny Bruce's highly publicized trials.) Their room had been forcibly entered, they had been made to strip and their legs and arms were examined for needle marks. The sheriff asked another guest, a young woman, whether she'd had sexual intercourse that night.[5]

It was almost dawn before we were all catalogued and the housebreakers had made off with family photographs, books, bottles of wine, my favorite fuchsia plant.[6] The sheriff escorted Tim to a black car with a firm hand on his shoulder while his minions guarded the rest of us. Tim grinned and waved a handcuffed victory sign to the photographers

---

(cont. from p. 49) district attorney's staff; he was not (as some versions state) the district attorney, an elected post Liddy actually ran for after the raid but did not win. He is best known for his later role in the White House Plumbers gang responsible for the Watergate burglary. As noted, in 1973 he was sentenced to prison for conspiracy, burglary, and wiretapping. He served more than four years in prison until President Carter commuted his sentence.

4. Michael Bowen (1937–2009) was a Visionary painter and psychedelic pioneer. He was one of the prime organizers of the Human Be-In in San Francisco in 1967. In later years, as a devotee of the Hindu goddess Kali, he used the name Baba Kali Das Acharya.

5. Another version has a deputy ask this question.

6. Another version has "before Liddy and the Sheriff finished listing everyone and photographing everything."

assembled on the lawn. In an orderly procession Fords and Pontiacs drove down the long maple-shaded drive and out of sight. For the first time in many hours the house was quiet.

Downstairs, musicians were already composing songs about The Raid. I ran upstairs to the office, found the address book under a pile of papers, borrowed pockets full of change, an old Studebaker and a driver, and set off in pursuit of Tim and a telephone. An all-night diner near Poughkeepsie had the only phone available at that hour. We paused at the door; the diner was unusually crowded. Inside were the Officers of the Law, laughing, back-slapping, eating homemade apple pie. We continued northwest toward town. At the red brick jailhouse we woke the bloodhounds in the kennel. The man at the desk shouted above the clamor that he could tell me nothing, didn't know a thing. Back at the now-deserted diner I called Billy Hitchcock and the defense fund lawyer in New York.

"Millbrook was raided, they took Tim, I don't know how much the bail will be."

Control of Dangerous Drugs![7] Adultery! Maintaining a Public Nuisance! Nevertheless Tim was released on bail later in the day. Unscathed, good-humored, and unworried, he seemed almost to have enjoyed this new confrontation with the law. It was as if he thrived on the response of the press, the need for more lawyers and funds, the threat of trial and prison, the invitation to climb onto the cross, the myth of the tragic hero: a sweet dream of oppression. It was his movie.

We made frequent visits to the village to shop and check local reaction to the raid. Our trade was appreciated and our eccentricities tolerated. A few wanted to see us "driven out of Dutchess County." They exercised their fears giving interviews to the *New York Times*.

Hippies will rob and rape to get their filthy drugs, women won't be safe in their beds from the lust-filled, sex-crazed addicts.

A grand jury was convened to investigate the Castalia Foundation.

---

7. The law actually forbade "criminal possession of a controlled substance." The statute was classified among "Offenses against Public Health and Morals," now Title M of the New York Penal Law.

I was called as the first witness. Marriage might be one way of avoiding the jury, but Tim was still married. I thought he might adopt me if I could go to California but he didn't like the idea. My lawyer, the Poughkeepsie attorney Noel Tepper, said that I could face a five-year federal sentence for evading a grand jury. Tim decided on a Hindu religious defense. We had as much chance as Christians in Nero's Rome.[8]

DISTRICT ATTORNEY: This is an application by the district attorney in connection with the refusal of one Rosemary Woodruff to answer questions that were put to her in connection with an investigation by the Grand Jury into certain alleged violations of law. She was subpoenaed, she was asked one question, and she refused to answer upon the ground that it might incriminate her, whereupon the record will disclose that the Grand Jury conferred immunity upon her for any crime that might be disclosed by her testimony. She persisted in her refusal to answer.

THE COURT: I would just like to ask you, Miss Woodruff, that, after listening to the testimony by the District Attorney, I would like to ask you why you have not answered these questions.

MISS WOODRUFF: Your Honor, no discourtesy is intended to the members of the Grand Jury or the District Attorney, but I feel that I must refuse to answer any questions on the grounds that immunity in the Grand Jury is not protection against federal or possible other prosecution. My psychological and religious beliefs and those of my spiritual leaders are not the proper subject of any inquiry. There is a constitutional and common law privilege against being forced to testify as to my religious beliefs and perhaps, by asking me to testify against my friends, you're asking me to violate my religious and moral beliefs in violation of the First, Fifth, and Ninth Amendments of the United States, and article 1,

---

8. Another version has "which was as effective as a pagan defense would have been in Salem."

sections 3, 6, and 8 of the New York State Constitution. I believe that the scope of the inquiry is too broad and vague and wider than immunity granted, and I do not feel you have a moral and constitutional right to ask me about my spiritual and personal life. I submit to you that my silence goes out for the freedom that all Americans adhere to and is not meant discourteously whatsoever.

MR. TEPPER: Would you tell the Court the basis for your refusal to testify before the Grand Jury?

MISS WOODRUFF: I am a member of a group which uses practices and beliefs which are closely allied to . . .

THE COURT: Oh, you can speak louder than that. Pretend you're at some football game.

MISS WOODRUFF: Our beliefs and practices are closely allied to Hindu beliefs.

MR. TEPPER: And what is the nature of the Hindu beliefs and practices that you identify yourself with, the tenets of these beliefs?

MISS WOODRUFF: Well, there are many sects, but our aims and purposes are to increase our knowledge of ourselves, of nature, and of God.

THE COURT: I'll have to admonish you, Miss Woodruff, will you please speak up a little bit?

MISS WOODRUFF: I'm sorry, I have a sore throat.

THE COURT: Well, you and I both.

MR. TEPPER: And what are these aims and goals of the religion that you subscribe to?

MISS WOODRUFF: To increase and expand one's consciousness and to know the nature of God and the Universe.

MR. TEPPER: When you say expand one's consciousness, what do you mean?

MISS WOODRUFF: I mean essentially to know God, to know more of oneself and the world in which we live, other than the usual daily way of perceiving things.

THE COURT: What is the name of this religion what you're talking about if it has a name?

MISS WOODRUFF: Well, we have yet to name it.

THE COURT: It doesn't have a name?

MR. TEPPER: Your Honor, we are prepared to prove that a basic part of Miss Woodruff's religion is the concept of nonviolence by not hurting a fellow human being by either word or deed, and requiring her to testify in an incriminating manner about a fellow human being is in violation of her deep-rooted sincere religious convictions and beliefs and would form what is considered in the Western world as sin, and we are prepared to prove that the relationship between Miss Woodruff and members of the Castalia Foundation is a private, personal, religious, spiritual . . .

THE COURT: They are not the rules or laws of this State, are they, Mr. Tepper?

MR. TEPPER: Your honor, if I may . . .

THE COURT: These are the rules of Pakistan or India but they are not the rules of the State of New York, are they or not?

MR. TEPPER: We are talking about the Constitution of the United States and New York, Your Honor.

THE COURT: I understand that, but I also understand there was a sect years ago who believed in this and polygamy, and the United States Supreme Court ruled it out. Now I'm not going to permit you to go into this, I don't think it's relevant to the issue here.

MR. TEPPER: We are prepared to prove that as a tenet of this religion as well as that of most contemporary civilized religions that the use of psychedelics is harmless and not harmful in pursuit of religious beliefs, and there is no public interest in disallowing the same.

THE COURT: You're going to prove to me that the use of LSD drug is harmless, is that what you're going to prove to me? You're not going to prove it to this Court because that's not the issue; the only issue before this Court is whether or not the questions that were put forth to this witness were proper and in which she was granted immunity to the answers, and if she refuses to answer them I'm to hold her in contempt of Court.

MR. TEPPER: Miss Woodruff, what non-drug methods are used to expand consciousness in order to obtain relationship with your religion?

MISS WOODRUFF: There are many, the use of mandalas, mantras.

MR. TEPPER: Could you describe that for us?

MISS WOODRUFF: Mandalas are a centering device, they are instruments used for centering and focusing one's attention in order to go within. They can be used in meditation and contemplation.

MR. TEPPER: And how is this practiced?

MISS WOODRUFF: By viewing the center. This is but one of many devices. The mantra is the spoken word, the name of God repeated. The mudra is the placing of the hands or the body positioning for centering one's self and one's energy and locating the source of that energy.

MR. TEPPER: And what is the basis of this approach?

MISS WOODRUFF: The basis?

MR. TEPPER: Yes, where is it learned and where does it come from?

Miss Woodruff: It's prevalent in all Eastern religions, primarily in Hindu techniques, yoga and such.

Mr. Tepper: What are the religious tracts or holy writings or the writings which you feel to be holy that involve your religion, if any?

Miss Woodruff: Well, there are hundreds of books, the Bible is used, the gospels of Ramakrishna and the writings of Aldous Huxley, Dr. Leary and Dr. Metzner, which is a book called *Psychedelic Experience,* and most of the inspirational texts of Hindu and yogi textbooks. There are many and it's not confined to any one particular book.

Mr. Tepper: Does your religion or religious belief have priests or ministers?

Miss Woodruff: Spiritual leaders.

Mr. Tepper: Rosemary, why did you refuse to testify before the Grand Jury?

Miss Woodruff: One of the most basic tenets is the sacredness of the relationship between pupil and guru . . .

The Court: That's a Hindu word, Indian?

Miss Woodruff: Yes.

Mr. Tepper: Who or whom would be considered your guru?

Miss Woodruff: I consider Dr. Leary as such.

Mr. Tepper: Now aside from the relationship between the teacher and student, are there any other bases within your religion which require you to refuse to testify?

Miss Woodruff: That my religious and spiritual beliefs are private unto myself and not subject to questioning or probe.

Mr. Tepper: Now can I ask you this question: what harm might come if you do testify, what would be the effect of your testifying?

MISS WOODRUFF: Inadvertently I might say something that could cause harm to Dr. Leary and my coreligionists. I think I've already said the relationship between the pupil and the teacher is of a private nature and are not to be disclosed.

THE COURT: Somewhat of a confidential relationship?

MISS WOODRUFF: Yes.

THE COURT: Privileged communication, all right. Do you feel that if you did testify about your religious group would you be subject to persecution?

MISS WOODRUFF: Persecution of my own conscience.

THE COURT: No physical persecution? No violence?

MISS WOODRUFF: No.

THE COURT: Let me ask you one question. Would you still exert this privilege and refuse to testify if a homicide were committed at the Castalia Foundation as part of the religion? I don't mean that the religion advocates violence, but as a trance or something that took place while in one of these subconscious states, would you still refuse to testify?

MISS WOODRUFF: I'm sorry, Your Honor, but such a situation is impossible to imagine.

THE COURT: Why, Rosemary, why is it impossible to imagine?

MISS WOODRUFF: Murder?

THE COURT: Because you don't believe in murder, is that right; you don't believe in acts of violence?

MISS WOODRUFF: Or harm to any living thing.

THE COURT: Well, suppose an act of violence arose because of some substance might have been given to some particular individual or some transient, would you still refuse to testify if it incriminated your teacher whom you already testified to be Dr. Leary?

MISS WOODRUFF: You're asking me to envision an impossible situation.

THE COURT: No, would you still refuse to testify on the grounds that it is a part of your religion that you shall not what we normally use, tell tales or squeal or inform on your coreligionists? You use a different terminology than I do, but would you refuse to testify?

MISS WOODRUFF: Well, may I go back to your statement about an act of murder being performed while under a . . .

THE COURT: Well, let's make it an act of intercourse or an act of adultery.

MISS WOODRUFF: I refuse to testify about the private life or actions of anyone.

DISTRICT ATTORNEY: Now I'll ask you what other grounds you base your refusal to testify as to the questions asked by the Grand Jury.

MISS WOODRUFF: The right to privacy.

DISTRICT ATTORNEY: Whose right to privacy?

MISS WOODRUFF: My right to privacy.

DISTRICT ATTORNEY: Are there any other grounds upon which you base your refusal?

MISS WOODRUFF: The possibility of incriminating myself.

THE COURT: Are you a college graduate?

MISS WOODRUFF: No, I'm not.

THE COURT: She appears to be a very intelligent young lady.

DRUGS, MURDER, SEX! Lurid headlines. The judge was rubbing his hands, the district attorney's large expanse of exposed neck was brilliantly red, my attorney patted his forehead with a handkerchief; the spectators leaned forward on the benches. Liddy lurked in the dim recesses of the courtroom whispering to his aides. The steam radiator hissed. The sky darkened behind the grimy windows. I didn't like my role. I wanted genius and domesticity, cerebral excitement and serenity. I wanted to be a freedom fighter and a peacemaker, to destroy injustice and pacify. I needed the appreciation of my lover and the privacy of a cloister; to be lustful, ever pregnant yet a very nun for solitude and habit. But this part called for a hypnotized convert, the potential victim of a mad scientist; white gloves and a pillbox hat, a serious expression and modest demeanor. I was a lover, not a devotee.

I felt psychopathic as the district attorney honed me down to a thin wire of stubbornness. The judge was having such a good time he granted a continuation of the proceedings until Monday. After court, the lawyer and I went to meet Tim at the local steak house. We were in low spirits—I because of the insane situation I was in (a cognitive dissonance), he because his golf partner the D.A. scored so well on legal points.

We silently waited for our guru. He entered the restaurant, scanned the room with an expectant smile, then bounced over to the table in his tennis shoes. He was ebullient and refused to let our depression affect his enthusiasm.

"Don't you realize this is the first test of LSD in the courts?" His hands punctuated the importance of the moment; faces turned our way in recognition. "You're making legal, scientific, philosophical, political, religious history."

His delivery made it difficult to remember how well the prosecution scored. "This case could go on for years! Beginning right here in Poughkeepsie we could change the world. Our grandchildren will be proud of you." I could see the lawyer's spirit lifting.

"We'll ask Dr. Mishra to testify, Lama Govinda from India, we'll get Allen Ginsberg, peyote roadmen from New Mexico.[9] We'll fill the courtroom with chanters, Tibetan gongs, flowers, incense."

My counsel was enthusiastic. We finished dinner buoyed by wine and the great importance of the trial in the evolution of the species. I had been primed again to leave the future to chance, to leap into the fire to prove my devotion, to submit all to his desire.[10]

The next two days I made calls to witnesses available in New York. We couldn't afford to bring anyone from California, much less India. A few friends would act as character witnesses for me.

Kumar's lilting voice and charming manner had the court enthralled. For me the dialogue was reminiscent of a Marx brothers movie written by a disciple of Kafka.

MR. TEPPER: What is your name, sir?

MR. KUMAR: Kumar Kumar.

MR. TEPPER: What is your occupation sir?

MR. KUMAR: I'm teaching Hindu studies at Columbia University.

MR. TEPPER: And how long have you been doing this?

MR. KUMAR: Two years.

MR. TEPPER: What is the position of the guru to his followers in the Hindu religion?

MR. KUMAR: With relation to guru, it means "teacher" in English, you

---

9. Rammurti S. Mishra (1923–1993), also known as Shri Brahmananda Sarasvati, was an Indian medical doctor who emigrated to the United States in 1955. He wrote many books on yoga and ayurveda (classical Indian medicine) and in 1964 founded the Ananda Ashram in Monroe, New York, some of whose members migrated to Millbrook (see page 78). Lama Anagarika Govinda (1898–1985), originally from Germany, was a noted sage and scholar of Tibetan Buddhism. He is best remembered for his books *Foundations of Tibetan Mysticism* (London, 1957) and *The Way of the White Clouds* (London, 1966).
10. In the Ramayana, as Rosemary certainly knew, Sita leapt into a ritual fire to prove to her husband Rama that she had been chaste during her time as a prisoner of Ravana, the demon king.

don't get the same connotation, but guru is someone who gives you rebirth. That is someone who takes you out of ignorance and takes you to knowledge. And in that sense it is important, because it is a higher relationship than parents. So the relationship between a disciple and guru is very close, very sacred and private. You see, as you might know, we don't have any psychoanalysis or psychoanalysts. There are very few, so a guru is a philosopher, doctor, teacher, and it's a very private relationship.

MR. TEPPER: Within the scriptures, the holy scriptures of Hinduism, is there protection against disclosure of communication between a guru and his confidant?

MR. KUMAR: You see, religion is not a constitutional thing, but the basic tenet of Hinduism with regard to the guru or any other individual (he may be of another faith), the basic tenet is nonviolence, and I hope you don't mind, this is not a seminar, but nonviolence is the most understood thing. Violence does not only mean to hit a person, but to be nonviolent through thoughts, speech, and words.

THE COURT: Like the Christian religion; acts, words, and deeds?

MR. KUMAR: Yes, nonviolence in words, being words that might hurt a person psychologically and not even think it. You may say it, but a religious person would not say.

MR. TEPPER: What about incriminating a person, a guru or a member of your household?

MR. KUMAR: No, you cannot incriminate a guru. You see, a member of your household doesn't mean a blood relative; anybody who is a guest is a member of your household, including animals.

THE COURT: I take it a member of this particular religion could never be a member of the Police Department?

MR. KUMAR: He could, yes, because he is enforcing the law. Like

Mahatma Gandhi said, we should not be violent to the British, and he followed it.

THE COURT: But if you make a decision that's contrary to the penal law of the state and in accordance with your religion, you stick to that one that's moral?

MR. KUMAR: The moral law is the highest.

THE COURT: That's not the law of the state of New York.

MR. TEPPER: In Western traditions, we've held that when a person commits a sin . . . is there anything similar in Hinduism?

MR. KUMAR: Well, in the Hindu religion, they don't believe that heaven and hell are geographically located somewhere; it's right here. But even in the West, Professor Huxley wrote these things: heaven and hell are right in us.

MR. TEPPER: And what is the relationship between the Hindu religion and the use of psychedelics?

MR. KUMAR: Well, in Hindu religion this whole entity which we see and you see consists of three things; existence, consciousness, and bliss. Now you cannot do anything to the existence, it is as we saw it, God created it. Bliss is a matter of feeling, how you hold yourself, and the third entity is consciousness, which has been discussed. Now this consciousness is when we are born, and some are born with very superior consciousness. Now this is how you evolve spiritually. Either you're born very high, people like Christ, Mahatma Gandhi, Buddha, or Moses, or you use drugs, and it is in the fourth chapter Hadai, which means "drugs or herbs"; or penance or through concentration. I'm translating this from Sanskrit as close as I can to English.

MR. TEPPER: What is the purpose of the use of drugs?

MR. KUMAR: The purpose of the use of drugs is that you disassociate yourself from the ordinary environment which pulls you down and in which you feel no communion. You see, the Hindu religion . . . a Hindu is not supposed to drink alcohol, and as in Bombay and most parts of India you cannot take alcohol and you are penalized.

MR. TEPPER: What about marijuana and LSD in India?

MR. KUMAR: LSD is a later thing. If an Indian gets a headache he does not take a pill. You see marijuana in India is called *bona ganga,* it is its stronger element. Some of these elements are as strong as LSD, but now it is being experimented with by certain Indian religions.

THE COURT: Do you testify that marijuana is legal in India?

MR. KUMAR: There is no law for or against it. Like milk, are there laws against milk?

MR. TEPPER: And is it used in religious groups for religious purposes?

MR. KUMAR: Yes, and also a substance called soma and other forms are found in India and they are used by some very prominent people.

MR. TEPPER: And is the use of marijuana harmful?

MR. KUMAR: No.

THE COURT: According to your religion in India?

MR. KUMAR: No, under the guide and instruction of a guru.

THE COURT: All right, how do you become a guru or a chief?

MR. KUMAR: Is not a chief. You see Hinduism is not an organized religion. It's when a person studies for years and writes about these things and teaches them and then he opens an order and people come to him.

THE COURT: You become sort of a saint?

MR. KUMAR: Yes, like Mahatma Gandhi.

THE COURT: And do you have temples?

MR. KUMAR: Yes.

THE COURT: And do they prescribe drugs?

MR. KUMAR: Yes, you can choose either of them or all of them. You are supposed to learn it.

THE COURT: And you said something interesting: depending on how it's used?

MR. KUMAR: Yes, in religious context it shall be used for personal evaluation and not what is called in America getting high. These are bad words. There are feast days in India, holy days, and all the family members have marijuana in their food and drink, and they meditate and do their services, and go to temple, and I have never heard of any harm being done to anybody.

DISTRICT ATTORNEY: Now in connection with your explanation of the relationship between the guru and the student, you said the relationship is private?

MR. KUMAR: Yes, like between parent and children.

DISTRICT ATTORNEY: And if the truth means that the student may say something which is true and which incidentally might hurt the guru, which is of greater importance, preserving the guru or protecting him?

MR. KUMAR: Well, the student is not supposed to say anything. This particular thing is called religious troubles; Hindus as you know do not eat beef, kill cow. Now if a cow is going in a street and a butcher is following her, and the butcher asked where did the cow go? Hindu does not want the cow to be killed so he would answer no or send the butcher the wrong way.

DISTRICT ATTORNEY: Are you saying that the protection of the guru is paramount and more important than any other concept than the truth?

MR. KUMAR: Yes.

THE COURT: Even if you had to lie for him? Lying would be involved if you told somebody the cow went the other way? Let's get on with some of the questions because practically all of this is an exposé. I'm learning something.

DISTRICT ATTORNEY: If a student was aware that the guru had committed a murder in cold blood and was asked by legitimate interest to tell about it, what would be of greater importance in terms of religion, to tell the truth so that the family or interested persons might benefit or be redeemed, or is his loyalty to the guru more?

MR. KUMAR: Now a guru would never kill anybody; if he did he is not a guru.

DISTRICT ATTORNEY: Well, we'll assume up to the very minute he was a guru; now does he become a guru if he kills?

MR. KUMAR: He would not be a guru if he does something that is antisocial.

DISTRICT ATTORNEY: He becomes . . .

MR. KUMAR: He becomes a hypocrite.

DISTRICT ATTORNEY: If he commits an antisocial act?

MR. KUMAR: He is not a guru.

DISTRICT ATTORNEY: If in this particular case, if Dr. Leary, Dr. Timothy Leary committed a criminal act according to the penal statute of our state, and he was a guru up to the time he committed that act, and Miss Woodruff was aware, having been advised by her lawyer that the act itself was criminal, does he suddenly become not a guru and she would be required to testify?

MR. KUMAR: The guru is supposed to follow his conscience and I don't think a conscience of any guru will ever commit murder.

DISTRICT ATTORNEY: Well, let's talk about the crime of let's say rape, involuntary rape.

MR. KUMAR: He's not a guru.

THE COURT: Or is he suddenly not a guru?

MR. KUMAR: He cannot rape anyone physically.

THE COURT: Then he ceases to be a guru?

MR. KUMAR: He never was one, he was a hypocrite.

The hearing went on and on. The judge finally suggested we should all go to India if we liked its laws so much. There were no gongs or flowers, just a few sleepy spectators. Only the judge found the witnesses interesting. Allen Atwell and Ralph Metzner were in an awkward and possibly dangerous situation, having to use the Fifth Amendment rather than answer questions about their predilection for illegal substances.[11] The last day in court everyone brightened a bit. It was time for orations and conclusions.

THE COURT: Rosemary Woodruff, you refused to testify and answer certain questions made by the Grand Jury presently sitting in Dutchess County. You did produce witnesses whose testimony, although enlightening, failed to controvert any of the material facts germane to this application for contempt. I respect your personal conscious feelings with respect to your religious beliefs, nevertheless they cannot in any way be used as a cloak to shield from law enforcement any violation of the penal law, the penal statute of this

---

11. Allen Atwell, a psychedelic artist, was a resident of Millbrook at this time. He designed the cover of the brochure quoted in the epigraph to chapter 2 (Horowitz L11).

state, particularly when you're dealing with narcotics which might undermine, although there are those who disagree with me and that's their right in this great country of ours, which still might undermine the foundation of this great democratic system and the great foundation and morality of this country. . . . Your contempt was committed in the presence and view of this Court. You offended the dignity of this Court; I'm not talking about me as an individual, I'm talking about the Court in fact. If people were permitted to refuse to answer questions when they were granted immunity, complete immunity in your case, you can see how hamstrung law enforcement would be. . . .

It is ordered and adjudged that you be committed to the Sheriff of Dutchess County at the Dutchess County Jail for the term of thirty days, that's the maximum I can give you, and that you pay a fine of $250.00. I deny any request to stay execution. In the meantime, you are confined. Court adjourned.

She was fifteen, five-months pregnant, kicking an amphetamine habit, locked in a cell for three months awaiting trial. The year before she'd given a small amount of something illegal to an undercover agent. He wore a beard, drove a motorcycle, carried a gun, acting tough around the kids; he kept bugging them for some dope. A year later he totaled up his arrest record, came up short, and put her name on a warrant. She was caught at the train station. Every night she'd moan, "Ma, I want to go home."

She was an elderly, good-natured black lady, allegedly a murderess. The matrons said she'd get riled up now and then, but I never saw it. I brought her food trays, washed the cell, helped her into the prison-made, clean-once-a-week cotton dresses we wore. We'd talk about what a crazy world it was. She'd sing "Sweet Jesus Set Me Free" till the matrons told her to be quiet. She read the Bible twice a day, was partial to Ecclesiastes and Revelation. They took us to court one morning, our wrists chained together.

She blinked in the sunlight but held her head high when she saw the photographers.

She was a black mother of three at the end of a three-month sentence for shoplifting. The day she left she changed from a drab prisoner to a spunky young girl, a gay wig on her head, stilted heels clattering down the stairs. "You've seen the last of me."

She'll be back in no time.

She was a lame, gray-haired, seventy-five-year-old great-grandmother, arrested for hitchhiking. She had a sad tale about repossession of her house trailer, Social Security payments, indifferent children. She was there three days, poor soul.

She was the Head Matron, a round brown woman with sore feet, looking forward to retirement. Her daughter was a matron too. She was more official in her outlook than her mother, liking the feel of a uniform and the heavy bunch of keys. The civil service gave them status, hospitalization, gossip, and eventually pensions. They were both good-intentioned women and kind within the confines of their work. The third matron was a henna-haired woman who'd participated in the raid on Millbrook. She liked that kind of work. A metaphysically inclined lady had the graveyard shift. She woke me in the mornings with a kind word and an inspirational message. It was hard to wake up.

As the only sentenced prisoner, I didn't have to stay in the cell all day. It was cold in there, no sunlight, frosted glass windows with iron bars facing a brick wall. Sagging spring bed, painted-over skylight with heavy metal screen, green concrete walls. Last cell on the row. Out at six to serve the other prisoners coffee and doughnuts, collect the trays, wash the dishes, then the cells and hallways; waxing every other day, doing windows on Tuesdays and Fridays. The lunch dishes, three hours off, dinner service, the dishes again, which were always greasy. Back in the cell at seven p.m. CLANG heavy key turns metal bolt. Three hours to read by dim lightbulb; Gideon Bible, *Gospel of Sri Ramakrishna*, *Reader's Digest*. Ten o'clock matron closes the peephole.

"Pleasant dreams, Rosemary." Panic desire to shout *No, let me out!* Retrieve hidden pencil, blind notes in the back of the gospel.

Third day. They won't let me do yoga in the corridor, too small in here. Do they put something in the coffee? I feel so listless. Cleaned the sheriff's office today. Matron stood in the doorway jangling her keys while I waxed. I'll have to clean it once a week, she said. Never while he's there, I pray, he looks like a closet full of whips and cattle prods. Eagle-topped flag next to his desk, framed photograph of a mean-looking nurse on his desk.

What am I doing in jail on a warm spring night? Bad dreams. Stubbornness, pride, and guilt got me thirty days. Does that balance Laredo when I went free? Free? His left hand should be under my head, his right hand should embrace me.[12]

Matron called me to the visitors' room this afternoon. I thought I was being let out, but no. She pointed to the TV where Ted Kennedy was shaking his finger at Tim. He answered with the need for controls, licenses, not a word about religion. Kennedy was making points for the folks out there, denouncing drugs; he sounded speedy to me. Quick shot of Susan and Jack looking spaced and bored. Tim was rather mad professorish, clearly rattled by Kennedy's aggressive manner.

And you admit that it can leave an individual so that he does not know the difference between right and wrong in the socially acceptable terms, is that right?

"Yes, sir." He did better with Senator Dodd's polite inquiries, even ventured to say *Gawd* in that unique Boston way. Weird life, watching Tim on television from jail. He said nothing about religion.[13]

First visitor, Fred Swain, my priest, come to bring me spiritual solace.[14] He brought my little Tibetan statue of Tara, sharp edges and

---

12. Rosemary is quoting from the Bible, Song of Solomon 8:3.

13. This Senate hearing took place on May 13, 1966. A transcript is available (behind a paywall) on scribd.com as document 44318247; Leary's testimony begins on page 239.

14. "Fred Swain, a former Air Force major turned Hindu monk, associated with the Vedanta ashram in Boston" (Robert Greenfield, *Timothy Leary: A Biography,* New York: Houghton Mifflin Harcourt, 2006, 180). Swain introduced Timothy to Hinduism.

heavy enough to be a weapon so the guards won't let me keep it.[15] I asked if the Holy Cow had any messages. I could see the matron was wondering what weird rites we'd perform. Fred hadn't seen Tim since he went to Washington for Dodd's hearings on juvenile delinquency. Before that he was busy with a reporter from *Playboy*. At the house he set up a shrine for me in the front hallway. They cut my picture from the newspapers and hold meditations in front of it. Every night at nine if I want to tune in. They sing a song Bob made for me, Fred said it was real pretty.[16] We ran out of conversation, the matron said he had to leave. Fred patted me on the shoulder and told me to take care of myself. I wish he'd worn his saffron robes and brought his conch shell; that would brighten this place up.

Sound of man in cell below, bellowing, tin trays crashing, curses, something heavy dragged across a space. Interesting as anything outside this space would be. Quieter now, I can hear the merry-go-round from the carnival and bats squeaking.

Matron almost found this pencil today. Sable-brown Maybelline: I love you, keep me from going crazy.[17] Going to California as soon as this is over. Court appearance today to hear bail denied. Tim gave me an impersonal kind of greeting, holding his cheek to be kissed, police and photographers all around. I look terrible, can't get out till the time is up, then I can get thirty days for each unanswered question. Meditate and I'll feel him, he said.

Lord of the Rings came in the mail today.[18] I licked the front page and a suspicious looking watermark but no one thought to dose it. I'm tired of playing this character in search of myth. No more lyricism from the cells. Get me back to the lakes and forest.

---

15. Tara is a female deity in the complex system of Tibetan Buddhism.

16. John Schewel relates that Bob was a member of the League for Spiritual Discovery at Millbrook.

17. Maybelline is a brand of eyebrow pencil.

18. *Lord of the Rings* is the collective title of an epic fantasy trilogy by the English scholar of Anglo-Saxon J. R. R. Tolkien (1892–1973). It was first published in 1954–55 and has remained immensely popular ever since.

The thirty days done, I was rearrested at the jail house door and taken back to court. Mikki, Susan, and Jackie and Tim were there with armloads of flowers for the police, who freaked and called for reinforcements.[19] Upstairs we waited for Liddy to come out of the jury room. It was close to lunchtime, the clerks were getting ready to leave, no one was paying attention to the hippies in the hall. Policeman looked at us, said something unintelligible and went back into the jury room.

I told the group, "It looks like I can go home today."

I knew I shouldn't but I had to get away from the jail if only for one summer day. In a flower-bedecked car we drove toward the estate. Everyone was singing Bob's song; I was nervous, expecting sirens and a police chase on to the property. It was wonderful to see the wooden gates swing open and then close behind the car. The trees that had been bare of leaves when I left were a tunnel of cool greenness; the fields were full of wildflowers.

But it seemed that religion interfered with love, and I was hopelessly, unhappily, jealously in love. Jealousy was prompted when Tim's wife arrived to talk about their pending divorce. After she left he said it would be easier to go back to her than put up with my unhappiness. She was a tall, perfect beauty of a girl, titled, famous.[20] During our infrequent LSD sessions I returned to a more balanced state of emotions. Then I felt free of guilt or jealousy, then he was devoted, trusting, and I felt tolerant, wise, knowing.

It was a beautiful June day, my first day of freedom in more than a month. At the end of the drive, the house loomed large, I remembered the raid, the police with guns, and all that followed. I told Tim I wanted to go directly to the woods.

I tried to talk of jail; he wanted to show me a tantric pose. I was

---

19. I have been unable to identify Mikki.

20. This was Timothy's third wife Nena von Schlebrügge, whose father was indeed a German baron (*Freiherr*). She was famous, as a fashion model. However, she was only titled in the most attenuated way. She was born in 1941, but German nobiliary titles had been abolished in 1919, and the nobiliary particle *von* became legally part of a surname rather than a title. Most German titles only descended in the male line anyway.

pale from lack of sun, his body was golden brown; I was fearful, he was confident. I couldn't leave; I'd be subject to a five-year federal charge. I said I'd freak if I had to have anything more to do with the law.

"You didn't learn anything in jail then?"

"I learned how to clean a jailhouse. Look, I didn't have permission to leave today; I just wanted to be with you."

"They probably have a warrant out now." Angry, he rushed to call the lawyer and forestall another raid. I walked familiar paths in the pine forests. They couldn't catch me; I knew places deep in the deep woods full of poison ivy.[21]

I had two days to roam the estate and explore all the changes. On Monday I would have to testify or go to jail. In the office on Sunday I read Tim's *Playboy* interview. He spoke of an LSD session spent looking into the blue eyes of his wife, seeing in her all women. He also said to my surprise that any woman could have a thousand ecstatic orgasms during an LSD trip. I could understand the aphrodisiacal exaggeration for his audience, though I wondered who would back that claim. *Blue* eyes of his *wife?* Well, I reasoned, he has a poet's bias for blue and wanted to pay homage where it was due. But I wished he'd said something for my brown eyes and our religion.

Under my bed I discovered the overlooked bottle of DMT. I asked Tim if I should throw it away or hide it in the woods. He suggested we use it as an injectable solution. I would go first.

The room was glowing, deep-hued and brilliant. Candles, incense, flowers. My feet on the paisley cover looked perfect, still, dead, like marble. They were marble. Blue veins of marble on white stone. In the shadowy recesses of the alcove an old woman beckoned to me. Her fingers warned, pointed, counted. She wanted me to know—wanted me to know—wanted me to know that dying . . .

"Hello, how are you?" Tim said.

"Dead, I was dead and laid out for my burial."

"Interesting, isn't it?"

---

21. Rosemary was immune to poison ivy.

"This room was a tomb, and I was going to be led by an old woman—I looked like marble, like stone, I felt like stone, and the air was horizons of shadows, the obliquity . . . veiled . . . thank God I wasn't this high the night they raided. How could I explain this to a grand jury?"

For the next thirty days I appeared before that grand jury, looked at pictures of the disorderly house, answered questions about my use of drugs and why I used them, heard myself accused of adultery, declared love and faith in the guru in countless ways before twenty-three farmers and housewives. They were polite and didn't question a thing I said. The D.A. was persistent, though: ". . . do you maintain?" I did, till it was midsummer. The charges were dropped; there were no indictments against anyone.

My religious beliefs were vindicated, the search warrant was invalid, a tithe had been paid to the right political god. Whatever the reason, *the Woodruff woman*, as the local radio stations reported, was out of the news. I could go back to the woods and gardens. Tim and I moved into a tepee on Ecstasy Hill on the Millbrook Estate. Gordon Liddy went to Washington. This was years before they went on the lecture circuit together.

FOUR

Celebrations

Millenarian sects or movements always picture salvation as:

(a) collective, in the sense that it is to be enjoyed by the faithful as a collectivity;

(b) terrestrial, in the sense that it is to be realized on this earth and not in some otherworldly heaven;

(c) imminent, in the sense that it is to come both soon and suddenly;

(d) total, in the sense that the new dispensation will be no mere improvement on the present but perfection itself;

(e) miraculous, in the sense that it is to be accomplished by, or with the help of, supernatural agencies.

NORMAN COHN

THE PURSUIT OF THE MILLENNIUM

Castalia's summer school was a success. The yoga classes, mandala and slide painting courses, meditation instruction, and afternoon lectures persuaded many of the guests to stay. A family of four sold their home and furniture by phone. A secretary, the mother of two boys, wired the bank she wouldn't be back. A nun from a Boston ashram gave up her robes and responsible position. Two artists moved their art from the city. A folk singer and a farmer joined forces. A stockbroker and his wife settled in. All wanted to live the utopian life. Some had come in the spring, some during the summer, some would stay, some would leave, others would join later.

Tim proposed that we secede from the Union, print our own money and stamps, issue passports, break up the asphalt of the driveway and plant flowers, close the gates of the estate. Utopian visionaries, millenarian seekers, guru chasers, light artists, health addicts, hopeful hangers-on, woodsmen, artful wordsmiths: we would form a sect, a clan, a commune, and "define and refine our goals, roles, rituals, rules, and mythic context."[1]

At summer's end the four-petaled lotus, a double infinity sign, was the seal. A small hexagonal building with stained-glass windows was the meditation house. A moonstone ring was ceremoniously handed to a keeper of the watch every twenty-four hours. One of us would be in the meditation house at all times keeping a log of our journey. The legally incorporated religion was announced on August 28, 1966 (full Aquarian moon) at a press conference in New York City. We—Jean, Cliff, Glen, Bhavani, Suzie, Edmay, Marshall, Pat, Nancy, Jill, Michael, Joel, Dora, Bob, Carol, Rudi, Jackie, Henry, Ruth, Susan, Alan, Tim, Jack, and I—were now The League for Spiritual Discovery.[2]

Susan and Jack had survived with varying degrees of equanimity all the mutations from Berkeley to Harvard to Mexico to the International Federation for Internal Freedom to the Castalia Foundation to the League. They'd learned to adapt to communal life. Tim was happy in the role of father confessor, psychologist, high priest, guide, Gandalf ringleader, and top banana.[3] I was out of time and out of step; the months in jail and the appearance before the grand jury left me feeling vulnerable and insecure. I was not prepared to sacrifice privacy and

1. Rosemary is quoting approximately from Timothy's tract *How to Start Your Own Religion* (Millbrook, 1967) (Horowitz A6), where he advises people starting a religion to "write down and define your: Goals. Roles. Rituals. Rules. Vocabulary. Values. Space-time locales. Mythic context." It was reprinted in *The Politics of Ecstasy* (New York: G. P. Putnam's Sons, 1968). The full text of the tract is archived at perma.cc/em92-6vz6.
2. Many of these people are profiled in chapter 21 of Art Kleps's *Millbrook,* archived at perma.cc/4map-6crL. The full text of this fascinating and entertaining memoir is available online at okneoac.org/millbrook.
3. Gandalf was the wizard protagonist of J. R. R. Tolkien's trilogy *The Lord of the Rings.*

pleasure to the demands of a large group dependent on Tim's attention.

A light and sound dramatization of Herman Hesse's *Steppenwolf* had been perfected during the summer.[4] Tim was a perfect Pablo, Ralph Metzner the unfortunate Harry Haller. I was a reluctant Hermine killed over and over again by H. H. behind a screen in our magic theater. Visitors from the city enthusiastically applauded our performances on the terrace of the bowling alley. We planned future trips: the League would stage light shows, lectures, demonstrations, religious celebrations, each week honoring a holy man, religious myth, or mind-changing concept. We would do Lao-tse, the Ramayana, the tales of Albert Hofmann and the Gospels.[5] *Steppenwolf* became *Death of the Mind* due to copyright laws; Buddha and Jesus presented no such problem. All that was needed was an angel and a theater.

Billy Hitchcock wanted to back us. He had a producer and a theater. Once a Yiddish vaudeville house, it had been vacant for some time. I'd watched movies there when I lived on the Lower East Side. Years later I waited for hours to see Lenny Bruce, but he'd been arrested and couldn't make the show.[6] The new owners called it the Village Theater. Later it would become a rock palace, the Fillmore East. We rented the theater with its 2,400 red plush seats and began rehearsals for our light show *Death of the Mind*.

Don Snyder, Jackie Cassen, and Rudi Stern had created hundreds of original slides that were projected from the front and back of the theater onto filmy panels extending to the sides of the stage. The col-

---

4. *Steppenwolf* (1927) is a novel by Hermann Hesse. A précis of its complex plot, featuring a magic theater, is archived online at perma.cc/m4s2-umad.

5. Rosemary is playfully conflating Albert Hofmann (1906–2008), the Swiss chemist and psychedelic pioneer who was the first to synthesize psilocybin and the first to synthesize and ingest LSD, with the German romantic writer E. T. A. Hoffmann (1776–1822), on whose stories Jacques Offenbach based his opera *Tales of Hoffmann,* first produced in 1881.

6. The theater, built in 1925 and originally called the Commodore Theater, was at 105 Second Avenue, near Sixth Street. In 2018 it was a branch bank. Lenny Bruce (1925–1966) was a stand-up comedian and satirist who pioneered a jazzlike, stream-of-consciousness delivery. He was repeatedly arrested under obscenity laws for his strong language and sexual candor.

ors and nebulous patterns seethed and shifted like the far outlines of a dream. From the shadows Tim walked through the interplay of light to center stage.

A great breakthrough in evolution is underway, a drastic change in the way we think. . . . With psychedelic drugs we are learning to use all of our brain, not just the cortical fraction in which our consciousness is centered. Along with the ability to expand the mind comes the danger of a chemically controlled robot society. To combat this we are testing our research, testing our ability to change minds the way we believe they should be changed. Those who have taken one of the psychedelic drugs may recognize the images behind me as part of a classic LSD sequence. Let me introduce to you Ralph Metzner as Steppenwolf / Harry Haller. And the beautiful Hermine.

That was me. After Harry Haller choked Hermine, I was free to enjoy the light show and sermon. Tim was engaging and humorous, the audience responsive to the now highly polished summer school lectures. The lights and effects were praised by New York's theater critics. The religious celebrations were a success, sold out for every performance.

Trouble developed in the middle of preparations for the next demonstration. The first Jesus found it uncomfortable to perch on a ladder, imitating the Crucifixion. After listening to a lecture by Krishnamurti, he decided it was also undignified and left to follow another guru.[7] The second Christ broke down and confessed that he should be playing Judas; he'd been asked by some police agency to spy on the League. He was forgiven and told to sin no more but to spread the good word, which he did.[8] The light experts got an offer from Hollywood.[9] The

---

7. Jiddu Krishnamurti (1895–1986) was an Indian spiritual teacher, originally a Theosophist and regarded as a new World Teacher in their tradition. But he broke with the Theosophists and taught, heretically, that everyone should follow a spiritual path independent of organizations and gurus.

8. "Neither do I condemn thee," said Jesus to the woman taken in adultery, "go, and sin no more." John 8:11.

9. Jackie Cassen and Rudi Stern.

group was diminished; there was a week's rent paid on the theater with no celebration prepared.

During the next few days I collected every slide I could find in the museums showing Jesus and his life as depicted by artists through the ages. The images changed rapidly: he was born, performed miracles, was tried, died, and ascended to heaven on a tape loop, on a tape loop.[10] Dalí's *Crucifixion* did backward flips off the screen while other projectors flashed madonnas, babies, angels. Censers with frankincense and myrrh swung in the aisles. Gregorian chants and gospel songs sounded through the theater. An eight-minute film of a pope's visit to New York—the motorcade, rows of dignitaries in the stadium—was overlaid on a film of the Hieronymus Bosch triptych *The Garden of Earthly Delights* (Creation, Eden, Apocalypse).[11]

I wanted to call my creation *The Vision of Hieronymus Bosch,* but Tim disagreed. The Second Avenue theater marquee read TIMOTHY LEARY: THE RESURRECTION OF JESUS CHRIST. He wanted to do a publicity shot—he would hang from the cross while I wrapped my legs around him. But the cross could not hold two of us.

During a weekend visit with Allen Ginsberg, the poet Diane di Prima told us that the Ananda Ashram in upstate New York had lost its guru, Dr. Rammurti Mishra.[12] The founders, wanting a peaceful weekend retreat, objected to the increasing number of dropouts who found the Ashram and its leader a welcome change from the acid streets of the

---

10. This phrase appears doubled in the typescript that is the basis for this chapter. If it is an error, it is an inspired one.

11. This famous painting by the Dutch proto-surrealist Hieronymus Bosch (ca. 1450–1516), now in the Prado Museum in Madrid, actually shows Eden on the left panel, Hell on the right, and the Delights of the Earth on the wide central panel. The scene of Creation is on the outer wings and is only visible when the triptych is closed.

12. Diane di Prima (born 1934) is a poet and teacher, active in the Beat movement and still working at this writing (2018). She was resident at Millbrook for part of the time covered here and was the first publisher of *Psychedelic Prayers* (1966). Rammurti S. Mishra (1923–1993) has already been mentioned.

city. The guru departed until the conflict could be resolved. The older members called the police to eject the young godseekers. Fourteen yogis were without a center, could they come to Millbrook? They would bring their leather shop, printing press, expertise in meditation and ritual. They arrived late one afternoon in two large trucks.[13]

The silk-coated, gray-haired, daft-looking brown little man bowing low to us turned out not to be Dr. Mishra or his representative. He was Tambimuttu: poet, publisher, Ceylonese heir to an Anglo-Indian drinking problem and literary tradition.[14] He stood aside to introduce the robed, sandaled, sashed, beaded, jowled, paunched leader of the ashram exiles, Bill Haines, who in turn introduced the twenty hearty souls with him. They included Bali Ram, a temple dancer from southern India; Saraswati, a bald, giggling girl; Susan, a *motorcyclista* in leathers; Jean-Pierre, a wizard from France; a wise man named Lewis; someone named Zen; a pirate with a parrot; assorted gay, young, brawny monks; a pretty woman named Karen and another called Wendy; Bill, a conscientious objector; four yapping Tibetan terriers; three pregnant cats; and (still in the truck) four geese and a gander.

The cavernous house was filled to the rafters. The unused servants' wing was packed and an unsuspected room above it became the abode of the small wizard and his giant friends. Two enterprising ashramites made a space under the eaves into a colorful den. The empty wine cellar was claimed by a man named Baron Otto who immediately began to sound the walls, believing the rumors of the kaiser's gold.[15] More people arrived daily and there were long lines in the pantry waiting to get into the kitchen. The League retreated to the third floor and to the city.

---

13. After internal discord in the ashram some of its members moved to Millbrook, where (as Art Kleps recounts in his memoir *Millbrook*) they became a faction, led by Bill Haines, often arrayed against Timothy's League for Spiritual Discovery faction. They occupied their own building at Millbrook (point C on the map on page 26).

14. See note on page 35.

15. Baron Otto is identified as "Otto H. Baron von Albenesius" in several chapters of Art Kleps's, *Millbrook*. The kaiser's gold was never found.

Michael Green made a poster, which we put in the few head shops in the Village, and a flyer announcing the new celebration.[16] Before the performance I stood by the ticket office of the theater giving the handbills to passersby. A familiar-looking woman approached and I smiled at her and gave her a handbill. She looked at Michael's rendering announcing the Resurrection, crumpled it and threw it into the street. "He's the devil, the devil, and you should beware of false prophets."[17] Tim walked up and hugged me.

"What was that all about?"

"You're the devil, didn't you know?"

"Just an ineffectual wizard mostly. How are the ticket sales?"

They were good. We were off-Broadway hits, lecture tour triumphs, sure of ourselves, glowing, in love, a hypnotized hypnotist and his assistant.

After a brief visit to Marshall McLuhan in Canada, Tim was arrested for leaving the country and not registering as a drug offender.[18] The new arrest added weight to the weekly packet of clippings from the news service and suspense to the evening's celebration.[19] Who would take his part? Allen Ginsberg, Richard Alpert, and various swamis were waiting in the wings, but Tim was bailed out in time to go on.

"If you study history, you know that once you are committed to the messiah game there are certain moves, as in chess, that you have to

---

16. Greenwich Village in New York, where the theater was, not the village of Millbrook. Michael Green was a commercial artist who had left that work and lived at Millbrook. An image of a flier for these "psychedelic celebrations" (Horowitz L21) can be seen in Michael Horowitz, *Annotated Bibliography of Timothy Leary,* Hamden, Conn.: Archon Books, 1988, 290.

17. "Beloved, believe not every spirit, but try the spirits whether they are of God: because many false prophets are gone out into the world." 1 John 4:1.

18. Marshall McLuhan (1911–1980) was a Canadian scholar and theorist of communications and their effects on society. His best-known works include *The Gutenberg Galaxy* (1962) and *Understanding Media* (1964).

19. In the days before the internet, people who were (or hoped to be) in the news paid services to search actual physical newspapers and magazines for mentions of them, clip them out with scissors, note the source by hand, and then send the annotated clippings to the subscriber by postal mail.

make. You know that you are going to have trouble with the establish-ment. I don't want to be a martyr," he said into the neck microphone, "but for thousands of years, wise men, holy men, prophets, have deliv-ered the message I bring to you tonight."

I'd heard the message so often I could click off and trip out on the light show, coming back when a cue was missed or Tim was too audacious.

"I don't want to run for president," he shouted. "I'd rather be the pope." Then he'd go back into the swirling images. I liked being part of the audience, it was a good show.

The congregation of celebrants grew larger each week. There was always a crush in the lobby with well-wishers, worshippers, and stoned freaks crowding Tim.

"How was I tonight?"

"I don't like that pope business, it gives you the pompous dignity of a high priest."[20] But he was in the midst of a thousand hands clapping, and unhearing. I held his coat and the messages, flowers, beads, dope offered in tribute. After supper at Ratner's, I'd drive back to Millbrook, a bottle of champagne between us. I liked those early morning hours when we could put off holiness for soft family love.

When there was a day free and clear before us we would often decide to have a session in the woods. We started down the stairs one afternoon after a dip into the Sandoz LSD bottle. Before we reached the front door I heard a thud and looked around to find Tim cruciform on the floor. I knelt by his side. His eyes were open, radiant.

"Too much, too much," he whispered. His head drooped to his shoulder, his ankles were crossed, a look of absolute bliss on his face. I sat down in the alcove seat, pulled my blue shawl over my head, clasped my hands, and stayed that way for an eternity. Jesus, Mary.

What a story, soap opera: Roman legions, Christian slaves, suffering

---

20. The High Priest (or Hierophant) is trump number five in the tarot. In the Rider-Waite deck he appears vested like the pope. Timothy was called the High Priest of LSD so often in the press, and enjoyed it so much, that in 1968 he published an autobio-graphical book under the title High Priest.

for religion. Wars go on, who's got the power? In Jesus's name, it's all sin and redemption. Holy man, warrior, tragic hero, jeered at, forsaken.[21] Or Mohammed, Islam's favorite son. Married a rich old woman, fought battles, not just like any man, he chose to be a hero. Or is it fate to be that way? What is fate anyway? Time spiraling. . . .

This seamless reverie was interrupted by Pontius Pilate and a group of Roman soldiers stepping not so carefully over Tim. Pilate, who looked like Bill when I concentrated on his face, looked at me, looked at Tim, rubbed his hands, shook his head.

"Holy mother, good god." He gave a thumbs-down signal and followed the soldiers out the door.

It took us hours to get to the woods, stopping every few yards in awe and wonder. Was this the road to Sodom or Golgotha or just the path to Ecstasy Hill where we'd planned to go? The heavy bombardment of Christian images during the celebration was having an effect on our private passion play.

"Roman soldiers," I said.

"Pontius Pilate," he said.

"You saw that too? Christ have mercy, must we always go barefoot? This gravel always hurts my feet."

It was a relief when the Buddha celebration started, no early martyrdom there.[22] A group of New York filmmakers staged the complex lights and sounds. Tim prepared a new lecture retelling the life of Siddhartha, Gautama Buddha. He took off his red socks and sneakers and went barefoot on the cold and dirty stage.

"Eccentric? For thousands of years men have been doing this, barefoot, sitting on the ground, contemplating to find the answers to the question of what life is all about." At his feet a beautiful girl picked up the beat on her vina.[23]

"If you shouldn't vote, picket, protest, play the establishment's game,

---

21. "And have ye not read this scripture?" asked Jesus. "The stone which the builders rejected is become the head of the corner." Mark 12:10.
22. The Buddha died of food poisoning at the age of eighty.
23. An Indian stringed instrument.

what should you do? What wise men throughout history have done. Retreat, withdraw. *Drop out.* Why shouldn't you seek to be the wisest, holiest man of the century?"

Allen Ginsberg invited us to meet one of his favorite gurus, a master of hatha yoga who'd gathered many disciples during his short stay in New York. We were greeted by one of the yogi's *chelas* and conducted into an incense-filled apartment.[24] Indian music played softly. A serious-looking group of young people was seated cross-legged on the floor before an impressive shrine of candles and flowers. Framed by this colorful display, the guru sat in serene majesty. We bowed before the gently smiling master—he looked so wise, so kind, so healthy. He motioned that we should sit near him. His disciples edged closer.

He began by saying that he was concerned that so many of his students used drugs and wished to continue using them. Tim replied that LSD and marijuana were sacraments, God-given benefits for the enlightenment of mankind. "It frees man, increases the range of his awareness, produces visions of grandeur and beauty."

"But surely it is not for everyone, this awareness?" The master's gesture was to open his arms wide.

"There is a religion growing around the drug, and it is the young people who are responding. For thousands of years old men have been telling the young what to do. It's time we listened to the young. Thousands of doses of LSD have been released in San Francisco. Haight-Ashbury is an unqualified success!"

"What is this Hate? I do not know it."

"You will, you will," Allen said, rocking back and forth.

The guru turned to Tim.

"Do you not think it best that this sacrament, as you say, should be secret? It is to the initiate only that we reveal sacred things, and even he should not know he is getting it. It should be like the master's hand on the disciple's head, a revelation."

---

24. A chela is a disciple of a Hindu spiritual teacher actively working in the teacher's service. The term comes from the Sanskrit word for servant.

Tim didn't agree and addressed himself to the guru's devotees when he spoke. I watched them all. The beautiful Indian man with his all-embracing gesture, Allen dovening in glee, Tim pulling up his shirt sleeves like a magician showing there was nothing hidden. The disciples looked like they were at a tennis match counting points. As for that, the hatha yoga teacher was the winner, just on posture alone.

We celebrated Thanksgiving at Millbrook. Under the direction of Bill Haines, the ashram made it a truly splendid feast. Allen Ginsberg was in the parlor tuning his harmonium, Bali Ram promised to dance after dinner, and Tambimuttu would read selections from the life of Rama and Sita.[25] Our local witch doctor was shaking potions and mixing bottles. It would be the first holiday that League and ashram members celebrated together.

One of the guests for the weekend was a television producer who'd filmed a documentary on LSD at Millbrook the year before. Tim was busy with the fire and I hadn't finished dressing, so our friend said he'd get the predinner drinks. I asked for a glass of sherry. He gave me a generous glassful, mixed a gin and tonic for Tim. We chatted for a while, then he went to talk to the other guests.

We sat before the fire waiting for the dinner bell. From below came an odd sound that reverberated through the halls. We rushed down to Bill's room on the second floor. Framed by beaded curtains, stretched out on Bill's white bearskin-covered bed, lay our friend the producer, all two hundred respectable pounds of him, quivering.

"Lyiyiyimn pblugged inn . . . Whaaatissss haaapppnniinngg?" We weren't sure, but made an educated guess.

"Well, I think you've accidently ingested some LSD, quite a lot possibly; we wouldn't have dosed you for the world, it's against our religion. But now that you've managed to have that session you said you wanted, you'd best lie back and enjoy it. You're in good hands."

Bali Ram entered the room and waved all six of his hands. He was

25. In the Ramayana. See chapter 2.

in full Kathakali costume, fan-pleated gold skirt, gold bracelets on his hands and arms, kohled eyes, rouged lips.[26] He shimmered before my eyes, a multilimbed deity. It was too much for the producer, who fled the room. I realized that I had had a large dose too and went to sit by the fire. I could hear the child-voiced phoenix of Allen and his harmonium below.

"I hope the chanting cools him out," I prayed.

"I might as well join you." Tim lifted the sherry bottle.

"I wonder who dosed it."

"I thought he always drank the scotch."

The dinner bell rang unheeded. We watched the ancient television show of flames flickering.[27] In relation to the act of ingesting a psychedelic substance, the results are extravagant. The rewards can be, to individual perception, a sense of oneself inhabiting a perfect world of love and harmony, a timeless moment of gratuitous grace, every moment having a "golden couch for sweet repose."[28] The reverse is a bum trip.

"What is that noise outside?"

"Sounds like a turkey come back to life, or a crow with a sore throat." We looked out the window. The producer was running across the lawn followed by a small man in robes playing a flute and a headshaven nun shouting that she loved him.

"He's headed for the lake."

"He'll hit the swampy part first." A football player joined the chase. They all ran out of sight trailed by a Great Dane and the six Lhasa terriers yapping loudly.

Covered with mud, Walt Schneider, an ex-naval captain and football player, returned in a short while.[29]

---

26. Kathakali is a South Indian classical dance form, with very elaborate costumes and makeup.

27. It is not clear whether this is memory or metaphor. But another version says "We watched the flickering flames on the traditional Thanksgiving television broadcast of the wood-burning fireplace."

28. I have not been able to trace this quotation.

29. Schneider's memoir of this period appeared as *Millbrook Thanksgiving* (San Francisco: Mad River Press, 1971).

"We had to tackle him, he was headed for Canada to tell his wife and the prime minister."

"Where is he now?"

"In the dining room by the fire surrounded by all the animals, the cats are rubbing against him and he's calmer." We weren't and decided we needed some of Allen's soothing mantras. Bill met us on the stairs and said the League and ashram members wanted to take a trip together. He thought it was a good idea to have a group session; it would resolve the little personal conflicts that had sprung up among the sixty or so people living in the house. Tim called together the League members for a meeting in our room.

It was decided that to preserve the unity and consciousness of the League, a mantra would be chanted and, as at a peyote meeting, a prayer object would be passed when someone wished to pray aloud. We would use a small metal statue of the Amitabha Buddha. We gathered in Bill's room; he was surrounded by members of the ashram. The League took their places opposite the shrine of a dancing Shiva that was placed before Bill.[30] The sacrament was handed around.

Eons later I woke.

"Oh me too bah ow."

"Oh ta, fa."

"Ah meat ah bahm."

"Oh tim sat." I opened my eyes, Tim was sitting in the center of the room, rocking back and forth, clutching the Buddha statue between his legs. Bill was walking around, calmly lighting candles, adjusting flowers with a practiced hand. He looked at me, winked, and said, "All gods suck."

I was shocked. I'd never heard that mantra before. I closed my eyes again and tried to sort out the cacophony of sounds. From the League came the chant Amitabha Om.

"Consciousness-ness-ness-ness-ness-ness-ness," whispered Michael Green.

---

30. Shiva is one of the principal gods of the Hindu pantheon, manifesting the universal power of transformation. He is often shown in a graceful dance, standing on one leg with the other one raised.

"OM TAT SUT." The ashram answered. It went on for hours. The League gradually joined the ashram: "THOU ART THAT" they chanted in unison.[31]

I untangled my legs and went down to the kitchen to see if there was any turkey left. The cats were licking the bare bones. Bill followed with a redolent package.

"You win the prize, you didn't flinch."

"What is it?"

"Irish ham."

"Where's the producer?"

"Back at the hotel. He said he'd see Tim tomorrow."

"I wonder if he's bringing a lawyer." I thought it possible.

"We're going to tie up the next freak-out. He almost got to the highway." Bill was true to his word—*get the rope* became an ashram refrain.

Not fully recovered, but forgiving, the producer returned the next afternoon. We met him at the front door.

"I should have asked you which bottle was all right."

"No, no, stupid mistake, LSD in the sherry, it should have been in the vodka." Tim gestured to the stairs,

"Why don't we go up to the office and we'll talk about your experiences over a drink." We led the way up to the third floor, but turned when the front door closed. We never saw him again, but he used to send a card every Thanksgiving.

We left Bill with a check for the upkeep of the house and took to the road with a ton of equipment. Advance press agents had announced our trip to Chicago as THE RETURN OF THE O'LEARYS. We were scheduled to pose with a cow and a lantern at a press conference.[32]

---

31. It is not clear what the mantras are that Rosemary remembered, but *Om tat sut* is likely *Om tat sat,* a Sanskrit mantra from the *Bhagavad Gita,* meaning roughly, "Om, it's truth." *Oh tim sat,* despite its appealing double meaning, was probably *Om tat sat* also. The mantra translated as "Thou art That" is *Tat tvam asi.*

32. The reference, clear perhaps mainly to Chicago people, is to Mrs. O'Leary's cow, who is said to have kicked over a lantern in her barn and thus started the Great Chicago Fire of 1871.

At the theater in Chicago I sat in a control booth above the audience of thousands, chanting in unison or echoing Tim's words.

Can you float thru the universe of your body and not lose your way?
Light . . . life . . . love . . . Fatal unity. Warning bliss.[33]

The screen undulated with mandalas, tantric paintings, dancing girls. The sound of bee-buzzing vinas, Tibetan gongs, and tambours droned through the huge amphitheater. Rockets glared, a rain of rose petals fell from the balcony onto the audience of the McCormick Theater. It burned down some days later. Some enthusiast attributed it to the high energy manifested during our stay. A racial conflict produced another conflagration a few days after, and Chicago burned.[34]

The next stop was the Santa Monica Civic Auditorium. Southern California tribes filled the vast hall. A rock band named The Daily Flash played for the restless audience. THE ILLUMINATION OF THE BUDDHA went on.[35]

Then he obtained the knowledge that unfolds the causes of existence. Rays of six colors spread far and wide from his shining body, penetrating to the uttermost bonds of space and announcing the attainment of Buddhahood. Not even a hundred thousand tongues could proclaim the wonders that were manifested.

Tim addressed the colorful crowd.

---

33. Passages from Timothy Leary, *Psychedelic Prayers,* Berkeley: Ronin Publishing, 1997, or perma.cc/8pa6-hmx6. The first part is from "V–1: The Eliminative Cakra," page 28; *fatal unity warning bliss* is from "II–3: Jeweled Indifference," page 9.
34. The McCormick Place Exhibition Center burned down on January 16, 1967. Rosemary may be misremembering the next fire—there were riots in Chicago in July 1967, during the so-called "Long Hot Summer," and riots and major fires on April 5, 1968, after the murder of Martin Luther King, Jr., but not a few days after the McCormick Place fire.
35. The date was January 20, 1967.

Those of you who have taken psychedelic drugs, who have made direct contact with the life process through a psychedelic or spontaneous mystical experience—I suspect that some of you here tonight are at a more expanded level of consciousness . . .

Cheers from the audience, tabs of acid, capsules of mescaline, packets of joints, and flowers were thrown at his feet. A little old lady from another community stood up to hurl eggs, but Tim dodged and they splattered on the stage. Richard Alpert and Owsley, a friend of the rock group waiting to go on, were watching from backstage.[36] Tim was in the middle of his sermon.

. . . turn off the television set of power politics. In every generation there are a few men who go outside the imprinted chess game of the mind, who lose their minds to use their heads, who bring to the world their revelations and discoveries. It's obvious that a very higher power wants to use us as an example. I see myself as an early Christian, an Islamic Sufi, as a Hindu reformer, as replaying the role of Copernicus, Bacon, Socrates. Right now Christ is being harassed by Pilate and Herod and the saints of our time are being busted right here in California.

"You sure you guys get high?" Owsley said. "He ought to stop talking so the Dead can play." The Grateful Dead from San Francisco was making one of its first appearances in Southern California, and for the enthusiastic crowd it must have been a welcome change from drive-in movies.

"You want to see Tim?" Two young men were squatting comfortably on the dressing room floor.
"We sure do, been wanting to meet him for some time now, called him at your place in New York awhile back and talked to him. We

---

36. Owsley Stanley (1935–2011) was the sound engineer for the Grateful Dead and one of the leading manufacturers of LSD in the 1960s.

think he's a saint." They certainly looked saintly: long, clean blond hair; bearded; bright blue purple-irised eyes. They wore embroidered shirts, soft cotton pants, and each had a small woven bag on a long strap across the chest. They were beautiful and obviously very high. Tim came from the stage, they rose to meet him. He shook hands with them and looked into their eyes.

"I'm John Griggs and this is my brother Mark. We have a church and meditation center in Laguna Beach where we take the sacrament."

"Does your group have a name?" Tim asked.

"We incorporated this year. We're The Brotherhood of Eternal Love and we have an art gallery called the Mystic Arts; it's right on the main street in Laguna Beach, next to the Amvets Club."[37]

"What do you do there?" I asked.

"We sell handmade clothes, our wives make them, and leather goods, rugs from Afghanistan, beads, candles, there's an art gallery with pottery and paintings and a juice bar and health food store and we have a bookstore, we've got all your books, can hardly keep them in stock."

"Far out." Tim looked at me, his eyes shining. These two beautiful men were a manifestation of one of his fondest dreams, a psychedelic community of self-supporting heterosexuals.

"Do you support the church from the store?"

"Mostly. If you would come back with us tonight, we're just finishing the meditation room and planning a special service. We'd sure love to have you there."

We looked at one another. We were tired, and we'd accepted such invitations before only to find ourselves stranded on a mountaintop with a tribe of tipsy revelers or trying to sleep in someone's rumpus room.

"We'll try when we get back from San Francisco."

"Well, we really enjoyed your services tonight. Give them your bag, Mark." Mark took the embroidered cloth sack from his shoulder and

---

37. John Griggs (1943–1969) is remembered as a near-legendary hippie saint. The gallery, called Mystic Arts World, was at 670 South Coast Highway, Laguna Beach, in Orange County; it burned down in 1970.

handed it to Tim. John and Mark put their palms together and bowed slightly.

"Om Tao brother, Om Tao sister. Peace be with you."

"And with you," we replied.

Tim looked in the bag after they left. "Oh wow!"

"What is it?" He poured the contents on the dressing room table. A plastic bag of purple grass buds, another of gold, a large round circle of dark hash and a vial of blue tabs lay on the table.

"Bonanza."

"Gold rush."

"Brotherhood of Eternal Love."

"Mystic Arts."

"Laguna Beach."

"Om Tao sister."

"Om Tao brother."

"How do you like California?" he asked.

"Should have moved here years ago. My family lives very close to here."

It was the first time home with my family since I'd joined Tim at Millbrook. I was a bit nervous about their reaction to him and his appreciation of them.

"Are you going to marry him, Ro?"

"I don't know. Did you like the celebration, Mother?"

"Well, you know, Ro, we don't know much about these things, and Daddy doesn't like the smell of incense, but Tim certainly is a fine speaker. You know, love, we'd always hoped you'd settle down and be as happy as Daddy and I." Despite two strange sons-in-law, they hoped I'd found a good man this time.

I carried the tray of coffee into the living room where Tim was watching television with my father. My grandmother held the family photograph album open, but Tim's attention was on the television screen.

My brother, in his red numbered jersey, bounced into the room from football practice. On TV the young son in the series entered wearing a red football jersey. We looked at the set and then at my brother Gary. Even the stage sets looked the same.

"Unbelievable." Tim looked a little strange, we'd overtaken a bit of hash on the long drive from L.A.[38]

"Hi, folks." Carol, a young neighbor, entered carrying a pie. The scene was repeated on the screen: Lucy's friend, carrying a cake, says "Hi, folks."

"Fantastic! Do you believe this is happening?" Tim looked around. I could see what he meant, the family comedy. The tired man in front of the television set, the woman and her crossword puzzle by the lamp, the teenage boy delighting in his strength, the aged woman talking proudly of her grandchildren, the neighbor's friendly gesture, the tiny tract house that contained them, the love that held them together, while outside freeways roared past glittering supermarkets.

After the last show we were feted at a party at Micki and Benny Shapiro's house high in the Hollywood Hills—celebrants among celebrities.[39] Dennis Hopper was entertaining in the dining room. Peter Fonda was in the kitchen describing the new movie script for *Easy Rider*.[40]

"Peter, it can't end that way, you can't kill them," I warned.

"That's the way it is, we have blown it."

"Not yet, please God."

Benny and Micki had a word of warning about a Hollywood producer who wanted to make a movie from the celebrations. But with a cast of sixty in the house back East and a troop of lawyers to support,

---

38. Another version says "over done hash. But overtaken is better."

39. Ben Shapiro was a Hollywood producer and had been the Los Angeles manager for jazz trumpeter Miles Davis. Victor and Jacob Maymudes, *Another Side of Bob Dylan* (New York: St. Martin's Press, 2015), 158.

40. In this film, which made a sensation on its release in 1969, Peter Fonda and Dennis Hopper play two acidhead motorcyclists; at the end they are murdered with a shotgun as they ride.

Tim couldn't hold out for artistic control.[41] Contracts signed, dates agreed to, we went on to San Francisco for the last live celebration.

While Tim was giving a press conference, Susan and I went to visit the house she'd lived in as a young girl. Tim built it when he was a young Berkeley psychologist. In the twelve years or so since, it had been rented to a succession of college students. They'd hardly altered the 1950s decor. It was a museum of memories for Susan, who remembered where she'd kept rabbits, finding old toys and games in the closets.

"Would you like to live here again?"

"Has Timothy asked you to marry him?"

"He did that a long time ago, we were hoping you'd approve." I did want to marry him. I wanted to have his child. I wanted Susan and Jack to love me. I wanted to be a family, a small family, live in a house that wasn't open to the public, prepare food for a few friends rather than hordes, have a quiet drink by the fireplace, write, plant an herb garden. I wanted Tim to be recognized again by the academic community, among his peers and away from sycophants and disciples.

We were silent on the ride down the hill. My imagination had been caught by a glass and wood house overlooking the bay. I could be happy there, I thought, as we drove through Berkeley.

We met Tim at Michael and Martine Bowen's house in the Haight-Ashbury. Martine had arranged for flowers to be delivered to the press conference announcing the "Summer of Love" the hippie community was planning for San Francisco.[42] Representatives from several underground papers had been barred from the prestigious hotel and were rather upset that Tim had addressed himself to the "straight" press who spurned the flowers but appreciated the free bar.

This was a strategy meeting, a love council held in a beautiful tapestry-covered room with Michael's paintings on the walls and the smell of Martine's bread coming from the kitchen. Most of the men

41. Another version says "we" couldn't hold out for artistic control, an important difference.

42. The "Summer of Love" was in 1967.

there were urban guerrillas in fringed buckskin and cowboy boots, or wore Indian shirts and beads; the women wore soft dresses and antique shawls. One looked at my nyloned legs under my street-length tweed dress and suggested that two coats of baby lotion would take the place of stockings. Not in an Eastern winter, I thought, but determined to adopt an easier way of dressing. No more trying to squeeze into the elegant couture costumes I'd been borrowing from Flo for public appearances. I'd had to buy white gloves and severe clothes for the grand jury trials while everyone else was discovering their mythic selves in thrift and antique stores or Indian boutiques.[43] Tim was still wearing his Harvard tie and a crumpled suit he'd had for years. Perhaps the Mystic Arts in Laguna Beach would have something suitable, but for tonight he could wear the long Indian shirt Owsley had given him.

While my thoughts were occupied with clothes, Tim was explaining to Haight-Ashbury residents the need for a religious basis for the psychedelic revolution. "Groups of young Americans will present and defend their new religions in the courts." Michael was enthusiastic and wanted to print up thousands of League membership cards for distribution in San Francisco. But *start your own religion* was the standard response to any expansionist ideas.

Winterland was a sports arena and ice hockey palace.[44] The San Francisco audience gave the Buddha Celebration a chilly reception. They'd tripped at the Acid Tests with Kesey and knew all about light shows.[45] The timing was bad, we ran out of rose petals, the Grateful

---

43. The grand jury proceedings were not actually trials, but they must have felt like trials to their star witness.

44. The Winterland Ballroom at 2000 Post Street, San Francisco, became one of the most important music halls in America when the impresario Bill Graham used it for rock concerts, beginning in 1966. It closed in 1978 and was demolished in 1985.

45. Ken Kesey (1935–2001) was a novelist and psychedelic activist who took a different approach from Timothy's. While Timothy regarded LSD in a quasi-religious way as a sacrament, Kesey held vast open parties and invited everyone present to drink from an acid-spiked punchbowl. The differences between the Leary and Kesey approaches are explored in Tom Wolfe, *The Electric Kool-Aid Acid Test* (New York: Farrar Straus Giroux, 1968).

Dead didn't play, the illumination was missing. The straight papers didn't review the show.[46]

"Looks like we lost San Francisco," one of the crew remarked.

There was still Hollywood and the movie. Its unwieldy title was *The League for Spiritual Discovery Presents Dr. Timothy Leary in: Turn On, Tune In, Drop Out.* The producer was unyielding. It was a low-budget film. We would do most of the scenes in a garage somewhere in East L.A. The studio shooting would be reserved for Tim's lecture.

There was a bit of the old Hollywood flair when we drove to the studio for his big scene. The gate man directed us to the soundstage with a genial wave. The assistant director was waiting for us.

"I'm expecting Dr. Richard Alpert, would you leave instructions at the gate?"

"Sure thing, Doc, let me show you to your dressing room."

I left him in the star-marked trailer and wandered through the prop-filled lot. A science fiction movie was being filmed in the next studio. A spaceship filled the stage, goggle-eyed monsters sipped Coke.[47] Someone officious hurried over. "No visitors on the set." I went back to our own science fiction flick.

Dick was in a director's chair watching the bustle of cameramen and crew. An amplified voice called: "Dr. Leary, Dr. Leary, we're ready for you now."

Tim walked out of his dressing room. We watched as he took a lei of flowers from the prop man. He was very brown against the pale blue Indian shirt.[48] The makeup woman arranged his beads, dusted his nose, then combed his long hair to a more graceful arrangement. He settled on the bright pillows piled in imitation of the old sofa cushions we'd hauled to the Village Theater, smiled at the rented hippies at his feet.

Richard looked at me with a quizzical smile, "What's he doing up there dressed like that?" I looked at Dick's ruffled gambler's shirt, hip-hugging bell-bottoms, Grateful Dead pin. "Saving the world, and

---

46. It was the Psychedelic Celebration No. 1, on January 28, 1967.

47. Another version has "google-eyed" monsters, which seems oddly better.

48. Another version says, "His skin was very tan."

stopping the war and paying the lawyers, of course." Actually I didn't know what any of us were doing out on the edge of the movie galaxy. Creating diversions for ourselves, perhaps.

Timothy was in Hollywood with a new movie and a new religion. We were invited to dinner by Laura Huxley, Aldous Huxley's widow, to meet a few old friends. I was seated next to Christopher Isherwood and across from Alan Watts.[49] Tim was dining in an adjoining room with Laura and Jayne Watts and some elderly Vedantists; I was nervous, separated from his social assurance.

I told Christopher Isherwood that I'd read his biography of Ramakrishna and he smiled kindly at me. I went on to tell him that I'd read the *Gospel of Sri Ramakrishna* while in jail and mentioned it as a source of religious teaching during my trial. He continued to smile but looked rather puzzled and I didn't finish the story of how the court reporter had understood me to say Roman Kubner rather than Ramakrishna and that now we had a fountain named for Roman Kubner.

Alan Watts saved the moment by talking about food, which he did brilliantly, and I mentioned Kazantzakis's descriptions of banquets in his novel about Ulysses[50] (which I'd also read in jail with much more enjoyment than the dour woman-hating tales contained in the *Gospel,* but I didn't say that). I silently blessed Alan for being so charming and amusing, but I could never quite remember just what it was he'd said so wittily. I felt socially inept, and it felt awkward to mention defending my religious beliefs and love attachments in the courts.

---

49. Christopher Isherwood (1904–1986) was an English (later American) writer, known for his *Berlin Stories* that were the source material for the musical *Cabaret.* Guided toward Vedanta by Aldous Huxley, he published many books about it, including *Vedanta for the Western World* (1949) and *Ramakrishna and His Disciples* (1965); he also published translations of important ancient texts. Alan Watts (1915–1973) was a writer and broadcaster; he moved to the United States from England in his early twenties. He was known for his witty, learned, and accessible popular explanations of "Eastern" religions and philosophy, including *The Way of Zen* (1957), *The Joyous Cosmology: Adventures in the Chemistry of Consciousness* (1962), and *The Book: On the Taboo against Knowing Who You Are* (1966).
50. *The Odyssey: A Modern Sequel,* an epic poem by Nikos Kazantzakis (1934), first published in English in 1958.

The studio rushes were embarrassing. The director slipped in a scene of a naked woman rolling on some artificial grass, clutching up fake daisies. All the while my voice is saying *can you lie soft-feathered in the thickets, offer your stamen trembling for the electric penetration of pollen?*[51] Tim wanted to reshoot the lecture scene but the producer wouldn't go for the additional costs. He said we could shoot it ourselves, he'd lend us the equipment.

A friend let us have the mirrored bedroom of his Hollywood home for the scene, an adaptation of Hesse's Magic Theater. Pablo, Harry Haller, and Hermine sat before their infinite images. In front of us was a crystal flagon of wine.

"Is this straight champagne?"

"Ask the prop department."

The cameraman said he was ready.

Scene Five: How One Kills for Love

Pablo poured the liquid into a silver cup. He drank, then gave it to Harry, who took a sip. He gave the chalice to Hermine, she took a long draught. I looked into the reflected eyes,

"You want to kill me with your mind . . . with your mind?"

"Cut!"

"Perfect, we'll put that on a tape loop with an echo."

---

51. From "The Sex Cakra," in Timothy's *Psychedelic Prayers,* page 29. The actual passage quoted reads: "Can you offer your stamen trembling in the meadow / For the electric penetration of pollen / While birds sing? / Writhe together on the river bank / While birds sing? / Wait soft-feathered, quivering, in the thicket / While birds sing?"

FRAGMENT: WE DIDN'T NEED YOUR LIGHT

> ❦
>
> ## Editor's Note
>
> It is not clear where to place this fragment, which appears in Rosemary's papers without context, but the Roman numeral IV above it in one version suggests it should go in chapter 4. It fits as well there as anywhere else. A lot of the symbolism is frankly occult. I added the title.

We didn't need your light, Prometheus.[52]

Four-square skipper. Passing ship. Almighty architect of space (time is feminine, don't you know). Honor and power, what a bore, holding globe and mace, facing west, one leg crossed for stability?[53] Inventor, founder, past master builder, begetter, originator, bastard, son of the magician or double virgin? What kingdom then, Oedipus? Back against the Sphinx,[54] squeak of gum shoes on concrete corridors, mace and rubber truncheon. Perfect martyr serene in your cells, smiling sweetly at the hardened walls. Rebel, risk chaos, secure a new covenant with power, tyrant or scapegoat, either way more blood-letting eagles.[55] Assume you are a butterfly, be anything, does your center have a brassy ring? Come in through the window, door, a needle's eye put you on the camel's back

---

52. In Greek mythology the Titan Prometheus stole the secret of fire from the gods and taught it to humankind. Zeus punished him horribly for his transgression, but he was revered by a grateful humanity as the symbol of enlightenment, knowledge, discovery, achievement, and control of nature and energy. Many cultures have similar myths about the theft of fire for humanity's benefit.

53. The Hanged Man in the tarot (trump number twelve) is suspended by one leg and holds his other leg crossed behind it.

54. The Sphinx, part woman and part lion, guardian of Thebes in Greece, died when Oedipus solved her riddle, and Oedipus became king of Thebes for a time.

55. Zeus punished Prometheus by having him chained to a rock, where an eagle would eat his liver forever (or as some tell it, until he was rescued by Heracles).

and off into the desert you must ride, fading sunsets as you go.[56] Golden dawn the memory of you and your eternal bliss.[57] Adios.

FRAGMENT: KEEPER OF THE WATCH

August 1966

I was keeper of the watch. A sky blue glow in Orion. "Wait for me." It does not return. Am I just to keep watch?

Return to meditation house, fire almost out, candles burning low. Still dark night. Who is outside the door?

Wind at the shutters and goats on the roof. My hands form mudras, gestures of protection, safety shaping the air, sowing, reaping. Virgin, wife, mother?

My left arm, caught above my head. Ruth opened the door, a water flower offering for me.[58] I leaned forward to grasp it.

---

56. "It is easier for a camel to go through the eye of a needle, than for a rich man to enter into the kingdom of God." Mark 10:25.

57. The Hermetic Order of the Golden Dawn was a British "magical" society in the nineteenth century. Rosemary's favorite occultist Aleister Crowley was active in the order.

58. Ruth was Rosemary's mother's name. In a later version of this fragment Rosemary changed the water flower to a lily; a lily appears later in this fragment too. Rosemary is invoking the iconography of the Annunciation, in which the angel Gabriel informs Mary of what is to happen. Luke 1:26–38. "Blessed art thou among women, and blessed is the fruit of thy womb." Luke 1:42 (Elizabeth to Mary, her cousin).

"A gift should be accepted with both hands." But I couldn't bring my hand round and down.

"Do not fear, do this." Wide breathing out, breathing in hands together. My hands held a golden lily.

The air is bright between us.

Arms outstretched, fingers touching, we hold a space, a sphere.

Her experiences flow into me.

Childhood, lovers, war, concentration camps, pain, childlessness, never-ending search for peace and joy. Wisdom and folly. Pouring a view of time, expanded to embrace me, contained in the touch of hands and mind.[59] A moment of radiance, accepted as a gift.

(cont. from p. 99) Although a lily does not appear in the biblical accounts, it has long been traditional to include it in Annunciation scenes in Western art, as a token of Mary's purity.

59. In a later version Rosemary changed *pouring* to "sharing," which makes more sense but is less poetic. It seems best to keep to her original conception.

FIVE

Initiations

Be anything you want—you took the drug; you're entitled to be translated into whatever pleases you. It's not real, of course. That's the truth. I'm letting you in on the innermost secret: it's a hallucination. What makes it seem real is that certain prophetic aspects get into the experience, exactly as with dreams. I've walked into and out of a million of them, these so-called "translation" worlds; I've seen them all. And you know what they are? They're nothing. Like a captive white rat feeding electrical impulses again and again to specific areas of his brain—it's disgusting.

PHILIP K. DICK,
THE THREE STIGMATA OF PALMER ELDRITCH

Hollywood hadn't solved the money problem. The cost of the appeal of the federal sentence, the heating bills (among others) for the huge house and host of characters inhabiting every nook and cranny had to be met by a college lecture tour that would take us from Pennsylvania to Idaho.[1]

---

1. Another version says "Utah" rather than Idaho. The federal sentence arose from the Laredo arrest described in chapter 2. In 1969 the Supreme Court held unanimously that the Marihuana Tax provision (eccentric spelling in the statute) under which Timothy had been charged and convicted was unconstitutional, because compliance would have required self-incrimination under the criminal law prohibiting possession of marijuana. See *Leary v. United States,* 395 U.S. 6 (1969).

On earlier lecture tours I'd seen a small but vocally appreciative group of supporters in the front row. Among the mostly button-down crowd, they were the ones with the longest hair, the most colorful and creative clothes. Obviously the campus rebels, they formed a bulwark of ten or so against the cautious-but-still-willing-to-be-amused audience. Then there were the scoffers and the unconvinced, and on the outer fringes, the believers of other sects, there to parade their banners and slogans, the new Puritans, adherents of Meher Baba, charismatic Bible-thumpers, or dominating athletic coaches.[2]

A change in the makeup of the audience was apparent in the early months of 1967. There were more people with long hair and beads, more babies, and always several men with suits and recording equipment. Raising his voice for their microphones, Tim would shout, "The homicidal drug is booze! There's more violence on a Saturday night in a neighborhood tavern than there has been in the whole twenty-year history of LSD."

The response from the audience was more vocal than in the past, when the silence of bewilderment would have met such a statement. Occasional outraged boos and hisses were totally overcome by the shouted refrains of *right on, out of sight,* and coyote yips and yells.

Before the lecture there was usually the obligatory faculty dinner or tea. The unrelieved boredom of these events convinced me I was glad that Tim was barred from an academic career. After the first courtesies, the rubber chicken or gray roast beef, the conversation returned to local interests and concerns and we were seen as strange beasts, rare birds to be looked at with amusement and concern.[3]

At one college we were told of the Andy Warhol lookalike who had, a year or so before, duped the college for the first few days of a photographic exhibition until unmasked by a faculty member who had seen Warhol at a gallery opening in New York. The art department was still very upset

---

2. Meher Baba (1894–1969) was an Indian spiritual teacher who claimed to be a divine avatar. He maintained complete silence for the last forty-two years of his life. Meher Baba opposed using drugs for spiritual development and in 1966 published a pamphlet about this called *God in a Pill?*

3. Another version has "meat loaf" rather than roast beef served at the faculty club.

by the deception. Later, deplaning in Pocatello, Idaho, expecting the usual welcoming committee of six undergraduates and a small Volkswagen, we saw only a group of television reporters and cameramen at the foot of the airplane stairs. We were preceded by a young executive type who was met by the TV crew. A returning congressman, I thought—I was concerned that there was no one to meet us as we literally had only two cents with us. While we were walking to the terminal the television crew caught up to us and told us that the man had said *he* was Dr. Leary and responded to their questions until a more knowledgeable interviewer spotted Tim.

I discovered then Tim's ability to shed a bristly, unshaven early-morning skin, the tired eyes and the coated teeth and tongue of the overnight traveler, for an incandescent *I never felt better, isn't it great to be here* smile and a radiant look of well-being for the camera and crew. Years before, in Toots Shor's restaurant in New York, I had seen a most wonderfully handsome, silver-haired, blue-eyed man, the Hollywood star Gary Cooper, and I thought then that people who spent a good amount of time being scrutinized by strangers and baked under strong lights seemed to have thicker skin, poreless, inches deep as though carved from something other than flesh and shining from within. In an instant, Tim had transformed himself from an aging, tired man into a star whose essence was the certainty that he could charm anyone. And he did charm, particularly after the lectures when, in an admiring faculty member's house, the dining room table of wilted canapés and lesser wines forgotten, he entertained and explained far into the night.

These were whirlwind trips: Salt Lake City one day, Pittsburgh the next. There were few moments for privacy. Our confidentiality was public, unspoken, meeting one another's eye, commenting on something amusing or weird by glances and a quick smile. Fueled by small doses of LSD, almost everything was amusing or weird. Part of the enjoyment came from the sad belief that we were infinitely superior to anything we might happen to meet.[4]

Our mental accord was deepening but we talked less. I was with

---

4. Other versions have "knowledge," but "sad belief" is better. All versions have them feeling superior to *anything* rather than to *anyone*, so I have kept the word despite its awkward fit.

him now as a silent witness to what he was becoming. Now there was an obligatory hour of meditation before a lecture, the adoration of a chosen few, the adulation of crowds, and a constituency, impossible to disappoint, which must be ever titillated and amused, taught to revere. I would guard the cloakroom or locker room or green room door against them. It wasn't a case of going to the city to sit before a small group of friends and discuss recent ideas and then talk and laugh our way back to Millbrook. Now, exhausted, we stayed in guest rooms or hotels—even on one memorable night in a psychiatrist's office under a frowning picture of Freud. We were troupers on a show-business circuit, and the applause and cheers were as necessary as the check we had to get before we left town.

My critical faculties were suspended by the need for watchfulness, checking for hostility that could turn to violence or disruptive over-enthusiasm. I scanned the audience to see if he was being appreciated or scorned. His exaggerations and gestures had now a comic-book-hero quality of largeness[5] against the static backdrop of audiences, a heroism I admired. I did admire his courage to stand alone on the stage and declare what I had fervently come to believe in as basic to our rights—that what or whom one chose to put into one's body was one's own business and not the government's. He had the presumption to make up his own statistics ("millions of young people"). He could have been quoting Aleister Crowley.

> You children are the flowering of the new generation. You have got
> to fear nothing. You have got to conquer everything. You have got to
> make use of drugs as your ancestors learnt to make use of lightning.[6]

He likened himself to Prometheus, Galileo, and more often to Velikovsky and Reich.[7] He predicted, to the cheers and jeers of his

---

5. Another version has "largesse" instead of "largeness." Not the same thing.

6. From Crowley's *Diary of a Drug Fiend* (London: W. Collins Sons, 1922), 158. Some versions have "fire" instead of "lightning," but this is a misquotation. Aleister Crowley (1875–1947) was an English occultist, countercultural pioneer, and self-described "drug fiend." Rosemary knew his work very well.

7. Another version includes "Socrates" and continues "among the most important men in the world." Immanuel Velikovsky (1895–1979) was a psychoanalyst and scholar best

audience, that LSD courses would be required at the universities of the future. He was never at his best when he predicted his own deification and subsequent martyrdom, but he was wonderfully amusing when he chafed the government and the powers of the world.[8] He gave expression to what more cautious popularizers of social unrest would have hesitated to say. He tried to live up to fiction instead of fact and I, besotted, applauded with the rest, though I often regretted his need to be such an ass, as Aldous Huxley said, "flouting conventions, cocking snooks at the world."[9]

We went everywhere together, as much as possible among the rich and famous where we could sustain the heady feeling of being celebrities. To Otto Preminger's for dinner with Helen Gurley Brown and Bennett Cerf, Patrick O'Neil, Carol Channing, and Gloria Steinem, whom I kept a very close watch on though she ignored my existence.[10] She flattered Tim outrageously and looked far too attractive in her Pucci miniskirt. Preminger asked Tim to do a promo for a new

---

(cont.) known for his book *Worlds in Collision* (1950), in which he traced the supposed effects on human history of catastrophic close encounters with other planets. This made him an academic outcast and he spent many years struggling against rejection. Wilhelm Reich (1897–1957), also a psychoanalyst, based his psychology on releasing the psychic power of the orgasm, a view that proved disastrously offensive to the government. His work was suppressed, and he died in prison.

8. Another version has him chafing "the government's war and drug policies." *Chafing* seems an odd choice of word here, but it appears in all versions so I have kept it.

9. *Cocking a snook* is British slang for thumbing one's nose. Rosemary is quoting from a letter from Aldous Huxley to the psychiatrist and psychedelic researcher Humphry Osmond, dated December 26, 1962. Huxley, English patrician that he was, wrote that Tim's nonsense-talking is just another device for annoying people in authority, cocking snooks at the academic world. It is the reaction of a mischievous Irish boy to the headmaster of his school. One of these days the headmaster will lose patience—and then goodbye to Leary's psilocybin research. Which is just what happened. The letter is found in Grover Smith, *Letters of Aldous Huxley* (New York: Chatto & Windus, 1969), 945.

10. All celebrities of one kind or another. Otto Preminger (1905–1986) was a very distinguished film director. Helen Gurley Brown (1922–2012) was the editor and publisher of *Cosmopolitan* magazine (another version includes her husband "David Brown," a film and theater producer). Bennett Cerf (1898–1971) was a publisher and media personality; Carol Channing (1921–2019) was an idiosyncratic singer and actress. The feminist writer Gloria Steinem (born 1934) is still active at this writing (2019).

George Burns film. Tim enthused: "George Burns *is* God."[11]

We went to Andy Warhol's studio to see the newest movie and to pose with his stars, among them Viva (known in another incarnation as Susan).[12] Warhol arranged the group for the photograph—Tim in the middle with his arms about Andy and Viva. I assumed I was going to be cropped from the final print, placed as I was at the very end.

Other photographers came to Millbrook on the rare occasions that we were there. Among them was Diane Arbus, who posed the League members before the main house. When I remembered the way we looked, rather dispirited or gamely smiling, and the instructions Diane gave for the posing, I wondered if the photo was meant to be included in her collections of freaks.[13]

A *Newsweek* reporter came up one snowy weekend, not to do an article but to collect material for a future obituary, as she told me, somewhat frightened, after I'd gotten her rented car stuck in a snowdrift in the back woods. Chemical experiments were taking place in the main house; it was imperative that she not witness.

Tim was in demand for television talk shows everywhere. We went to Chicago, had dinner with Hugh Hefner, and stayed at the Playboy Mansion. The bunnies were really nice to me.[14] There was twenty-four-hour

---

11. This memory is somewhat distorted. No one thought George Burns was God until he appeared years later in the title role in the film *Oh, God!* (1977). It was produced by Jerry Weintraub, not Otto Preminger. Preminger produced a very heavy-handed satire on 1960s psychedelic folkways, called *Skidoo* (1968), in which Groucho Marx did a cameo turn as God (it was Groucho's last film).

12. Andy Warhol (1928–1987) was an artist known for elevating advertising and other banal imagery into "Pop Art." Rosemary seems more interested in his experimental films, which were of equally deliberate banality. Viva's birth name was Janet Susan Mary Hoffmann.

13. Diane Arbus (1923–1971); people usually looked dispirited in her haunting photographs.

14. Hugh Hefner (1926–2017) was publisher of *Playboy,* a magazine that combined cultural aspirations with pictures of naked women. He was an advocate for personal freedom and a libertine lifestyle. Timothy's 1966 interview in *Playboy* was an important step in popularizing LSD and Timothy himself in nonelite circles. Bunnies, found in large numbers at Hefner's mansion, were what the waitresses in Hefner's Playboy-themed nightclubs were called—they wore bunny ears and little cotton tails.

room service and Hefner really did walk around in robe and slippers.

William Buckley asked Tim to join him on his show in Chicago.[15] Buckley picked us up in a limousine and treated us with great courtesy. He exuded from his pores a consciousness of and desire for power. His voice was an instrument he stroked fondly, no voice was so cultivated, charming, confident, and self-consciously upper class, totally lacking in humor. I had never seen teeth quite so yellow. He and Tim got on amazingly well.

Dick Cavett was not so gracious, interrupting Tim's monologue to say that he was full of shit, a first for live TV and a foretaste of the hostility and disbelief that was gathering in the wings. It was time to return to Millbrook.[16]

A new drug appeared at this time. STP were its initials, corresponding to a widely advertised motor oil.[17] There were constant reminders of it everywhere. Though it was a short-lived phenomenon among mind-altering pharmaceuticals, it was to have some devastating effects. We took a small dose and went to see the preview of our movie produced in Hollywood. We arrived late and didn't have time to greet the friends gathered in the small screening room.

The movie was to be a short-lived phenomenon too. It was awful. The effects of STP were primarily somatic, and uncomfortable at that. An uneasy greasy feeling was pervasive, a discomfort heightened by extreme embarrassment at our amateurish attempts at moviemaking. Tim's reputation as a somatologist was being ruined before our very eyes.

He did not photograph well, his enthusiasm looked like a madness that would have worked in a Boris Karloff movie, but not in this

---

15. William F. Buckley Jr. (1925–2008) was a conservative Catholic intellectual who used his long-running television interview show *Firing Line* to taunt and sneer at liberals, who knew to expect this.

16. Timothy appeared on Cavett's ABC show *This Morning* on April 22, 1968. Cavett later said he told Tim he was full of *crap*, a distinction perhaps without a difference.

17. Actually an additive for motor oil and gasoline. The drug STP was really DOM (2.5-Dimethoxy-4-methylamphetamine).

"evolutionary art film" that would be seen for a brief while on the campus circuit along with *Romeo and Juliet*.[18] I looked ridiculous. The falsies I had padded myself with for the scene when Ralph Metzner choked me made my chest look like the prow of a ship. Impossible to believe that Ralph could have overcome so powerful a silhouette. The visuals, which also had been Ralph's responsibility, were the only redeeming feature. They would be seen, amplified, in Stanley Kubrick's film *2001: A Space Odyssey*.[19]

The lights came up in the theater. Our dog Fang, whom we'd brought to the city with us for the first time, yawned widely and groaned as a dog does after a long sleep. That was the only sound except for a rustling of coats. The audience, our friends, reluctantly turned to face us. We cowered in the back row. They passed by in a rush, their comments inaudible. Billy Hitchcock paused by our seats, started to speak, ruefully shook his head and left.

Someone else stopped. I looked up and was caught by the sight of an intricate turquoise belt buckle set in silver. I raised my eyes to a face that contained the same color in its eyes, one of which rolled a little wildly. Tim leapt up and he and the owner of turquoise belt and eyes embraced.

"Well, Tim, let's all go have a drink in my suite and I'll tell you about *my* movie."

Alan Watts swept us off to his suite in a private residential hotel, settled us in our chairs with glasses of silvery icy straight vodka, and described the movie he wanted to do. It would be projected on a curving overhead screen; the viewers would lie down to see it. It would open with bird song "warbling, burbling"; odors of "ferns and crushed flowers"; shapes of "leaves flowing into caterpillars, grass into clouds, bodies into worms." Tim and I laughed with each description of form and shape and accompanying odor. Alan's humor was irresistible and

---

18. Franco Zeffirelli's very popular lush film adaptation of *Romeo and Juliet* was released in 1968. Boris Karloff (1887–1969) was an English actor known for his roles in horror movies, most indelibly as the monster in *Frankenstein* (1931).
19. Kubrick's film came out in 1968.

his Eton-accented voice stroked and guided us further and further into the realm of his imagery.[20] "A trace of ripe gorgonzola, a woman's new leather glove, perhaps hooting monkeys"—it left us howling with glee.

After another vodka, which seemed to still some of the unfortunate side effects of the STP, we left Fang at the hotel and Alan took us to one of his favorite Japanese restaurants. He was greeted with great deference by a small, beautiful woman dressed formally in robes and sashes. She bowed us to a table and exchanged twittering birdsong sounds with Alan. Warm sake was brought, and hot towels. Then the food that Alan had ordered for us: delicate, otherworldly shapes and forms, colors I had never seen in food before. The STP was having its way, for a while I felt as though we had been transported to another planet: Venus perhaps, where everything was light, delicate, imbued with good humor.

The manager was not good-humored when we returned to Alan's hotel to fetch Fang. We were told he had howled and "bayed constantly" since we'd left, and the bell captain was afraid to enter the room. Alan calmed him with an assurance that the dog would not be brought to the hotel again. We collected the bad dog, declined a late-night vodka, thanked Alan for everything and arranged to meet with him again in Sausalito later in the year.

Fang, with Tim's old Harvard tie as a leash, walked as though obedience-trained through the city streets. He had never had any experience with city traffic, yet he kept to my left knee, protecting me from the honking taxis. Would that he could have protected me from Tim's ill humor on the drive back to Millbrook. I suspected that the STP and ordeal of watching the movie were the cause of his bad temper, but it was not the first time I had been the recipient of it, and it was devastating as always.

---

20. Alan Watts *was* an Englishman, and he *did* have a posh accent, but he did not go to Eton—he did his secondary education at The King's School, Canterbury, another highly selective school. Another version of this chapter calls his voice "ecclesiastically trained," and he was indeed an Episcopal priest for five years in the 1940s, but he was trained at a seminary in Illinois. All this is entertainingly developed in his autobiography *In My Own Way* (New York: Pantheon Books, 1972).

We quarreled and reconciled all that winter. But even our reconciliations were becoming banal: cheap champagne, a perfunctory embrace, and he was gone into his work. When he voiced his complaints he accused me of not helping him enough, which meant editing. I enjoyed that work but could not do it for very long as it prompted more arguments. He would not stand for my comments or objections, which for the most part concerned the flattery he poured onto others or himself.[21] I resented the intensity he reserved for himself or for visitors but denied to me.

I wanted to get him into the woods and back to the quick understanding of our drug experiences. I wanted us to have a sense of exploration, to have courage to find out more about ourselves together than we could alone, but he was reserved, distant, and busy with writing and plans that seemed grandiose and impractical to me, and I was alone.

I felt that in some way I had lost my individuality. I could not even think of myself but only of him. I felt ensorcelled, that there was a spell, a riddle that I must figure out to regain myself. But at the same time I rather enjoyed the trap I felt myself in, the sense of being dominated by this man, not by his body but by his mind, his will. To think only of him meant that I could avoid the inner emptiness of the knowledge of myself, the sense of not existing. I often thought of leaving him, but then such a sense of despair would come at the thought. I could not think of a life without him and I could barely stand the life we had together when he was with me only in sleep, when I would match my breathing to his, wait for him to turn to me, to want me even though the waiting had chilled me so deeply that it needed eons of tenderness to warm.

But he was too busy, the weather was too cold, and there was no sanctuary in the house anymore, no privacy. All grace had fled. Perhaps it had left with Flo and Maynard on their gaily decorated bus going west, or evaporated when the ashram, and Diane di Prima and family,

---

21. Another version says "he wouldn't tolerate my objections, which for the most part concerned the unearned flattery he would pour onto undistinguished rock groups or the ideas that seemed, to me, grandiose and impossible." Part of this phrasing appears in the next paragraph.

moved in. There was something nasty in the feeling of the place, something furtive, sarcastic, and hostile. There seemed to be shouts and cursing or sibilant whispers lingering in the air. Sounds of breaking glass from the kitchen, cats yowling in the back hallways, unfinished arguments in the dining room. The place smelled of sour stews and burned sauces, moldy bread and goat shit. There were unrecognizable figures in unlit corridors. Bulb snatchers were rampant, and book and record thieves. My jazz collection and speakers had vanished along with Burton's *Arabian Nights*. The washing machine was broken and the costume exchange box in the laundry room was depleted. The house looked ravished, raided. Lists of grievances, injunctions, and admonitions were posted everywhere. KEEP OUT: MEDITATOR AT WORK. DO DISHES OR DON'T EAT. NO LEFTOVERS IN THIS REFRIGERATOR. Rumors were rife, plots were being hatched, knives sharpened, a king about to be dethroned.

Susan Leary was locked away in a corner room with her cats, playing Donovan's "Season of the Witch" over and over loudly.[22] Jackie Leary was unreachable in the tower room. Homework, he said, but the smell of DMT wreathed down the stairs along with Jim Morrison's voice screaming *father . . . I want to kiiilll you!*[23] Jean tried to stay aloof from the mess, meditating in the woods. Bhavani was involved with her lover and avoided us. Carol and Bob were busy making dandelion root coffee. Ed and Marshall kept busy supplying the thirteen fireplaces with wood.

Diane di Prima and her husband Allen were occupied destroying the seventy-five-year-old lanes of the bowling alley where we had once bowled by candlelight. Drunken Art Kleps, the creator of the Neo-American Church, had crawled in at some point and set up house

---

22. A popular song in 1966. "You got to pick up every stitch, yeah. / Beatniks are out to make it rich. / Oh no, must be the season of the witch." Susan thought Rosemary was "a witch of darkest pitch" who wanted "to destroy everything she could lay her spells on" (Art Kleps, *Millbrook: A Narrative of the Early Years of American Psychedelianism*, Burlington, Vt.: Neo-American Church, 1975, 130).
23. From Morrison's song "The End" (1967).

with one of the ashram maidens.[24] His barroom brawler's face overlay the mean bleared features of a mean and angry man. His shouts shook the halls. His saving grace was his outrageous humor and intelligence.[25]

The other strong male figure in the set-up, Bill Haines, radiated good humor when he wasn't in a shrewish, bitter mood, venting his bad temper just out of Tim's hearing but not mine. He had the demeanor and dress of a self-important cardinal.[26] Then there was Billy Hitchcock, the feudal lord of us all, finding the Kleps-Haines act much more entertaining than anything the League had to offer. It was beginning to feel as though the nobility, the Vatican, *and* Luther were ganging up on the wizard and his mate.

I knew myself to be unhappier than I'd ever been, could ever be—unending dismal sadness that only death would end, my death, unknown to anyone, a pit to swallow me up, a hole to hide in forever. I would dig it in secret, fit a trap door of loam and moss with a stick I could kick as I drifted off from an overdose. What would an overdose be? I would think about that later. Meanwhile there's the hole in the ground to dig, hide the shovel, arrange the trap door. I'd be gone from sight and never found again. *Disappeared,* they'd say, *perhaps California.* No one would think of a self-made grave deep in the woods where the deer shed their antlers. No. Fang and Obie would dig my body up and drag my grinning skull. How he grins at me. Smiling into my eyes saying "what relationship" when I asked him what was wrong with ours. The daily coldness is driving me mad with grief.

Susan's love for her father was fierce; her dislike for me was equally

---

24. The Neo-American Church, of which Art Kleps (1928–1999) was the founder and Chief Boo Hoo, was established in part to assert a constitutional right to the sacramental use of LSD, analogous to that extended to some American Indian religious use of peyote. This was unsuccessful (see *United States v. Kuch,* 288 F.Supp. 439, D.D.C. 1968).

25. Both of which are clearly and indeed riotously displayed in his remarkable memoir *Millbrook: A Narrative of the Early Years of American Psychedelianism,* 3rd. ed. (2005), often cited in these notes. It can be read in searchable full text online at okneoac.org /millbrook.

26. Kleps described Haines as "for the first time since Watts, someone who knew what he was talking about discuss[ing] the religions of the East." *Millbrook,* 87.

strong. It made my tongue clumsy when I wanted to speak with her, my smile stiff and false, kept my arms at my sides when I would have hugged her, kept me immobile and awkward when I wanted to be light and loving.

Why didn't they love me anymore? Though almost every night he loved me with a hurried obligatory before-I-go-to-sleep bucking fuck of an elderly careless man who in his mind is young and innocent and fucking the bejesus out of me. Will I always have to seduce him, satisfy his quick whims, and forever make the morning coffee? God, help me. My body was committed to his touch long before my mind, compelled to be receptive.

What a wonderful mother you'll be.[27]

The strings on my body are cut and it's my mind that's enchanted by a magician who smiles at me so coldly. Please, God, let me be free of this pain of loving, this second-rate actuality—retribution for I know not what sins. He grins at me as though I were just another freak-out that he can outstare, outshine, uplevel anytime, as though I were just another burnt-out case who'd lost the vision of the harmony of things, who couldn't see the radiant grace all around, just another dark cinder while there he was blazing away with white energy. Why must he be the center of my imagination and the rest of the world not exist? How did he come to be the focus of my life when I was once indifferent to him? The past is insignificant, anemic, there is nothing except this man, this pain, and death is the only way out.

Christ have mercy, No Lord Jehovah.

"Be the resident goddess," he said. This with a look of good-humored concern, a look that said part of my attention is on you and that is all you deserve right now because you are not giving off positive energy, a look that he would give to anyone and if they'd smile back at him he'd stare them under control again, the force of his personality rendering everyone else pale and unimportant, or dark and dreary as I

---

27. This line, spoken by Timothy, is chronologically but not emotionally out of place here. Rosemary places it in a narrative context on page 133.

had become. Why did I want to kill my body when it was my mind that was making me miserable, unable to think except of ways of stilling the unending grocery list of grievances?

I had run away from every previous relationship. Brad beat me . . . I ran. Mat was unfaithful . . . I ran. Charles drank too much. Kenneth wanted to get married. Jesus met the woman at the well. She said Lord, I've had five husbands, and the Lord said but the one you have is not your own.[28] I wouldn't run this time. I would love him, and he would love me and we'd live happily ever after, after the problems with Jackie and Susan and the government were solved.[29]

Lunacy Hill was some miles away from the Main House.[30] I don't know how it got that name. I had planned to camp there till I decided to leave Millbrook.[31] I was really confused, half-convinced there was a serial number and manufacturer's imprint somewhere on my body—

---

28. "The woman answered and said, I have no husband. Jesus said unto her, Thou hast well said, I have no husband: for thou hast had five husbands; and he whom thou now hast is not thy husband: in that saidst thou truly." John 4:17–18.

29. In a difficult-to-place fragment Rosemary says, "I did leave him, and he brought me back. My face was green in the dirty train window, gray snow outside. Florida—making me kneel for forgiveness. I returned to his indifference, Susan's unremitting hostility." In another version of this fragment, following the word *Florida*, she says, "It may be a third-rate world without him but I can't go on always being wrong."

30. In another version Rosemary calls this place "Ecstasy Hill." Both were on the Millbrook estate, somewhat beyond the main compound. Point G on the map on page 26 shows the entrance to the path that led to these hills. Art Kleps described the scene in *Millbrook*, 102:

> There were two major hills. Lunacy had a magnificent sweeping view of the Hudson Valley and most of the League clustered there in their tents. Ecstasy was further back by a mile or two. In good weather, Tim and Rosemary lived there in a tent with a view of a sequestered bosky dell full of tall grass and wildflowers.

If Rosemary went there to be away from Timothy, Lunacy Hill seems more likely than Ecstasy and matches other references in this chapter.

31. It is not clear from this whether Rosemary's plan was to camp there *until* she decided to leave, or whether it was an open-ended plan only to be changed *when* (and *if*) she decided to leave. Maybe the second reading is better, because in another version she wrote: "Till I freaked out and wanted to leave Millbrook."

that I was a robot. Time slowed down, it took hours to get out of the house. And it seemed I was invisible—as people passed me in the halls, I heard them say, "She needs a good smack" or "He needs a strong woman." I hid in the dining room till they went past. The hall phone rang, Tim spoke to a reporter, I guessed—he was answering questions. *The highest yoga is the union between a man and woman.*

Considering our quarrel and his coldness, that confused me even more, so I fled to the bowling alley. I got a fire going, the Tibetan devil mask winked its good and evil message. It was peaceful away from the main house. Then League members filed in all solemn, carrying candles. They were there to pray for me; they said he'd sent them. I escaped to the meditation house. The next morning Tim said I should stay there. "Be the resident goddess, prepare yourself for love."

"Be the resident goddess," he'd said. What humiliation! Pat McNeil watched with a wry eye. Bhavani and Susan giggled. Jean seemed concerned. How could I put up with such trashy stuff? It was stupid—it had some other intent. What was it?

I couldn't go back to California where I'd been just the week before.[32] I'd flown back when he called, expecting a reunion, love, but there'd been an ugly scene. I took some LSD to find out how to get away from the triad of jealousy, love, and anger, the mean stepmother game.

I stayed in the meditation house for a month. Morning and evening group meditations, lonely nights hoping he'd come. Then a couple of League members decided to marry and the happy couple wanted the meditation house for their honeymoon. After the ceremony I moved to the woods.

In the woods I was completely alone for a while. Even the dogs didn't visit very often. I put a shelf bed in the small pump house, whitewashed the walls, cut a skylight in the roof and inserted a glass window with a painted bird.[33] Candles, a small brass camping stove, a

---

32. In another version Rosemary says, "He said I shouldn't go back to California."
33. In another version, Rosemary says Timothy's son Jack helped her make these improvements.

fire outside the door were warmth and company. The poison ivy around the shack didn't bother me, I was immune to it.

At first I waited for him, but after a while I liked being alone and hoped no one would come. I got up with the sun and washed at the spring.[34] I'd found a small puddle of water and dug till water came bubbling up. It was closer than the waterfall and warm in the morning, a nice place to bathe in the sun. Then I'd collect wood and start a fire under the kettle for yesterday's soup or a fresh one. Michael might bring sorrel, or Ed might stop by with some mushrooms. We'd sit by the fire and drink sassafras tea. I didn't mind their company. Ed never talked much and Michael had taken a vow of silence. When visitors drove out to see me I'd hide in the woods till they went away and the birds came close again.

Chickens scratching around the door or a goat tied to a tree would have completed the picture: old iron kettle, stirring the broth with a wooden stick in front of a gingerbread house on the hill.[35] It had been called Lunacy Hill for some time, a high meadow of stunted and twisted pine trees, planted in irregular rows. A project of some years before—Christmas trees they were supposed to be. But the hired labor from the mental home, lacking skill and supervision, trimmed them so they grew up all bent and askew.[36]

The pump house was above that meadow, and beyond it were thousands of acres of woods; lakes, one hidden and overgrown. I was alone, learning which way the wind would blow, listening for the screech owl or the deer. They'd scratch their antlers on tree bark, the sound of tearing silk. Moths and June bugs—a wild and plaintive sound, flying

---

34. In another version Rosemary says she washed at the well, or what had been a well at one time.

35. Rosemary is imagining herself as the witch in the Grimm Brothers' story "Hansel and Gretel," who lived in a gingerbread house in the woods and ate children.

36. The "mental home" labor had been procured by Art Kleps, who had been a school psychologist. In *Millbrook,* 42, he writes: "I went to a nearby state school, picked up three young retardates to help clean the Big House, supervised their work, and brought them back. High-grade morons. They enjoyed the experience enormously, particularly the opportunity to ogle so many pretty girls."

against the harp in the corner, put there to prevent their immolation and extinction of candle flame.

It was a time of waiting: for Susan to get over her anger, for Tim to love me again. Meanwhile the woods, the silence, being alone on Lunacy Hill.

Editor's Note

A fragment from the materials for chapter 5 seems too important to omit, but too difficult to place, so I reproduce it separately. It is only one paragraph, about an intimate moment, but it is not clear when this happened or who Rosemary's companion was. The last line—*it was a grace junk gave him*—echoes her description near the beginning of chapter 2 of an old lover she reencountered at Millbrook. But the reference could be ironic, and the passage could refer to someone else. It is just possible that it was an incident on the trip back from Florida mentioned in the note on page 114 above.

FRAGMENT

We were lying on a creaky bed in a room at the macrobiotic center in New Jersey. We'd taken 1,000 micrograms of LSD. Our heads were touching, our arms were about each other, our hands clasped as though to dance. The night was very hot. Moths flew through the broken window screen and died in the candle flame—wax images of death. I went with him; wherever it was it was a cold dark space; a very cold, dark space; a lonely, cold, dark space. I felt his despair. I could not help him. It was a grace junk gave him etc.

SIX

The Lovers

marry *v.t. 1: to join as husband and wife according to law or custom.*
2: to unite in close and usually permanent relation.

I left the woods in September and moved back to the main house. I found it was overrun with painted cowboys and Indians. A new movie was being made, a "psychedelic western." Day-Glo painted tepees were sprouting on the grounds, the house was full with a camera crew from the city. Tim would play the benevolent sheriff, he posed for publicity pictures wearing a cowboy hat and silver star, joked with reporters that he would be a peacemaker as opposed to the sheriff of Dutchess County, who was again denouncing the "public menace" of the League's camp in the woods.[1] We had several visits from the Public Health and Safety Office. They said they were interested in our latrines.

There wasn't a part in the movie for me, though I felt like a lonesome cowgirl. I had lived at Millbrook for two years as mistress, housekeeper, companion, administrative assistant, office manager—but wife was what I longed to be. We discussed marriage for some time—he and

---

1. Another version has the supposed public menace as "Dr. Timothy Leary's residency in the state."

his wife had been divorced for months. Susan's continuing hostility lay between us like some gloomy fog that I could not see through. She avoided me as much as possible. Spending most wanting guarantee of love a permanent religion.[2]

We quarreled; I went to California. Home again, I waited for the phone to ring; when it didn't, I called him to wish him a happy birthday.[3] Told he was unable to take the call, I wondered. He'd be out in a month, he said. Meanwhile the influx of hippies from the city was causing problems in Dutchess County. The movie would never be finished, the producers were quarreling, and several of the cast had reported to the local hospital for penicillin. And the newspapers were saying that the county's VD rate had tripled.[4]

Meanwhile, why didn't I go to the house in Berkeley to wait for him? Ralph was there and an Indian fakir and his family,[5] and a group of Baul singers who were enjoying a successful tour.[6]

The house overlooking the Bay was transformed by shrines and Indian hangings.[7] Asoka was a master storyteller, and the women of his family were gentle and kind.[8] I woke to the sounds of Krishna hymns, the gentle swish of a broom, and the soft patting of Apurna making

---

2. This paragraph has been heavily edited, by whose hand is not always clear. I have restored some deleted language to preserve content not found elsewhere. The last line is partly obliterated, and while its best reading is still not entirely coherent, because of its emotional force it seemed better preserved than discarded.

3. Timothy's forty-seventh birthday was on October 22, 1967.

4. Elsewhere in the same version Rosemary gives essentially the same account of Timothy's report from Millbrook but places it after his arrival in Berkeley. It seems better placed here; I have combined slightly differing elements.

5. Rosemary used *Harry* here as pseudonym for Ralph Metzner. I have replaced it with his correct name. Fakirs are mendicant ascetic Sufi holy men. They do not ordinarily have families with them—perhaps this one was not a regulation fakir. Mendicant saints in India are sometimes called fakirs even though they are not Sufis.

6. Original has "Ball" crossed out and "Baal" written in. *Baul* seems the best reading— the Baul are Indian mystical minstrels. I have omitted the phrase "from Southern India" because the Baul are from Bengal.

7. Another version has "and the gentle presence of the Indian women."

8. Rosemary has *Asoke,* but that is not a generally recognized Indian name and *Asoka* (pronounced *Ashoka*) is.

chapatis for breakfast.[9] The house was now part office for Ralph's psychological practice and part ashram, but full of memorabilia from Tim and the children's long residency here.[10] I pored over old scrapbooks full of pictures of them, and Tim as a young father, and longed to recreate that family scene.

On Halloween, Ralph and I drove to Billy's house in Sausalito for dinner before a concert in San Francisco. As I was sipping the liberally dosed punch, a sly gossip asked me, "Great, isn't it, about Tim and Peggy getting together again?"[11] I agreed that it was simply great and went off for a refill of punch.

The rock palace at which [*illegible*] Grateful Dead and Janis and Big Brother and the Holding Company were rock bands that night. The rock palace was full of costumed [. . .].[12]

Ralph and I made love that night, sweetly, simply, till Jack opened the door and saw us. Ralph followed him downstairs to the living room.

"Hit me, if you feel like it," he said to Jack. But Jack tried to punch his way through the plate glass windows instead. He wasn't angry, just testing reality in his own unique way. He'd had some of the punch too.

We tested a new drug a few days later and under its influence decided we were in love. Ralph thought we ought to call Tim in Millbrook and tell him of our discoveries. Tim was interested in the new love drug MDA and wished us happiness.[13]

---

9. Chapatis are soft Indian flatbreads, sort of like tortillas but made of wheat flour.

10. The house was at 1230 Queens Road, Berkeley.

11. Rosemary used *Maggie* is a pseudonym for Peggy Hitchcock, with whom Timothy had a long but intermittent liaison. I have replaced this with her correct name.

12. This sentence is badly mangled in the surviving manuscript and ends abruptly in midsentence. Above this fragment, in what seems like Rosemary's hand, appears the note *insert John's version,* but no corresponding text appears in the version provided by John Schewel. Following the passage is written *Crowley* (presumably Aleister Crowley) and the typed words INSERT THE [illegible] OF THE BALL FROM *STEPPENWOLF*. It is quite obscure what all this means.

13. MDA (3,4-methylenedioxyamphetamine) is sometimes called a *love drug,* but Metzner himself called it an *empathogen* because "the single most obvious and striking

He arrived at the house in Berkeley the next evening. We went for a walk in the woods above the house. He said he wouldn't be happy with anyone else and said I couldn't be either; we should get married, he said, and get away from communal life. We'd live quietly, privately, work on the new book. He wanted to get away from Millbrook and publicity, live simply with me somewhere by the sea. It was too late, I told him; we'd had several chances and lost them. I thought I could be happy with Ralph. "In that case," he demanded, "you ought to leave my house." I said since we were all friends, surely he'd rather we live there than some stranger's. We parted amiably, I watched him as he walked away and blew a kiss.

Ralph and I took MDA again a few days later and this time he decided that he was torn between his love for Tim and his love for me. He felt he'd betrayed his friend by making love to his woman. I promptly developed an alarming fever and astonishingly painful stomach cramps. Ralph left for his three-day work period at a mental hospital up north. Apurna was loving, consoling, she rubbed me with warm scented oils and crooned Krishna hymns over me during the two-day illness. She feared the white-haired man, she said, and cautioned me I would be unhappy with him. But the I Ching insisted "the way of a husband and wife should be long lasting."[14] And surely I was more Tim's wife than Ralph's. I called him the next day and said I wanted to be with him.

We started up the mountain well before sunrise. The wedding march was a symphony of retches and curses. The party of friends from the city stumbled into cactus and rocks, stopping from time to time to cope with the nausea brought on by the altitude and synthetic mescaline.

We separated from the rest of the group, wanting to be alone

(*cont.*) aspect of [empathogen drug] experiences . . . is the relatedness, the feeling of connectedness or communion with others, that ability to feel what others feel—in short the empathic resonance that is evoked." See the letter from Metzner in Newsletter of the *Multidisciplinary Association for Psychedelic Studies* 4, no.1 (Spring 1993), archived at perma.cc/dn63-nx58.

14. From the Sequence of Hexagram 32 (Duration): "The way of husband and wife must not be other than long lasting." Wilhelm-Baynes edition, 545. Timothy was a white-haired man.

together. We found two yucca trees growing side by side and sat before them facing east. The earth turned, the sunrise was glorious. "I marry you," and "I marry you," we said. Our friends brought flowers and kisses and beads. Then someone shouted that we'd blown the whole ceremony, the medicine man was leaving.

Down to the desert we wandered hand in hand, desiring love. At the end of the trail, in the shade of a Joshua tree, Samu sat in the back of his weathered car, wrapped in a sunrise-colored blanket. He was sorry, he said, not to have performed the wedding ceremony, but he'd been overcome by the "white man's medicine." Habituated to the ritual use of peyote, he'd found the synthetic compound too harsh.

"I was too angry to say the words this morning, but if I had, this is what I would have said." We turned to face him, listening attentively.

"The man says to the woman: Here is my blanket, it is your home. I will bring meat for you to cook and keep you warm. Then the woman says to the man: I will cook for you and walk behind you to protect you from harm." We repeated these words after the medicine man.

That night we were in Laguna Beach at an admirer's house in a hippie ghetto. Word spread quickly through the canyon that Tim was there and the house filled with devotees. An apprentice masseur arrived, wanting to practice, and the bridegroom was the recipient of his ministrations.[15] I went to bed early with a fever. We liked the small resort town and the younger residents seemed happy to see us. A religious group called the Brotherhood of Eternal Love suggested we spend our honeymoon there.[16]

We rented a cottage by the sea but it wasn't all moony nights. Every local paper wanted an interview.

The man who almost changed the world . . . drops out . . . in Laguna Beach for his honeymoon.

---

15. One version has a "masseuse," but that doesn't fit the masculine pronoun.

16. Laguna Beach, California. Either Rosemary did not remember having introduced the Brotherhood in chapter 4, page 90, or that chapter had not yet been written, or something has been incorrectly placed in the confusion of competing drafts. On one version of this passage Rosemary wrote in the margin "Confirmation of the vision."

I fed the seagulls while he answered the same old questions.

When used properly, it is a sacrament aimed to produce love of God and Man.

The same old gulls, marriage hadn't changed anything.

We had a week or so of relative quiet, working on the new book that would pay the lawyers' bills and the rent. Then Jack Leary was arrested. The police had put him in the mental ward of the local hospital and he'd been kept strapped to a table till we got him out. He'd been wandering around the neighborhood looking for our dogs who'd ended up at the dog pound once too often. Looking into people's houses too, perhaps, for it had been a scared old woman who'd called the police to check on a prowler. When he was arrested he wouldn't give his name, fearing to get us into trouble. The local papers blared our names and photographs again. Jack went east to Millbrook; we went to Berkeley to get away from the reporters and the curious.

The Indian fakir was still living there. He wanted to marry us; he'd read of our mountaintop wedding and said, "You are Hindus, I will marry you." Malaka and Apurna dressed me in a sari and their prettiest jewels, then led me to the small shrine room where Tim and Asoka Fakir sat before a tripod of incense. Asoka blew a conch shell, then anointed us with oil. He directed Tim to place a line of red powder on the center part of my hair and a red dot between my eyes. Tim's hand shook and a cascade of powdered rouge covered my head. I looked like the victim of a scalping.

We spent a few days in San Francisco meeting the Diggers and wandering around Haight-Ashbury.[17] Kids who recognized Tim gave a friendly greeting or pressed grass and LSD into his hand. Others whispered "speed, speed."[18]

---

17. The Diggers were a radical anarchist collective active in San Francisco's Haight-Ashbury District in the mid-nineteen sixties. They were led, to the extent anarchists can be led, by Emmett Grogan, Peter Coyote, and others. They offered free food, medical care, crash pads, "free stores," and provocative street theater. They took their name from a proto-socialist radical movement in seventeenth-century England.

18. Amphetamine.

We returned to Millbrook to close the house and finalize our vows before the League and ashram members. Bill Haines had moved the ashram and some of the League members and most of the furniture to the former chauffeur's house behind the main building. He'd used the signed checks that Tim had left behind to good effect, and the once decrepit building was warm and comfortable.[19]

While we were at a party in New York, the League's tepees in the woods were raided by deputies from the sheriff's office. They'd used helicopters, walkie-talkies, men on horseback, bloodhound dogs. They found a little bit of grass. There was an arrest warrant for Tim and several League members were in jail. Everyone was bailed out and Tim turned himself in at the courthouse.

An hour later we applied for our wedding license. We were met at the justice of the peace's office by reporters and the district attorney, who wanted to know if we'd had a civil ceremony in California. "Most civil, thank you," I replied. Tim was telling the reporters about our plans for a quiet life.

Our return to Millbrook was also marred by Susan's refusal to bless our marriage. And we found that a former resident and would-be holy man had stolen all of my furniture and wrecked some of the rooms by ripping out stained-glass windows and mirrors. It was said that he made enough out of the sale to pay for a visit to his guru in Sikkim. We were left with seven file cabinets full of history and a few worn mattresses to furnish the house in Berkeley.

On the twelfth of December, 1967, surrounded by friends and covered with flower leis, smiling with the effects of the wedding gift from Alan Watts (a large-sized tablet of THC), we listened to the words of the marriage rites as interpreted by the leader of the ashram, Bill Haines.[20]

"You, Timothy, are a guru, which means bringer of light, and you

---

19. These two sentences, which had been an unmoored fragment, seemed to fit best here, but it may not be where Rosemary intended them to go.
20. Rosemary calls him "Gil Baines." THC is tetrahydrocannabinol, the principal psychoactive ingredient in marijuana.

Rosemary, though once an independent woman, are the wife of a guru.
I enjoin you to be as Sita to Rama.[21] A husband is a woman's god, her
friend and guru. By the power invested in me by the State of New
York, I pronounce you man and wife." Then he told a long priestly
tale about the impossibility of living with a woman or without one.
Bali Ram, the ashram's temple dancer, performed. Tambimuttu recited
a tender verse or two: "The blood of the woman is a form of Agni and
therefore no one should despise it. So say the Vedas."[22]

Our friends came forward to embrace us. Zain, newly released
from jail that morning, wept when he kissed us, Kate refused to meet
my eyes. I thought of Susan, still angry at us, alone in the city. I hoped
that at least there was to be "a total love of the whole heart and body,
day and night, in an uninterrupted embrace, sensual enjoyment and
mental excitement."[23] I hoped that marriage was the key that would
turn me on.

We spent the next few days packing and cleaning the house. The
local newspapers continued the story of the raid on Millbrook. A
bearded League member (Michael Green) was shown handcuffed, his
arms cradling a statute of the Amitabha Buddha. *Religious presence at
Millbrook ended,* the papers said. Another grand jury investigation was
underway; I was immune this time but Tim's secretary Jean and several
other League members weren't. They went to jail, refusing to testify.
The house was closed, Castalia finished. The League had lost its home
and center; police maintained roadblocks outside the gates. Tim and I
left for Laguna Beach to continue the winter of our honeymoon.

---

21. This was an unfortunate precedent to have cited, as in the Ramayana Rama consistently, repeatedly, and brutally mistreated his blameless wife, Sita, to such an extent that finally she left him to return to the womb of her mother, the Earth.

22. The translation is from Friedrich Max Müller, ed., *Sacred Books of the East: The Upanishads* 1:232 (Oxford: Clarendon Press, 1879). The Vedic citation is to Aitareya-Aranyaka: II Aranyaka, 3 Adhyaya, 7 Khanda, 3. The idea is that men and women give their bodily essences (including semen and menstrual blood) to each other and thus grow together. *Agni,* meaning "fire," was the name of the ancient Vedic fire god.

23. From Albert Camus's novel *The Fall.* The quoted passage continues, "all lasting five years and ending in death. Alas!"

SPRING 1968

The first light of the sun woke me. Something glittered near my head, something I hadn't noticed in the twilight. A pair of high-heeled golden sandals was neatly placed on the rock that had been my bed. Just my size. I'll pick them up on the way back.

We'd started from Laguna Beach the day before, hoping to climb to the waterfall before sunset. But a stop by the highway police outside of Palm Springs delayed us. They'd walked around the beat-up old van a couple of times and checked the papers. We'd been respectful, quiet, but disinterested when they indicated by their look and manner that we were a bunch of no-account hippies and they could arrest us if they chose. Individually we'd blocked the moment, when we were all in the van and moving again, the brief interruption of police held suspended, not imprinted by fear or anger. They let us go and we picked up the thread of our journey to the falls.

The canyon walls narrowed as we climbed. Metal loops for a rope were attached to the rocks in difficult places where we had to swing across the deepening gorge or climb hand over hand to a higher spot. The falls widened out suddenly and we were near a pool, a perfect blue oval. A tall rounded rock thrust up from the center, a Shiva-Shakti shrine, but defiled, polluted by mounds of debris in and around the water.[24] We hurried past the pool and the large cave in which some people seemed to be camping. A few bearded men lay before a smoky fire, a mound of beer cans and wine bottles by their side. Amazing, the things people had chosen to haul up the mountain and then discard. Broken shoes, every kind of plastic and aluminum wrapper littered the landscape. Discarded knapsacks, sun-faded underclothing caught in the bushes or in a swirling eddy of water. They grew less as we climbed higher.

The sun rose above the mountain, lighting the water cascading into

---

24. I have changed *spherical* to *rounded*. A stone marking a Shiva-Shakti shrine would more likely have been cylindrical or pillar shaped, as stones marking Shiva shrines tend to be, rather than spherical.

the pool below, which regained its lost beauty. The rounded rock was touched by the light. "Just a little higher," John called out, "we're almost there." One last haul on the rope and we stood in a small clearing.

John passed round the gelatin capsules of LSD.[25]

"OM TAO."

"OM TAO."

"Peace be with us this day."

Each couple found a place to wait for the vision that would surely come. Brennie and Lil crossed the stream to a sandy beach in front of a water-worn cave. Inside the natural grotto was a chalk drawing of Christ with the motto *Jesus Saves.* It winked at me fitfully all day. Carol and John settled their knapsacks and dogs under a willow tree near the stream. Adrianne dove into the pool from a high rock. I found a flat sunny spot near a laurel tree and lay down to watch the sky and slanting walls.

I felt the roar of the falls through the rock beneath me, then heard the echo. It blended with the chanting, a continual AUM filled the air. But no one was chanting, it was the sound of the place. *Tahquitz,* the Indians called it. Tahquitz, the spirit of the mountains, was speaking.[26]

I looked to the others. Lily laved Brennie's feet before the Jesus shrine. Calvin and Adrianne stared happily into one another's eyes, Carol gazed pensively into the gently moving stream. Tim came near. "How are you?"

"Happy," I told him. "My body is a hammock for my soul today." I thought I'd found a peaceful answer to the meaning of our being together.[27] It was to protect him perhaps, to love him all of our lives. Bhakti yoga, surely that was the message of the golden sandals.[28]

---

25. One version calls them "extra large."

26. Tahquitz was the spirit deity of the Soboba Indians of California. Tahquitz as the local spirit places this episode in the San Jacinto Mountains of Riverside County.

27. Another version has "to the problem of not being able to conceive a child, and the meaning of our being together."

28. Bhakti is the yoga of adoration, sometimes expressed by veneration of the feet or sandals of a god or guru. A mantra called the paduka-mantra says: I worship the sandals of the guru.

Goddess be my guide, would I wear a crown of stars or thorns?

John came from the upper falls, he said he'd felt heat above.[29] We kept still, listening. Muttering and cursing, two men appeared. Intent on the slippery path, they didn't see us till they were very near. They looked at Lily, then looked away—naked beauty was too much for them to stare at. They hurried past, slipping awkwardly on the rocks; one gave a hefty tug to his gun-heavy shorts. In black city shoes and socks, holding their suits in clumsy bundles, they stumbled by. "Peace be with you," John said as they passed; they did not answer.

We stopped at the foot of the falls to break our long fast. Carol gave us bread, rich with nuts and raisins. We passed a bottle of grape juice. Brennie squatted before Tim, looking straight into his eyes.[30] "We got it made this time, I tell you we're going to make it this time around." His conviction erased for a time the police stalking our Way.[31] Maybe Brennie was right, perhaps we would move on to a better brighter world than we'd known before. It was a hope we shared that day.

The sound of Tahquitz was with me all the way to the desert floor, and even in the van it combined with the motor to sound a gentle AUM as we drove through Palm Springs.

Zain was waiting for a lift back to Laguna. "I know a ranch for sale, in a valley five thousand feet high, five miles in from the nearest road, midway between Palm Springs and the coast. It's beautiful, Robbie and I used to trip there. His father wants to sell it." Land, a garden, orchards, space for the children, a bit of earth to belong to. Peace, Eden perhaps? I wanted to be with them, brothers, sisters, kin. The Brotherhood of Eternal Love.[32]

---

29. "Heat" meaning police.

30. In another version Rosemary says Brennie squatted before "her" and looked into "her" eyes.

31. Another version says "stalking through our day." But *stalking our Way,* capitalized as Rosemary has it, is better.

32. Zain is a pseudonym for John Griggs, founder of the Brotherhood of Eternal Love. Robbie is his brother Mark. We have met them earlier—see chapter 4, page 90. I have left the pseudonyms in place so as not to confuse John Griggs with other Johns in the story. The Brotherhood bought the property, which they called Idyllwild Ranch.

SUMMER 1969

But if thou shut up thy Soul in the Body to abuse it and say, I understand nothing, I can do nothing, I am afraid of the Sea; I cannot
climb up into Heaven, I know not who I am, I cannot tell what I
shall be; what has thou to do with God?[33]

Sharon, Lily, Carol, and I wanted to see God. We'd never climbed
the mountain by ourselves before. Always we'd been in a group, with
the men; spending the day or several on top of the ridge, a round sandy
place ringed by tall pines. Above it, the mountain rose to a flat rock
large enough for two to sit and watch the play of clouds and sky. An
eagle lived up there.

We walked through all the seasons that morning. Spring at the ranch
with the garden planted, summer taking hold in the lower pastures,
autumn leaves, a bit of snow on the northern slopes in the acorn groves.
Groves that had once passed from mother to daughter,[34] the tribe making
the ascent from the desert in the fall to gather the acorns, leach the bitter
acid, dry them in the sun and then grind the meal in the stone metates
that could still be found.[35] There was a natural grinding stone on top of
the mountain; after a rain it would become a shallow bowl of blue water.

The Indians didn't come to the mountain anymore to carry acorn
meal to the desert. We were the Indians and the cowboys. Settlers, living a

---

33. Rosemary is quoting from a Hermetic text called *The Divine Pymander of Hermes
Mercurius Trismegistus,* book 8, verse 131. It was first published in English by Robert
Everard in 1650 and has often been reprinted since. A digitization of the 1884 London
edition is archived at perma.cc/g7gb-m2zz. A pymander (modern *pomander*) is a per-
fumed ball used to purify and sweeten the air. It could be a hollow ball of metal filled
with spices, or an orange studded with cloves, for instance.
34. During the time of the Soboba Indians and their matrilineal society. The Soboba
are now officially known as the Soboba Band of Luiseño Indians, because during Spanish colonial times they were attached (however unwillingly) to the Roman
Catholic Mission of San Luis Rey.
35. Metates are stones with natural or artificial depressions in which grains or acorns or
other substances are placed to be ground by other stones.

fantasy of a hundred years before, with kerosene lamps and butter churns, tepee fires and tribal ways. The electric generators had been traded for two black mules. The barn had a shelf full of blenders and electrical gadgets gathering spiderwebs. We were the newest comers to the remote valley, five miles of government land between the ranch and the highway.[36]

Reservations to the north; east the grazing land of an old mountain family; west, the property of a cattle syndicate. There were eighty acres of rich meadows and dry mountain to belong to. Seven springs of sweet water. Willow and manzanita, yucca, datura everywhere, stumps with wild honey; yarrow, mint, and red clover; eagles, hummingbirds, hawks, deer, coyotes, and rattlers.

We got to the top and stretched out in the sun, grateful for warmth and ease from the long climb. Carol felt her breasts and wondered aloud how long she'd be able to stay away from her baby, left for the first time since he'd been born the summer before. The men had had many sessions together on the mountain, but for the women, it was difficult to get away from chores and children. It had been a long while since we last took the sacrament. Lily opened the book of prayers and read aloud.

May all beings have happiness and the causes of happiness,
May all beings be away from sorrow and the causes of sorrow,
May all never be separate from the sacred happiness that is sorrowless.
May all leave attachment to dear ones and aversion to others.
And live believing in the equality of all that lives.[37]

We decided it was time to begin. I got out the matchbox, it was full of matches, nothing else. We laughed about it, both disappointed and

---

36. Rosemary is speaking of the Brotherhood of Eternal Love's remote ranch in Riverside County, one county to the east of Orange County, where Laguna Beach was on the western coast.

37. Lily is quoting a traditional Buddhist prayer called the Four Immeasurables (*brahmaviharas*). The translation is by Freda Bedi (archived at perma.cc/8wvd-xw8u). This teaching is found in the Buddha's sermon called the Metta Sutta (Benevolence Sutra).

relieved that we wouldn't have to test our endurance on the mountain—
there was something too still, too brooding about the day. The sound in
the pines made the ranch seem very far away. We cast the coins to see
what the I Ching had to say about the situation.

There is no water in the lake:

> *The image of EXHAUSTION.*
> *One sits oppressed under a bare tree*
> *And strays into a gloomy valley.*
> *For three years one sees nothing.*[38]

It wasn't our fault the lake was empty. God was simply absent from the
mountain that day.

FALL 1969

> *For a woman to work herself up to a point of . . . apparently*
> *presumptuous spiritual independence often costs a great*
> *deal, especially because it can so easily be misunderstood or*
> *misjudged. But without this sort of revolt, no matter what*
> *she has to suffer as a consequence, she will never be free*
> *from the power of the tyrant, never come to find herself.*[39]

We climbed through the barbed-wire fence, circling round the cattle that wandered freely through the valley. We were following a narrow
trail of water south, upstream to the falls. It was a perfect campsite
there: flat rocks to lie on in the sun all day, a clear stream for bathing.

---

38. This combines two passages from Hexagram 47 (Exhaustion). The Image says (in
the Wilhelm-Baynes translation, 182): "There is no water in the lake: The image of
Exhaustion. Thus the superior man stakes his life on following his will." The next three
lines quoted appear in the section for the moving line *Six at the Beginning,* which applies
only if the coins fall in a particular way.
39. Unattributed in the manuscript. But it is from Emma Jung, *Animus and Anima,*
translated by Cary F. Baynes and Hildegarde Nagel (Zurich: Spring Publications,
1972), 23–24.

Pine trees surrounded the clearing, giving protection from the strong east winds.

A pine tree lay across the falls. Broken boughs and pine needles covered the area for yards around. The tree had fallen on the rock where so many had sat through vision-waiting days and nights. It would have to be cut up and hauled away before the falls would be clear again.

We went downstream to a small meadow by the stream. I had a short manual on pranayama yoga and wanted to practice the complicated breathing exercises in the sun.[40] Tim took off his clothes and I did the same, though I felt exposed and helpless in the open meadow. The black long-horned cattle were grazing very near. I joked that I'd hate to be high, chased by my own astrological symbol through the chaparral.[41] But it was good to feel the sun after weeks of courtrooms and trials.

I stood by the water holding the book, counting in-breaths and exhalations. He wandered upstream, his skin so white against the thorn trees and sage.[42]

A plane circled overhead and flew low over the meadow. There had been a number of planes and helicopters over the ranch lately. No one bothered to look up after we'd seen the cameras snapping pictures of naked hippies bathing. Sometimes it was the forest rangers on patrol, who dipped their wings; sometimes it was a private plane from a nearby ranch. More recently it was a government helicopter or the sheriff's black-and-white Cessna that swooped so low over the horses and the ponies and the women by the shore.

A few months before, at a drug conference, we'd encountered a militant group of young people. *Motherfuckers* they'd called themselves.[43] He'd told them to get out of the cities, it was the city that was

---

40. Pranayama is the yoga of breath control.

41. Rosemary was born on April 26, 1935, under the sign of Taurus, the Bull.

42. Another version says, "against the harsh desert land."

43. They were an anarchist group whose proper name was Up against the Wall Motherfucker, if that can be considered a proper name. It derives from Amiri Baraka's angry 1967 poem "Black People," which contained the lines, "All the stores will open if you say the magic words. / The magic words are: 'Up against the wall motherfucker this is a stick up!'"

responsible for their anger and anxieties. "Get back to the land, start commures, plant seed, forget about the city and its politics."

"But," they said, "the government's got planes, helicopters, they can bomb your mountain out of existence."

"You are the warriors, we are the priests, it has always been that way," he said.

I tried to ignore the harsh sound of the propellers cutting the air. Concentrating on the intake of breath, counting. Overhead the plane swooped low over me, naked by the water. Vulnerable. Cactus and thorn trees, horns of cattle. Binoculars searching the clearing. I wanted to curl into a ball or hide in the shallow waters.

A rattlesnake held lazily in the stream, mouth open, tongue flickering, almost invisible, a length of crystallized water, body curving with the current. The plane flew lower. I panted in fear, I couldn't breathe, I'd forgotten how. Smiling, walking slowly upstream, he came, a yucca blossom behind his ear, unaware of the many dangers.

"You were made to be a mother, beloved, what a beautiful child we'll have."

"And what if I can't have children?"

"You can have children, I know you can if you really want to."

"Your eyes, my nose, your smile. I'd like a son of yours."

"What a beautiful mother you'll be."

The setting sun flattened into red rays, two horns of flame. Across the horizon a shark-shaped plane bit through the air. Screeching, it passed over us.

"What's the matter, beloved? Why are you frightened?"

"Stop the war, stop the war if you can. Mothers, children, that plane, hiding from a rain of fire."

"I felt it too, and for a moment saw the seat of power, all black leather and chrome. Women seek it too, in gold, in jewels."

"Stop the war, it must stop."

I thought then of another woman, another time. A woman gamboling in the Alpine meadows while beyond the Austrian retreat horrors raged. The memory is not pleasant.[44] Am I as mad and uncaring as she? Ignoring the realities of the world outside, a world of madness and cruelty?

It was twilight when we walked back from the waterfall. Only the brightest stars were visible. "What's that bright light in the east?"[45]

"It might be Mars, I'll check the star book when we get back to the house."

I'd been seeing UFOs[46]—not saucers, but quick-moving lights. Planets, cross-country jets from L.A., high-flying jets from the air base catching the last sun. There had been a few sightings that were strange. Three bright lights moving in unison, closer and closer to the house then abruptly winking out. I'd seen the same lights from the mountaintop when we were camping and again when crossing the valley late at night. They seemed as though they were going to land in the pasture, then shot straight up and disappeared.

I thought I was ready for a visitor from another galaxy till the day one floated over the top of the mountains. I'd been sunbathing and looked up to see this white filmy-looking sphere coming at me. I called to Tim; when he saw it he fell to his knees and prayed: *We greet you in love and peace, O brothers.* But I felt silly and fearful, maybe I wasn't ready to leave this earth. I ran and got the binoculars and tried to get the thing in focus. It kept disappearing. I started to pray, too: *Let there be love and clarity in my heart to greet the unexpected.*

It kept tantalizingly out of reach of the magnifying lens. Then in focus: white, round, markings on the side, numbers, a weather balloon. I didn't give up though. I was sure they were there somewhere. If I just got high enough, and if I were pure enough, they'd appear.

We were encouraged when we found evidence of a visitation: fine

44. Indeed not. Rosemary is remembering the Austrian singer Maria von Trapp (1905–1987), whose story was the subject of the highly popular 1965 film *The Sound of Music.* But it was the Trapp family rather than the Austrians who retreated—they left Austria soon after it was annexed by Germany (without resistance) in 1938.

45. "Where is he that is born King of the Jews? for we have seen his star in the east, and are come to worship him." Matthew 2:2.

46. Unidentified Flying Objects.

shredded metal foil caught on the manzanita bushes on top of a previously unexplored range. It looked like Christmas tinsel, though it was heavier and the metal would not burn. Tim was going to send it to be analyzed till someone told us that the air force used it to blanket the radar at the nearby base.[47]

I spent a lot of time watching the sky, learning jets, the satellites, knowing their direction and pace. I could still be surprised by an unexpected light moving across the night sky, a planet rising in the clear desert air.

Others at the ranch had seen and heard strange things in the mountains. Travis and Ann claimed they'd been chased off the peaks by three strange lights. Zain said that during a session he and Robbie had heard a sound in the valley that sent them off the mountain, back to the safety of Palm Springs. Michael said he felt them near, when he was spending the night in Milarepa's Cave.[48] He knew that if he went to the top of the mountain he'd see something he'd never seen before (and he wasn't sure he wanted to).

Spirits, gods, messengers. Several times I called to Tim to look at an unfamiliar light, but when he turned it was gone. It seemed he never saw them; perhaps they were for me alone.

Tim built a fire. I made tea, we settled on the bed before the large window facing south. The brightest light of all flashed in the sky. "Oh look, quickly." But it was gone. I turned to Tim: a joke about the light he never saw was never said. A stranger had taken his place. An unfamiliar, unrecognizable being looked at me from less than a foot away. I

---

47. This is chaff: Mylar (or aluminum, or glass or plastic fibers) dropped from airplanes or fired by rockets as a countermeasure to confuse radar. The radar "sees" a cloud of radio-reflective chaff and cannot identify the plane or missile near or within the cloud.

48. Milarepa's Cave sounds like an unofficial name for a physical feature at the ranch or the nearby wilderness. The original Milarepa (approximate dates 1052–1135) was a Tibetan poet and sage, known for having repented and transcended his early violent sins. He wrote many famous songs, founded a lineage of sages, and is regarded as a bodhisattva. He lived for many years in a cave in Tibet. There are caves in Tibet and Nepal called by this name, but Michael's comment about going to the top of the mountain suggests that this one was in Riverside County.

was frightened. I looked at the stranger who looked at me and thought for a long while: What should my greeting be? "Peace." I said, finally. "What do you wish?"

The visitor from another space smiled. Hungrily, I thought. Teeth glistened, lines radiated from the corners of bright unfamiliar eyes. Licked its lips, slowly. "New Life," it thought at me, a hollow voice followed after: *New Life.*

I thought about that. Was it an unreasonable request? Flesh that had to be fed to this strange guest.

PEYOTE EQUINOX

Peyote was the second mind-changing psychoactive plant that I encountered (after grass)—it changed my mind about taking it in a Lower East Side tenement in New York City. It also helped to change my mind about the relationship with the man with whom I shared the low-rent flat, a Southern composer and madman who'd introduced me to beat poets and real poverty. His drugs of choice were alcohol and the interiors of Benzedrine inhalers. Our immersion into books about Native Americans, and his writing a symphony based on the life of Chief Crazy Horse, led us to send away to Brown's Nursery in Texas for the fresh peyote buttons.[49]

Despite the symphony's dedication to me and my appreciation for all that he'd taught me, I left him and the Lower East Side, vowing that the next time I experienced the drug I would be in an environment that would enhance the glimpse I'd had of the awesome power of the plant to brighten and clarify and that I would never, ever again

---

49. The composer was Charles Mills (1914–1982). He was from North Carolina, and his Crazy Horse Symphony (Symphony no. 4) is dated 1957, when Rosemary was twenty-two, about right since she says her next peyote experience (dated in her time line to 1968) was "ten or more" years after the first one with him. Crazy Horse (1840–1877) was a leader of the Oglala Lakota Sioux in their resistance to the Americans. He was the victor at the Battle of the Little Big Horn, where Custer was killed, but was eventually defeated and captured soon afterward. He was killed while in U.S. Army custody.

take it ground up, cooked, and mixed with orange juice. The memory of that taste was sufficient to induce nausea at the thought of it for many years. While flying as a stewardess, during a conversation in the cockpit, the pilot asked what was the worst taste I could remember. The memory of the abused plant sent me to the loo even though the skies were calm.

Despite the awful taste, I knew I wanted to take it again but in natural surroundings with ritual and ceremony. I got that wish some ten or more years later in the late nineteen sixties.[50]

A bumpy road, dusty landscape, the high tablelands of New Mexico, a Navaho reservation. Roadman invited us into his home.[51] Inside the large wooden room, his wife was preparing the evening meal of meat stew and blue maize porridge. We drank hot strong coffee from metal cups, then went outside to watch the sun pass.

Ted handed around peyote snuff. We leaned against the cars watching the stars appear, waiting for the others to arrive for the beginning of the meeting. Trucks drove up raising dust, greetings were exchanged. Roadman spoke to Ted, he arranged us in a line before the hogan. We walked sunwise twice around the building, then entered while Roadman directed us to our places. He sat before a crescent-shaped altar, Drummer to his right, Cedarman to his left. They prepared the water drum. Fireman brought coals for the wood placed before the altar. A sack of tobacco and dry corn husks was passed; we would each roll our own prayer cigarettes.

Roadman spoke of the purpose of the gathering. Two children were sick, their mother and father were sponsoring the meeting. They spoke briefly, welcoming us and our desire to pray with them. We smoked the cigarettes and Fireman collected the remains, placing them on the altar. Roadman poured peyote tea; it was handed around the circle. He explained his way for the ceremony and the sunwise path we would follow when passing the prayer drum, eagle fan, sage, staff, and rattle. Sunwise all the instruments would go.

---

50. This prologue to the peyote episode is dated 1998.
51. Roadman is the title of the officiant at a traditional Native American peyote ceremony.

An old woman seemed to be complaining of our presence. Roadman talked quietly to her and she seemed to agree. A young couple across from us smiled their amusement; we exchanged smiles. They were Native American, beautiful, young, and obviously experienced peyote takers.[52] Two small, bundled children were curled behind their mother next to Drummer. We had not yet drunk the tea.

We were eight from Los Angeles. Long-haired Anglos in cowboy boots with turquoise beads purchased that afternoon in the pawnshops of Gallup. Red-eyed men leaned against the lampposts. Police in county cars patrolled the streets, keeping a watchful eye on every Navaho man reeling tipsily from doorway to lamppost. Now, deep in the reservation, we sat in the hogan with the peyote church members, short-haired, hard-working people in sober clothes, neatly pressed jeans and plaid jackets.

Roadman prayed while Drummer played. We drank the tea. It was not bitter. Roadman spoke again in English. He prayed for sons lost in the wars, for those who drank whiskey, for those who did not know the Road, or who'd lost it, following the white man's way, forgetting their fathers. He prayed for those in jail, arrested for bringing peyote home,[53] for understanding and goodwill between all people, for the sick children here with us, for all children, for all beings. His prayer ended.

Drummer spoke while Roadman drummed. The peyote buttons from the altar were passed around the circle. They were much less bitter than I expected. Drummer spoke with his drums, the air hummed, the sound was oceanic. Cedarman placed sage on the fire, then passed the prayer instruments in our direction. One of the group attempted to sing but truth stopped him. Left hand, right hand,[54] we handed sage, staff, fan, and rattle, those with songs sang them. The young couple had many songs. The drum went round again. The peyote came: it was sweet, it was sweet. All prayed, sang aloud. I wept not unhappily.

In the middle of the night, Fireman spoke in his native tongue; I

---

52. Another version says they "smiled in friendship."
53. Another version says, "bringing people peyote from Texas."
54. Another version says, "From right hand to left hand."

understood him.[55] The fire flamed with his words, they were strong and full of courage.

Water Lady opened the door and passed the water gourd. We tasted water for the first time in many hours, then left the hogan. Everything outside in the still dark night was changed. There were tunnels of light coming from my eyes, illuminating everything I looked at. Everywhere I turned the air and the earth glistened from reflected starlight.

We returned to the altar, the comforting smell of sage, cedar, more peyote and praying. The fire spoke, from somewhere there was an answering rumble. The drum passed me again; I had no song but thought of a chant I'd read in a book of Navaho sand paintings.

> *I am being instructed, talking to God*
> *With God's little whirlwind touching the tip of my tongue*
> *I am being instructed, talking to God*
> *Pollen from my hands and feet should fall*
> *A way is opened to me, talking to God*
> *It has become beautiful again, it has become beautiful again*
> *A way is open, the world is restored in beauty.*[56]

Morning came through the eastern door. Dawn Lady[57] brought food and her blessing. Fireman arranged the coals in the shape of an eagle glowing before the altar.[58] Roadman asked if anyone had special prayers, it was time to say them. We prayed for children. He fanned us with cedar smoke, then gave us his blessing and a special button of peyote. Drummer spoke, then opened the drum; its water was poured on the altar. We left the hogan one by one, to greet the morning, Easter.[59]

---

55. Another version says Roadman spoke "in tongues unknown," which doesn't seem right.
56. I have been unable to identify the book or verify the authenticity of the quoted chant.
57. Another version has "Water Lady."
58. Another version has "an eagle glowed before the altar." Better, but less clear.
59. Another version ends with greeting the morning not of Easter but of the spring equinox, 1968. Indeed, there this narrative, titled "Peyote Equinox," is dated Fall Equinox 1998 and is dedicated "For Anita" (meaning Anita Hoffman). That later version

EPILOGUE

After a flight to New York for a lecture engagement, Tim and I visited a former League for Spiritual Discovery member at his apartment in the East Village, just a few doors away from where I had first encountered peyote. My hair still smelled of cedar and sage.

Peyote stayed in my life as mescaline, often taken on a mountaintop in Joshua Tree National Park. It was there a Native American married Tim and me. And I had a brief meeting with Carlos Castaneda, whose books confirmed and illuminated the experience in the hogan.[60]

It was only recently, more than forty years after encountering peyote for the first time, that I took it again, as a tea, in preparation for a healing ceremony. We arranged the room with pillows in a circle, gathered wood, and lit candles. There was a fire, sage and cedar, and five dear friends. The purpose of the meeting was to give our love and healing thoughts to one of us who was gravely ill.

Peyote was not the only sacrament that we used during the night, but it was the peyote that suggested the rituals that we used: the use of sage to clarify, an eagle's feather to fan the smoke, cedar to give fragrance to the carefully tended fire, and the focus of our attention on the one who needed us. And it is these rituals that have been recovered from our Native American ancestors that we of the sixties continue to use in the important rites of our lives.[61]

(*cont. from p. 139*) is fuller and in some ways clearer than the basic version in the Blue Binder that is the core text of most of the chapters, and I have taken text liberally from it. But Easter did not fall on the spring equinox in any of the years from 1964 to 1970. In 1968 the spring equinox fell on March 20, and Easter on April 14. Perhaps the answer is that the ceremony described here took place on one of those dates in 1968, but that the 1998 ceremony for Anita Hoffman, described below, took place at the fall equinox (September 22/23) that year.

60. Carlos Castaneda (1925–1998) was a Mexican-American anthropologist whose very popular 1968 book *The Teachings of Don Juan: A Yaqui Way of Knowledge,* describing dramatic spirit-world experiences using psychoactive plants, was one of the foundational texts of psychedelic exploration.

61. Perhaps the word *ancestors* in the last sentence is imprecise—*predecessors* seems better for most of us. Like the prologue to the peyote episode, this epilogue is dated 1998. I have set both passages off typographically to mark their separation from the rest of the text. As mentioned, the later ceremony was held for Anita Hoffman, who died on December 27, 1998.

SEVEN

Enchantments

*Pan, Bou Jeloud, the Father of Skins, dances through the
moonlight nights in his hill village, Joujouka, to the wailing
of his hundred Master Musicians. Down in the towns, far
away by the seaside, you can hear the wild whimper of his
oboe-like raitas; a faint breath of panic borne on the wind.*[1]

BRION GYSIN, LINER NOTES FROM THE ALBUM
BRIAN JONES PRESENTS THE PIPES OF PAN AT JOUJOUKA

Timothy and I spent September 1969 in Tangier. One night Paul
Bowles and Brion Gysin told us about the musicians of Joujouka, who
lived high in the Rif Mountains of Morocco.[2] The Master Musicians
were priests of Pan, who celebrated the ancient rites of the goat god and
the local goddess, Aisha the beautiful, the blue-faced one.[3] Brion told us

---

1. A raita (more usually *rhaita*) is a double-reed wind instrument of North Africa.
Unlike a Western oboe, it has no keys to cover the holes—those are opened or closed
with the fingers, like a recorder.
2. Paul Bowles (1910–1999) was an American writer, translator, and composer who lived
in Tangier on the northwestern coast of Morocco. He was a leader in the effort to preserve traditional Moroccan music. Brion Gysin (1916–1986) was an English avant-garde
painter and poet whose "cut-up" assemblage techniques influenced William Burroughs.
3. This Aisha is of course not the historical Aisha, Mohammed's youngest and most
favored wife, who after his death played important religious, political, and military
roles in early Islam.

that his friend, the Moroccan artist Hamri, could take us to the Master Musicians, the Ahl Srif, as they were the tribe of his mother.[4]

We started from the sea, at Tangier, on a clear fall afternoon. In a succession of taxicabs, each more decrepit than the last, we headed toward the Rif Mountains. When one driver had gone as far as he would go, we'd find another. In villages, Hamri disappeared into crowded marketplaces and reappeared within a few minutes laden with oranges and packages, trailed by the owner of the taxi that would take us to the next outpost.

We reached a checkpoint at a dusty fort on a barren plain where he reported our presence and destination to a "cousin," the local *commandante,* who allowed our passage. Our driver was reluctant to continue, but Hamri harangued and cajoled him until at last he agreed to take us into the foothills of the mountains, blue and smoky high above us. After miles of jouncing on a steeply climbing rutted road, he stopped and would not continue. We gathered our packages, paid the driver, and started on foot up the mountain path in the early evening light.

On the slope of the mountain across from our path, a shepherd boy watched us. He stood on one leg, the other leg bent and resting on his thigh, his arm crooked around his staff.[5] Hamri called out to him. The boy leapt into the air, waved his staff, and took off running up the mountain. "A cousin," Hamri told us. "He'll tell the village we're on our way. Perhaps they'll send animals. We'll rest here."

We waited on a broad section of the trail, and soon a group of villagers descended the trail to meet us. A woman offered us golden apricots from a fold in her cloak. Hamri exchanged greetings with everyone, waving his arms to include us. The villagers insisted on carrying our bundles and packages up the mountain.[6]

The sun lit the distant peaks.[7] Soon we saw the village, whitewashed

---

4. From 1954 to 1958 Brion Gysin operated a restaurant in Tangier called the 1001 Nights. The Master Musicians of Joujouka performed there, and Mohamed Hamri was the cook.
5. The shepherd with his leg crossed over his thigh is standing in the reverse of the position of the Hanged Man on trump number twelve in the tarot deck.
6. Another version has, perhaps better, "We gave up our bundles to insistent hands."
7. Another version adds "beyond the village."

walls of low houses turning blue in the darkening light. A few dim lamps glowed from the doorways. I heard a child's laugh and the distant bleat of a goat. The men of the village stood waiting: robed, silent figures. The women and children, in a group, stood farther away. Hamri led us to a long, low, white building with a porch. He said it was the schoolhouse, built with funds that he and Brion had given to the village.

We left our shoes on the porch as the men did and ducked our heads to enter the schoolhouse. Hamri introduced the men, but it was impossible to keep up with their names, until the last man stepped from behind a taller companion. "Berdu," Hamri said with emphasis. Berdu, the smallest and surely the poorest among the village men, shambled forward. He reached up and took off an imaginary plumed hat and made a sweeping, courtly bow to me. Startled, I involuntarily dropped a curtsy, and everyone laughed. The village idiot, I thought—he looked simple, small and ragged. We were invited to be seated in a corner of the room that was heaped with embroidered pillows.[8]

A kerosene stove hissed in the far corner, and shortly we were served sweet mint tea in small glasses. Hamri talked quietly with the men. Their clothing was simple: shirts, pants, a mix of European and handmade, always a ragged cloak, and one could occasionally glimpse the embroidered bags the men wore beneath their cloaks. Eggs and flat bread were served all around. After we'd eaten and the tin dishes were collected and cigarettes exchanged, the men opened the embroidered bags and pulled out simple reed-stem pipes and, to our delight, packages of finely cut kef. Hamri and Berdu shared their pipes with us. The kef was fresher and greener than any I'd had in Morocco.[9]

---

8. Another version elaborates: "each decorated with a bit of lace or embroidery, donated perhaps from different households."

9. Kef is a powerful preparation of the crystallized resin from the trichomes (hairlike structures) of cannabis flowers. It is the raw material of hashish. In Morocco, however, where this chapter is set, kef is usually a mixture of cannabis and local tobacco—not the same thing, but still powerful. Another version omits the kef, but says, "after the meal the men rearranged themselves against the walls of the narrow room, facing one another, while we sat at the end of the room against the pillows." My guess is both happened.

A man took a violin from its case and placed it upright with the point on his knee. Hamri told us the man had been a sailor, and that he'd brought the violin back from England. The violinist smiled and began to pluck out a reel. Everyone laughed. Pennywhistles joined the violin, and Berdu stepped into the aisle. He hitched up his cloak and held it with one arm. With the other arm behind his back he danced a sailor's jig until the violinist turned the reel into flamenco. Berdu became a self-important torero[10] who, with a twitch of his cloak, became an imperious woman trailing flounces as the music became a Gypsy wail. She opened her mouth to sing an impassioned lament. The violinist rose, swaying to accompany her, then interrupted the voiceless song to correct the glowering opera singer who stood before us. The violinist was now Paganini, enraptured by his own music.[11]

Berdu picked up an imaginary baton and rapped for attention on the nearest head. As the violinist unheedingly played on, Berdu snapped the baton in disgust and stalked away. He returned as an old woman carrying an invisible heavy bucket. With great effort, he lifted the bucket and dashed the contents onto the head of the violinist, who continued to ignore him and finished the real and wonderful music. The violinist then wiped his brow and sat down to everyone's laughter and applause.

Tim and I looked at one another. I reached into my own embroidered bag and discreetly took out two tabs of LSD. I placed one into his mouth as though I were placing a kissed fingertip onto his lips, and I put one into my own mouth. We swallowed the LSD with sweet green tea.

Berdu began a prayer in a surprisingly deep and resonant voice: *La ilaha illa'llah.* The men responded *Muhammadun rasulu'llah.*[12]

The prayers continued in a conversational tone, Berdu comment-

10. A Spanish bullfighter.
11. The original has "Paderewski," but this was likely a slip of the pen as Paderewski was a pianist.
12. This is the Shahada, sometimes called in English the Two Testimonials, the basic statement of Islamic belief. "There is no god but God; Mohammed is the messenger of God." I have corrected Rosemary's transcription.

ing, it seemed, on the village, the animals, and Hamri, who bowed his head to gentle laughter. Berdu directed us through prayer to laughter to a sense of closeness. There was a time of silence. We heard a few gentle coughs, a distant tinkle of bells. People stirred, shifting positions, and Berdu sat down among us.[13] We could no longer see him.

"Who is he?" I asked Hamri.

"Berdu, the Master," Hamri replied.

"The Master?"

"The Master Musician of Joujouka."

I needed to step outside. I found my boots on the porch lined up with the men's backless leather slippers. I started to put on my boots, but a man I had not noticed before waved his hand dismissively and pointed to the men's slippers. I nodded my thanks and put on the nearest pair of slippers. He motioned to my left, and I followed a path out onto a gently sloping field. I was facing a star-filled sky. There were no electric lights to dim the stars. Everything I saw was as it had always been, timeless.

I could hear the goats' bells, and their strong smell told me they were nearby. I pulled a cluster of white wool that had been caught on a bush. As I walked back to the longhouse I rolled it between my fingers, effortlessly drawing the silky tuft of wool into a fine strand of thread. When I returned to the longhouse I was reluctant to go back inside to the room of men, to the air heavy with kef and tobacco smoke and kerosene. I wondered what the village women and children were doing.

Hamri stood in the doorway, backlit by the kerosene lamps inside. He beckoned to me to join him and the men. He led us out over a slight rise to a small clearing between the hills where brush was being piled onto a crackling fire. "Stand here," Hamri said, placing us ten or so feet from the fire, before a clearing of packed earth. To our left, a row of hooded men took long wooden horns from patchwork bags.[14] Behind them stood a group of men with drums, each drum aslant across the

---

13. Another version has "Berdu disappeared behind his tall companion."

14. These are the raitas mentioned in the epigraph.

chest, held with thongs. They carried curved slender rods in their right hands, and in their left hands, heavier wooden sticks, the top ends carved in relief spirals like rams' horns.

All was still except for the fire throwing sparks into the dark night. The hooded men lifted their horns, and a thin piercing sound from the oboe-like instruments was sustained incredibly long, maintained by the subtle joining of one horn to another; no single breath could be that long. I traveled the reedy seamless breath to a star that seemed to grow brighter, larger, and then the horns went higher, taking me almost to the point of pain; the music swirled into a skirling bagpipe sound whose rhythm the wind had torn away.[15] The drums, silent until then, boomed into a thudding heartbeat of rhythm. My breath was caught by the horns; my pulse by the drums. Was this music, or the thunder of mammoth hooves, screams of birds of prey? It seemed the very tempo of life in my body. Eardrums could be shattered. Hearts could burst from these sounds. The drums built a wall to contain the reed instruments, which descended into a weaving ribbon of silver notes, playful to the drums' assertive tempo, seductive, cajoling, demanding rhythms.

A creature leapt over the fire to confront the musicians. He was tall, powerful, barely covered by a tattered robe. His face was concealed by a deep straw basket antlered with leaves.[16] He pounded his feet to the drums, caught by their rhythms, his arches curved so high they were like hooves. Trailing branches in his hands, flailing the air, his pelvis thrusting, he was goaded by the music. He whirled around the fire, pausing once to glare at me with a goat's horizontal eyes. The creature struck me, lashed me with the branches. Struck me or anointed me, I don't know which.

"Bou Jeloud," Hamri said.

Pan lives, I thought.

A slender figure in a blue-spangled dress came from the shadows. Arms curved, veils aswirl, her hips swaying with seduction, she turned

---

15. Another version has "cold as a star one stares at until it seems to grow brighter, larger."

16. Another version has "adorned with antler-like branches."

before Bou Jeloud. Hooves pounding, he followed her dancing form, leaping before her as she teased him with her veils, playfully turning him around and around, mocking him. Abruptly she was gone, and the creature confronted the musicians, but they taunted him with their rhythms. He danced before them, controlled by them. The drums reverberated through the mountains. The horns' high notes seemed to come from everywhere. Bou Jeloud bucked convulsively, howling in anguish.[17] The drums slowed; the horns were one pure fading note. Bou Jeloud scattered the fire with his flails and disappeared into the black night.

Later, at the schoolhouse, Berdu brought former Bou Jelouds and Aishas to the center of the floor to demonstrate and mime their styles. He made fun of all of them, showing how one of them had grown too stout, another too clumsy. Hamri said they were chosen for training while very young and that the characteristics they showed as children determined which role they would play.

And then I danced for them. Not that I wanted to, or even thought that I could, but my usual inhibitions were lessened by LSD, and there seemed to be silken threads tied to my ankles and wrists that Berdu controlled ever so surely. And the music was irresistible. Pennywhistles, violin, and softly tapped drums drew me to my feet. For a few moments I was Aisha to Berdu's gently mocking Bou Jeloud. There were shouts of *musicienne* and *encore* when I sat down. I rose again, but the magic that had descended upon me was fading and I had become self-conscious. I pretended to stumble and fell back into Tim's lap; we all laughed.

We left on muleback the next morning. All the way down the mountain I could still hear the drums in my head, and I could hear them at will for many years. The memory of the music that night reminds me that for a brief, magical time, I was a *musicienne* among the Master Musicians of Joujouka.

---

17. Another version has "howling in anguish that Aisha had left him."

EIGHT

Holding Together

The interpersonal effect of bizarre behavior is to provoke exasperated rejection from others. Marked eccentricity flaunts to the world the message, "I do not want your approval." This usually guarantees to the subject the disapproval of others. In the extreme case (psychosis) it provokes society to punitive incarceration.

TIMOTHY LEARY, *THE INTERPERSONAL DIAGNOSIS OF PERSONALITY* (1957)

Tim was behind thick glass. A visiting child's balloon bobbed above his head, the balloon and my hair reflected on the bulletproof window separating Tim and me. The phone connecting us didn't work. His lips moved, but I couldn't hear him. He was crying. I'd never seen him cry before.

Permission to visit him had been delayed over and over again. I was a convicted felon, released on my own recognizance pending appeal. The sentence was meaningless to me. The reality was that my husband had been handcuffed and led away. Jackie and I were stunned by the suddenness of it all. It seemed that one moment Tim had been telling Jackie to sit up straight, that the jurors were coming back in, and then the judge was calling him a menace to the community, and then Tim was gone. One last wave to us, and he was gone and the courtroom was empty.

Soon Jackie would have to serve three months. If my appeal failed, I would have to serve six months and be on probation for four years of a ten-year sentence. We were ordered to report to the Probation Department in San Francisco immediately.

Mother Mary, comes to me, speaking words of wisdom . . .[1]

The music on the car radio played as we drove away from the court-house, leaving behind a small group of friends. Among them I saw Jas waving a palm frond.[2]

I slept most of the way back to Berkeley, waking when Jackie stopped for a red light in front of the Black Panthers' headquarters. They were a mysterious organization, I thought. I'd seen Kathleen and Eldridge [Cleaver]'s photographs in the newspaper.[3]

The probation officer was a pleasant woman who had known Tim when he'd been at the Kaiser Institute.[4] She seemed sympathetic and arranged to schedule appointments that would allow me to return to Laguna Beach. Our lawyer was convinced that if we appealed to the judge through telegrams from prominent people, he would be forced to release Tim on bond.

I spent days in Laguna Beach in the lawyer's office, calling names from the list I'd stayed up nights to prepare, running up enormous telephone bills. Almost everyone I contacted agreed to follow the form that had been selected for the protest: "Dr. Timothy Leary is being denied his constitutional rights . . ."

There were other details to attend to in Laguna. Some adventurous Canyon People had put together a plan to spray the steering wheels of

---

1. Quoting from Paul McCartney's song "Let It Be," released in March 1970. Timothy was sentenced on March 16 (Robert Greenfield, *Timothy Leary: A Biography*, New York: Houghton Mifflin Harcourt, 2006, 371–72).

2. I have not been able to identify Jas.

3. The Black Panther Party was a radical black political organization founded by Huey Newton and Bobby Seale in 1966. It had a revolutionary socialist orientation and an aggressive commitment to self-defense. Katherine and Eldridge Cleaver figure prominently in chapter 9. See footnote on page 153 below.

4. The Kaiser Permanente hospital in Oakland, where Timothy had worked in the Psychology Department in 1951–52, and with which he later continued an association.

local police cars with a mixture of DMSO and LSD.[5] No one was sure if it would work, but they wanted to try it, and I had to persuade them not to. It was against our religion.

For the moment Susan was safe with her husband, so she wasn't a worry. I felt, perhaps unfairly, that her report to the Probation Department about Tim had prejudiced them against him. I was concerned about Jackie. The prison he'd been sentenced to was notorious for attacks on young men, and I worried about him being there, if in fact he turned himself in at all.

Money was an ever-present problem. The lawyer told me that the bail for Tim could be enormous and that I'd have to find some way to raise it.

We'd never been separated for so long.

The phone went on suddenly, and Tim was saying to me, "You've got to free me. You've got to get me out of here." And again, "You've got to free me." I tried to tell him about the telegrams to the judge and then he said, "No. You've got to free me. Don't trust the lawyers. You do it."

"How?" I asked.

"I don't care how."

"I will," I said. "I'll free you, my love. I promise."

The guard shook Tim's shoulder. Tim held my gaze. The child's balloon tapped gently on the window.

❦

Editor's Note

There is a hiatus in the narrative here, marked in the manuscript "To Be Continued," followed in Rosemary's hand on one copy with Planning the Escape and The Escape, and so on. Presumably Rosemary did not wish to publish (or even write down) the details of the planning of Timothy's escape from the prison in San Luis Obispo. Rosemary resumes the story with the escape already underway. I have had to

---

5. *Canyon People* refers to Laguna Canyon, partly a wilderness reserve and partly included in the City of Laguna Beach. DMSO is dimethyl sulfoxide. It was supposed to facilitate absorption of LSD through the skin, but it is far from clear whether this works.

rearrange some elements for a narrative clarity the surviving manuscript does not completely allow.

The feeling [that she could not bear to be with Timothy] started after his escape from prison, when we were at the farmhouse hideaway with Bernardine Dohrn and other members of the Weather Underground.[6] Waiting for him in the isolated farmhouse, I baked bread and made soups; outside by the river, I bent willow trees and gathered rocks to make a sweat lodge to purify ourselves. When I'd been told that we were going to stay in the old and not very comfortable farmhouse, I asked to stop at Pier Cargo where I bought an orange paper lantern and an orange cloth to cover the window.[7] I bought pillows to match the silk robe I had packed so he could forget the feel of prison denims. Our room glowed warm and welcoming with candles and color and incense, and me.[8] I had fulfilled my promise and helped to free him from prison.

Downstairs it was all bare light bulbs and rickety chairs and grim political posters. No comfort. No home.[9] These college students, children of privilege, had no use for creature comforts.[10] I could understand their need to avoid a bourgeois environment, but coming from a poor family I found this disdain for the barest comfort puzzling. Didn't they need cheerfulness and light? Was it all lived in the mind and in the hope of revolution?

---

6. Bernardine Dohrn (born 1942) was a radical lawyer, working with the National Lawyers Guild, Students for a Democratic Society (SDS), and finally the supposedly revolutionary Weather Underground. Her brilliance and beauty dazzled a generation of left-wing activists. After years underground and a time of imprisonment, she became a law professor.

7. Rosemary probably means Pier 1 Imports, a chain store that at that time had many California locations and stock just like that. Pier Cargo was a small clothing retailer in Provincetown, Massachusetts, where Rosemary lived for some time many years later, including the time when much of this memoir was written. This may account for the confusion of names, if there was one.

8. Another version adds "waiting for my man." It is better without that.

9. Another version has "Nobody home."

10. Another version reads, "Poor white trash would have a sense of creature comforts that these privileged college graduates had no use for."

When I was running around with Pam (as she called herself to me),[11] getting a wig and having photographs made for a passport, I only knew that she was part of a group that wanted to help free Tim from prison. I said that I wished the Weathermen would free prisoners rather than blow up buildings. About all I knew of them was what I'd read in the newspapers during the Democratic convention in Chicago, and later when they claimed credit for bombing university and government buildings. They had once been leaders in the SDS (Students for a Democratic Society); then the most radical faction split from the organization. They had become Weathermen after a line from a Bob Dylan song,[12] and then "Weather Underground," and their communiqués were regularly printed in the alternative press. I really hadn't paid much attention. I wasn't interested in armed insurrection and bombs and radical politics, except for Jonathan Jackson's attempt to free his brother George from prison.[13] Anyone who has had a loved one imprisoned unfairly understands that rage and the sense of helplessness.

They picked him up outside the San Luis Obispo prison where he had been for seven months.[14] Pam waited until Tim made his escape and was on his way to the farmhouse before telling me that it was the Weather Underground who had spirited Tim from the prison gates. I was grateful and impressed, and worried that the $25,000 I had raised to free political prisoners under Holding Together's name, that I had given Weather for the escape, would be used to buy dynamite.

I ran into Tim's arms when he stepped out of the car. But he was

---

11. Actually Bernardine Dohrn.

12. The song, "Subterranean Homesick Blues" (1965), contained the line, "You don't need a weather man to know which way the wind blows."

13. Rosemary refers to the attempt on August 7, 1970, by Jonathan Jackson, then seventeen, to free some prisoners on trial at the Marin County Courthouse in San Rafael, California, and take hostages for the release of his brother George Jackson from San Quentin Prison. Jonathan Jackson and several others were killed during the incident. George Jackson was killed at San Quentin about a year later in an unrelated episode.

14. The prison was called California Men's Colony. It consisted of two separate prisons, CMC East (Level III: medium security) and CMC West (Level I: minimum security, and Level II: light security). Timothy was at the Level I facility in CMC West.

changed. Prison had altered him, and I did not like the alteration. He was testy and uncertain, and not particularly grateful that he was free. I did not like our lovemaking either: perfunctory, without passion or tenderness. It didn't help that Bernardine was caterwauling most of the night in the embrace of her very handsome lover. The next morning we waited for news from the outside world, to hear what was being said about the escape. Tim was really upset that the messenger didn't bring the actual newspapers, just the report of what had been printed. The authorities were looking in the wrong direction, toward Laguna Beach, and for the moment we were safe at the farm near Seattle.

While Bernardine, bare to her waist, bathed at the old porcelain sink, we talked about Eldridge Cleaver and his situation in Algeria.[15] The Algerian government had accepted him and his party as the forerunners of an American liberation movement. Bernardine and the other Weathermen felt he would welcome us there, that he would be happy to see some Americans. Tim and Bernardine had both met Eldridge and liked him. No one knew Kathleen Cleaver or the other Panther women, but I thought we should bring some presents if we could. Bernardine suggested birth control pills—probably a good idea but impossible without a prescription. Perhaps some good soaps. I decided to look for some in Paris, where we would make our first stop.

At the kitchen table we also talked about Weather's change in their stance on armed resistance. The notorious bomb-making explosion in a Greenwich Village townhouse that left several of their group dead and others missing had changed their thinking. (My old apartment on Ninth Street was just one block south.)[16] They now convincingly espoused peace and love and community service. I felt we were with

---

15. Eldridge Cleaver (1935–1998) was a leader in the Black Panther Party. He became famous for his book of prison essays, *Soul on Ice,* published in 1968. That same year Cleaver, accused of attempted murder, jumped bail and fled first to Cuba and afterward to Algeria. He later returned to the United States and became a Republican and a Mormon.

16. The explosion, on March 6, 1970, was at 18 West Eleventh Street, *two* blocks north of Rosemary's old Ninth Street apartment.

people who shared a vision of the harmony of life and a dream of a world unified by freedom and justice for all. I liked them. And they had just risked their lives and their own freedom to help Tim.

I wished he was less grumpy over the missing newspapers and less hesitant about getting a false passport. I had done it. Getting the false passport had taken nerve but was amazingly simple as long as I kept my wig on and remembered the new name. At the passport office I forgot the name and had to drop my handbag and take time to recover the scattered contents while I frantically tried to think of it.

Within two days we had his passport. His head was shaved to a bald stubble, and he had a salesman's brown suit and vest. We were ready for the flight to Paris and airport scrutiny. The last night we all went to see the movie *Woodstock* and shouted and sang along with Richie Havens's "Freedom" and cried at the end of the movie when Jimi Hendrix played the national anthem. Jimi died in London the night before we saw the movie.[17] It was a fitting end to what was perhaps our last night in America.

In those days of frequent hijackings, federal sky marshals were conspicuous in the airports, standing near the gates, watching while the passengers were scanned with metal detector wands.[18] We stood apart from one another in the line leading to the plane. The Weathermen were behind the barrier watching us. What would they do if we were stopped? What could they do? But we didn't fit the hijacker or dope dealer profile, and we passed inspection. For the first time we were invisible to the powers of authority.

The flight was uneventful. We flew from Seattle (where the Weather Underground saw us through the security gates), I with my blonde curly

17. Another version says he died "a few days before," but Greenfield agrees it was the night before (*Timothy Leary*, 393). Hendrix, a guitarist of astonishing virtuosity, died on September 18, 1970, at the age of twenty-seven, five days after Tim's escape. The highly successful film *Woodstock,* about the famous rock festival, was released in March 1970 and won the Academy Award for best documentary feature.

18. Perhaps these were other officials—the sky marshals were not supposed to be conspicuous. They were covert agents, and their job was not to staff the security lines but to mix, armed but unnoticed, among the passengers on the flights.

wig and false passport and Tim with a newly shaved head and equally dubious papers. I believe we stayed over for a night in Chicago.[19] I remember waiting while Tim signed us into a hotel and being furious and scared when he called my real name loudly and angrily in the lobby of the hotel. He seemed to have forgotten our disguises and was ill-tempered and careless. We had so much of our escape left to do, and I could not trust him not to blow it.

Months of sneaking around, clandestine appointments with clever young people who wanted to free Tim but wouldn't tell me who they were had kept me alert and cautious and justifiably paranoid. There was always a strange car or two parked near our house on Queens Road in Berkeley. Men showed up frequently to make mysterious repairs to our telephone lines. Odd types appeared at the house offering us dope or guns. Some claimed to be prison buddies of Tim's and said he had sent them to get false papers or money or whatever. And then I'd visit him at the prison and he'd say yeah, someone told him that they would look me up, and then he would tell me of his latest escape plan where all I had to do was get a helicopter and a yacht offshore. Sure.

In the five years that we had been together, I had been arrested three times, jailed twice, spent thirty days locked up for contempt of court, and testified before a grand jury for twenty-five days. I had spent endless hours in courtrooms and lawyers' offices. I had gone from an operation and a week in a hospital directly to a pretrial hearing.[20] I traveled ceaselessly, first on lecture tours with Tim and then alone trying to raise money for bail. In the nine months since he was imprisoned I had been constantly on the move. I followed him to Texas when he was

---

19. Greenfield says they stayed more than one night in Chicago and got their passports at the Chicago passport office (*Timothy Leary*, 394). Rosemary's account here suggests that they got their passports in Seattle and just stopped over in Chicago. Greenfield is a careful scholar; Rosemary was there, but her words *I believe we stayed over* suggest a measure of uncertainty. It is hard to imagine they would have stopped for a while in Chicago in the midst of an international getaway without a good reason. Greenfield has them leaving Chicago for Paris on September 23, 1970.

20. In another version Rosemary adds that this operation was undertaken "to improve the possibility of conceiving a child."

moved there to face another trial on the old Laredo bust. I hitchhiked from Big Sur to the prison in San Luis Obispo every week, flying back to the house in Berkeley. Then I begged rides to Big Sur and the little stone house that the Esalen folks had found for me so I could be closer to the prison. I hitched to the prison and back to Berkeley or Laguna Beach, always circling, trying to keep the funds coming in and my probation officer appeased, trying to keep depressed Susan out of the hospital, to keep angry Jackie from tearing down the house, to keep my friend and her family in food while they stayed at the Berkeley house, to stop angry young hippies from dosing the Laguna police, and to keep Tim hopeful that escape plans were progressing, helicopters and an oceangoing yacht in the middle of the largest collection of army and navy and coast guard and air force bases in the country. And I had done it all, plus fundraisers and interviews and radio talks, living on carrot juice and not much sleep and growing wiser and stronger with every moment away from him.

And then Paris. By the time we got there we were exhausted and quarreled superficially, old lovers,[21] when really it was something other than what we were or were not saying. After our prison visits I would talk myself into believing that when he was free, I would be able to relax. Then he would know what we should do; the wild schemes he concocted were just the result of the unreality of his locked-up life. He would understand why I couldn't rescue him with a yacht and a helicopter, or get false papers for his prison friends. He would be free of jealousy and old recriminations, and despite the shaved head and altered appearance, he would once again be the strong and confident man I loved.

We arrived in Paris to find all the hotels filled, the tourist bureaus crowded, and the taxi drivers indifferent. This was my first trip to Paris, and I could not see its charms; my head itched unbearably from the wig, and I wanted a bath and some privacy more than anything else. Tim remembered some cordial correspondence with a French psychiatrist—

---

21. Another version says, "quarrels over old loves or something"; another says, "bickering like old lovers." It sounds like a stressful time.

perhaps he would have some idea where we could stay. He found his address in a telephone book and with characteristic optimism had a taxi take us through the September streets of a golden Paris afternoon to this stranger's apartment.

While Tim waited in a café, I asked the concierge for Dr. Pierre Ben Sousan. She directed me to the third floor. An attractive silver-haired blue-eyed Frenchman let me in. His profession, I decided, must have prepared him to deal with distraught, stammering, eccentric-looking women. He was charming and comforting and asked how he could help me. His office had a bohemian ambience—there was an incense burner, and paisley shawls draped over the furniture. I decided to trust him.

I asked whether he'd perhaps heard of the escape of Dr. Timothy Leary from prison in America. He said that he had. I asked whether he would like to meet with Dr. Leary, and he said that most assuredly he would. Then I told him that Tim was downstairs and should I fetch him? But of course. So there we were, welcomed by Doctor Pierre and his friend Anita to a comfortable room where we could be private and refresh ourselves. Alone at last, and I could not bear to be with him.[22]

Tim wanted to buy a car and just cruise around for a while. It was as though he believed that careful planning and facing the difficulties before us would draw some doom onto us. I just wanted to be alone and safe and think. Maybe I wanted to go back to the Weathermen. I called one of their contacts and suggested that I return and work with them. He asked if I could type. I didn't think typing was needed, but I couldn't think of what else I could do. Certainly I could not go back to Berkeley and my role as wicked stepmother, or report to my probation officer as returned felon facing ten years on my sentence plus more for aiding and abetting an escape, plus whatever extra for a false passport.

Tim couldn't deal with my depression and low energy and my inability to say what was wrong. I just knew that everything he did

---

22. In another version Rosemary says, "So there we were, welcomed, comfortable, and I could not bear to look at Tim." In chapter 10 Rosemary calls Anita the doctor's "wife" rather than his friend.

or said seemed wrong, crazy. In the civilized comfort where we had been offered refuge, I was on the verge of a nervous breakdown and where better to break down than in a Parisian psychiatrist's more-than-luxurious apartment in the 16th arrondissement?[23]

He decided he would go on to Algeria and check out the scene with Eldridge and the Black Panthers, and if it wasn't a good place he would come back and we could decide what we could do. We split the remaining money so that he had a couple of thousand dollars and I had a thousand plus plane fare, and then he was gone. I felt an overwhelming sense of peace and relief that I could be alone again for a while.

Pierre and Anita were kind to me, entertaining me with dinners and good wine and a secret meeting with a patient of his, Keith Richards of the Rolling Stones (and his wife). Richards was as mystified by the introduction as I was, because who was I supposed to be? If I stayed for another week I could go with them to the Stones concert in Paris. They took me to the flea market and I spent time with Anita, appreciating her warmth and beauty. She and Pierre seemed so compatible; I envied their easy, loving friendship.

I called the only person I knew in Europe and decided that a trip to Spain at this point was not a very good idea.[24] After several days I started to wonder how Tim was doing in Algeria with Eldridge and the Panthers. I missed him again. I could remember him as he'd been before prison—confident, strong, knowing what to do. And then he called.

I still can't answer the question why I was in Algeria except there was nowhere else to go and Tim was there waiting. We quarreled in Paris—not a quarrel exactly, I just couldn't stand to be with him anymore.

---

23. The 16th arrondissement is one of the richest and most elegant districts in Paris, on its western edge, and includes the great park called the Bois de Boulogne.

24. This was the Visionary artist Mati Klarwein (1932–2002), with whom Rosemary kept in contact during her fugitive period. Thanks to John Schewel for making this identification. Rosemary says when she called him in Majorca "he was dubiously welcoming to the idea of my flying there."

Editor's Note

The following untitled fragment was marked in Rosemary's hand for chapter 8. It seems best to include it here, but separated from the main narrative. Although the episode actually takes place in California in 1970, during Timothy's imprisonment in San Luis Obispo, her time line dates their encounter on Maui to September 1968. I added the title.

FRAGMENT:
TARQUIN AND PENELOPE

It was Tarquin and Penelope who reminded me of Big Sur. I'd found them camped under a bedraggled eucalyptus tree in the back end of the canyon, sitting around a little fire where they were broiling steaks. Tinkerbell, their three-year-old girl child, was leaning on my lap; Penelope was just finishing nursing their firstborn boy. Tarquin, with precise unhurried gestures, was fanning the fire on one side and carefully adjusting the meat on the grill.

"We'll be going up there as soon as we can get this old bus repaired. I need $20 for the parts, so we'll be here for a while yet."

I sighed, wishing I had the $20 to give them. I wouldn't mind making the long trip from Laguna Beach up the coast with them in their comfortable traveling home.

The last time I'd seen them they'd been camping on a little spit of land just beyond _____, Maui.[25] They'd lived for months on pineapples filched from the local plantations and coconuts brought down with a long pole. A family of three then, full of stories of Tarquin's heroic rescue of Penelope from the devil himself, who'd promised her rule of all the universes and all that was in them. "All except love,"

---

25. The place name is deliberately left blank in the typescript.

she'd said, describing her fifteen-year-old self three years later.[26] A Los Angeles child, grown up in tight pants and flame-colored shirts, trying out all the drugs and finally meeting the devil just as she'd prayed for.

Tarquin took her away from the city and the devil after a roaring night when the house shook and a large angry black cat screamed through the dark. They'd gone to Mexico, and Tarquin had been kept busy throwing away all the beads and amulets and strange-looking roots that had been found by Penelope or given to her by the witches of Mexico.

"She still had the mark on her of the devil, and all the brujas could see it."[27]

"But then I realized I was only a poor weak woman, and not a queen of the powers of darkness," Penelope said, smiling as she tipped another mescaline capsule into the hole of a coconut. She grinned even wider as she passed it to me, and more so when I passed it on without sipping from it. I'd had enough that night on Maui, already I was seeing and hearing things that didn't seem to affect the others in the party that had sprung up around their tent.

A strange red light flashed on and off in the darkness. It seemed to me there were ominous, unfriendly voices in the darkness beyond the campfire. But the drummers were lost in their rhythms, and another group was demonstrating different ways of opening a pile of coconuts, and no one seemed disturbed by the tenseness of the air.

A man named St. George arrived and greeted us. Under the cover of talk I asked if we might go back to town with him. He seemed to understand my feelings, and in a few minutes we were in his comfortable home, preparing with his good advice for a trip to the extinct crater of Haleakala that is the eye of the head of the island of Maui.[28] Tarquin

---

26. Satan tempted Jesus by taking him up the highest mountain and showing him all the kingdoms of the world. "If thou therefore wilt worship me," said the devil, "all shall be thine." In the next verse Jesus rejected this offer, saying "Get thee behind me, Satan: for it is written, Thou shalt worship the Lord thy God, and him only shalt thou serve." Luke 4:5–7.

27. *Bruja* is Spanish for "witch."

28. Haleakala is not extinct, only dormant.

was full of stories about this crater too: how he and Penelope spent weeks in there at a time, how he'd prayed at the bottomless pit *O Lord, let me find peace,* and a voice had replied *Then be a peaceful man.* And so he was a peaceful man, and this little family traveled from one peaceful place to another.

But most of their stories were from Big Sur, which even in the pleasant lushness of Maui they yearned for: its cool drinking water, the musicians of the forests, bright days and green fog. They had told me then of Big Sur, and now I was with them again, and again Tarquin was speaking of Big Sur—how I could find a house there and still be not as far from the prison as I would be in Berkeley or Laguna Beach.

I sat at their campfire and listened to their stories and wondered again if I'd have the courage and stamina to live the life they did: camping, traveling, making instruments from bamboo and gourds, making music, making love in their Volkswagen home, making babies to be born by the side of the road, making a life of little pleasures and goals, a bottle of wine carefully saved for or carefully stolen.

I thought of them through the four days and nights spent in the Eden of the crater. The first night was a terror of winds that crept through the door of the ranger station, cats yowling in the rushing air.[29] When Tarquin leapt over me he scratched my right shoulder with his toenail and the scratch grew infected. That first night in the crater was uncomfortable and frightening, full as I was of their stories of black magic and *Rosemary's Baby.*[30]

But the next morning was so crisp and clear, the black cinder landscape so lunar and new, that I forgot my fears. At the lip of the bottomless pit I laughed at Tarquin's heroics and Penelope's valor as she stood poised, ready to leap in after her man if he should decide to die.

---

29. Rosemary probably means not the actual ranger station, but one of the basic cabins provided for visitors to Haleakala National Park.

30. *Rosemary's Baby* is a terrifying film written and directed by Roman Polanski, which made a sensation when it appeared in 1968. In it a young woman (Mia Farrow) bears a child perhaps fathered by the devil. The protagonist's name, Rosemary Woodhouse, is chillingly close to our Rosemary's own name.

The pit didn't seem bottomless; there was even a ledge, an overhang where one could have second thoughts. I stayed away from the lip, though, and sat on the ground next to a silversword plant and watched the fat red bumblebees as they droned in the energy-charged air.[31]

I told Tarquin about those days and nights in the crater, how the wild goats sounded like Tibetan horns, the cry the seabirds made as they came through the gap to the sea. They asked if we'd take the path to the Seven Falls, but I said no, my feet were too torn by new sneakers and the lava, and we climbed out the way we'd come. I wished I'd taken St. George's advice and bought the two-toed Japanese fishermen's shoes, but they looked too much like the devil's feet and I couldn't stand the sight of them.

I asked why they'd left Hawaii, and it turned out that St. George had been a real rescuer after all.[32] After we left, a group of angry Hawaiians in a truck with a flashing red light crashed the party, beat up several of the guests, and made Tarquin and Penelope move their camp. So here they were in Laguna Beach, traveling up and down the coast, always trying to get back to Big Sur, where for some reason they weren't allowed to stay all the time until Tarquin proved himself in some unaccountable way. "But I'm sure you'll be able to get a house, and there ain't no finer place to be."

❦

Editor's Note

Another fragment is dated Summer 1970 and also fits the period when Rosemary was traveling to visit Tim at the prison in San Luis Obispo. Presumably the little house is the one mentioned on page 156 and having been provided by "the Esalen folks." Perhaps it is at least poetically the one suggested by Tarquin in the preceding fragment. Again the title has been added.

---

31. The Haleakala silversword grows only on the higher slopes of this one mountain.
32. In the legend of Saint George of Lydda, a Roman officer turned Christian rescued a maiden from a dragon. The legend is an archetypal one, conflated with pre-Christian stories, and has nothing to do with the historical St. George, if there ever was one, who became the patron saint of Christian chivalry.

FRAGMENT: AT THE STONE HOUSE

A large black bird walked into the house, looked at me, shook its head and hopped out into the sunlight. I sprinkled pot and sesame seeds outside the door, hoping it would come back. This morning my sleeping bag was full of nuts and crumbs. I must have slept very still and the mouse thought I was a good nesting place, how nice.

It is so peaceful here, this small stone house above the sea. Big Sur. There is a good feeling to it, something about the birds and the wind in the bamboo grove, something kind and helpful about the atmosphere. I wish I never had to leave.[33] I thought I'd clean the spiderwebs, but last night by the fire, looking up, I saw them as veils, filmy threads of lace. Today Betsy told me that her mother had asked that I leave the webs intact.

I must hitchhike to the prison tomorrow; I hope there's no fog. It is so strange to have found this measure of confidence, certainty, freedom in a way. Will this be the weekend that he tells me what to do? I pray not, I want to see my family one last time. But if I do, I might break down. No, I must be strong and sure, then we can both be free.[34] It is so strange to have found this measure of certainty, confidence, freedom in a way. Yet I miss him.

I don't want to die a violent death, God knows what will happen. There is so much more I have to learn, so many things left to do. Susan must be away from here, Joan and the children in another house. Jackie will be all right. The new babies, the garden in the lower meadow, the pear orchards, the view from Santa Rosa, will I never see them again? Walk to the café, call the lawyers, I'll do yoga by the spring, then.

---

33. Rosemary's peaceful feeling in this little house at Big Sur will remind the reader of her similarly peaceful stay at her hermitage on Lunacy Hill at Millbrook, described in chapter 5, pages 114 to 117.
34. There is an undertone here of the judgment of Holding Together, quoted in I Ching, chapter 8, note 1: "Inquire of the oracle once again whether you possess sublimity, constancy and perseverance."

NINE

Behind the Veil

*I reached the Southern Zone with the intention of finding
out about the Resistance.[1] But once there and having found
out, I hesitated. The undertaking struck me as a little mad
and in a word, romantic. I think especially that underground
action suited neither my temperament nor my preference for
exposed heights. It seemed to me that I was being asked to do
some weaving in a cellar, for days and nights on end, until
some brutes should come to haul me from hiding, undo my
weaving, and then drag me to another cellar, to beat me to
death. I admired those who indulged in such heroisms of the
depths, but couldn't imitate them.*

ALBERT CAMUS, *THE FALL*

I

We quarreled over old loves. Seven months of prison visits and there I
was with a grumpy desperado, running from the law. I couldn't handle
it, so we parted for good. Goodbye, good luck.

---

1. During the French colonial period the vast Southern Zone of Algeria, which included
the northern stretches of the Sahara Desert, was administered separately from the more
intensely occupied and colonized Northern Zone, where the cities, main agricultural
areas, and most of the French settler population were located. The Northern Zone was
administratively part of France.

Be free now, I said to myself, *get out of this mess if you can. Yes, but I've got ten years over my head. They'll put you away, and who's going to help you get out? How long do you think you can run? I don't know anyone in India or anywhere else for that matter. Do you really think you can hide out in the canyons with winter coming on? They'd spot me by helicopter easily.*

Then the phone rang. "It's great here; you've got to come right away. It's a perfect, perfect new life and I miss you."

II

Not knowing what to expect (an award? a decoration?), I crossed over to North Africa. The steward kept my champagne glass full and provided a deck of cards. I wished I'd brought the tarot pack. Tim said Algeria would be like Morocco only a little more military. Kathleen's picture in the newspapers, *Soul on Ice* on the bookshelves, were the repeating images. Perhaps I'd live in the desert and go to Timbuktu or Timgad.[2]

The airport was a neoned space anywhere, there was no one to meet me. Immigration gave me a three-day visa.[3] I changed dollars into dinars and was thinking about going home with the steward to meet his family when Tim arrived. He was wearing a new leather cap, which made him look rather like a thin Russian poet. His jauntiness was the same, his embrace familiar, and I felt a wave of affection. I was happy to see him. We collected my luggage, and he propelled me to a car parked in front of the empty terminal building.

"Where are we going now? When will I meet Eldridge and Kathleen?"

"Baby, we're starting a new life, and we have to meet Eldridge at his house right now!"

What I could see of Algiers through the rainy windows of the car did not look like Morocco. In Tangier the streets would have been full

---

2. Actually Timbuktu is in Mali.
3. Another version says, "a 24-hour visa."

of people, the little cafés brightly lit. The streets of Algiers were empty, the houses and other buildings tightly closed. Lonely sentinels of the dark boulevards, palm trees were bent by the wind, dripping with rain.

"What is Eldridge like, can we stay here?"

"It's so fantastic! It's so far out! The day I escaped from prison the Algerian government gave the Panthers an embassy! There's a brass plaque on the door with a drawing of a panther! Eldridge has meetings with the president; Kathleen is the guest of Kim Il-Sung's wife in North Korea; she and another Panther wife are having their babies there![4] The North Vietnamese sent a delegation to Eldridge," he said enthusiastically, and then in an altered tone, "Did you bring some money?" A familiar question.

"I have what I had before, except for plane fare, what you left me with." In fact it was chafing me raw, I had it in my panty hose. "Why, don't you have any left?"

"I had to give it to Eldridge, and he expects a lot more."

"Where will we get it?" A familiar worry.

"We'll write a book about the escape, we'll make a lot of money, don't worry love, we're free and together." He grinned at me reassuringly.

Free? I'd learned in Paris that I was afraid of freedom and ready to hand it back to him the moment he called. I still dreamed of total love. I was mated to him.

I wished we were not meeting Eldridge. I suddenly felt very tired. I wanted to take off the stupid wig and brush my hair, strip off the panty hose holding up the money, lie down on a soft bed with my husband and smoke a little pipe of hash. Instead I was going to meet the man who met with heads of state, who ran an embassy and would decide if Algeria would be our refuge. I knew so little about him, just what I'd read: his imprisonment for rape, the enormous vitality of his book *Soul on Ice,* his escape from the States, his wife Kathleen's beautiful and militant photographs in the newspapers.

---

4. Kim Il-Sung (1912–1994) was the founder of the North Korean state and remained its semidivine dictator until his death.

All I knew about the Black Panthers was that their confrontations with the police had been harrowing, the harassment and brutality extreme, their leaders imprisoned or slain, their numbers decimated by fusillades of police machine-gun fire. Huey Newton's visage from the popular poster, seated in a wicker chair, a rifle in his arms, and Bobby Seale chained and gagged in a courtroom in Chicago, were repeating images. The only personal thing I could remember about Eldridge was that his eyes were said to be green.

We stopped before a large white villa. It was an imposing place. Cleaver opened the gate; he was a very large man dressed in a military-looking tunic. I reached for his hand but shook his thumb instead. Eldridge told Tim to put my bags in the hall and follow him into the living room.

I was introduced to the few people there and offered a beer. Except for a big man called DC who was talking to Tim about a fund-raising party in New York, no one was very friendly.[5] It seemed a somber gathering. There was a beautiful girl sitting next to Eldridge. She ignored me. Eldridge had earphones on his head, his eyes were closed. I looked around and tried to relax. Familiar music was playing, there were red leather chairs and white walls and gray posters of people with guns.

I asked Eldridge about Kathleen, he waved me away impatiently. The other conversations also obviously irritated him, he grunted with disapproval whenever anyone laughed. I asked Tim if we were going to a hotel, he beamed at me and said we'd stay at the hotel by the beach where Kathleen and Eldridge had lived when they first came to Algeria.[6]

---

5. DC was Donald L. Cox (1936–2011), the "Field Marshal" of the Black Panther Party. Wanted for murder, he lived in exile in Algeria and France from 1970 until his death. The fund-raising party in New York might have been the famous event held for the Black Panthers on January 14, 1970, at the New York apartment of the composer and conductor Leonard Bernstein (1918–1990), which DC attended and which was described by Tom Wolfe in his article "Radical Chic: That Party at Lenny's." The article was reprinted in Wolfe's book *Radical Chic & Mau-Mauing the Flak Catchers* (New York: Picador, 1970).

6. The hotel was at a place called El Djamila (Robert Greenfield, *Timothy Leary: A Biography,* New York: Houghton Mifflin Harcourt, 2006, 397).

"Yeah, Kathleen, Barbara, and the children are coming back from North Korea tomorrow," one of the men said, looking at me. "Why don't you help in here?" I followed him into the next room and watched as he leaned over and inspected the bed; I looked for clues as to what to do. He took some linen from a closet.

"You'd better change the bed, Malika's been staying here."

Far out, here I am with the Panthers in Algeria and I'm changing the sheets and looking for stains on Cleaver's bed. What have I gotten myself into this time?

When I finished that little chore, Eldridge put the earphones aside to tell us he thought it would be better if Tim went to the hotel alone, our passports didn't have the same last name. I could stay at the house. "We go together," I insisted, holding tightly to Tim's arm. After a little more playful cruelty with the threat of separation and the insistence that I part with the small amount of hashish I'd brought from Paris, we were allowed to leave with the promise of an early return the next morning.

We drove through silent shuttered streets, past sandy beaches, east and away from the city. The hotel was quiet, comfortable. Our quarrel forgotten, I was happy to be with him again. We woke to the sound of the sea, the day was sunny. We had breakfast at a restaurant on the beach—fresh croissants, hot milk, and coffee. Tim was funny, practicing fractured French with the waiters.

The streets were crowded with men and boys, the few women were covered with gray sheets. We were in the traffic rush of a Sunday soccer game. Curious faces peered at us through the windows of the rented car, a policeman waved us through. We arrived at the Cleaver house just as midmorning prayers were broadcast from the mosque. I loved the sound, though it was no longer live but a scratchy record of a serene and confident voice praising God.[7]

When our ring went unanswered, we guessed that everyone was at the airport. Tim led the way to an open basement entrance. Seeing the mess in the kitchen, he said we should clean it up; I thought it good

---

7. Another version has "praising Allah."

of him to think of that. After traveling such a long distance, Kathleen shouldn't have to face a dirty sink. Tim went into the living room to catch up on back issues of the underground papers. I started to work on the greasy pots but dried my hands when I heard cars stop in front of the house.

Kathleen was far more beautiful than photographs of her. The two new babies were serene, sleeping little bundles. I reconciled myself to Eldridge when I saw his son laugh to see Poppa again. DC's wife Barbara had a friendly voice and manner that put me at ease. She said they'd had a natural childbirth, the Koreans didn't use anesthetics. She'd been so waited on that her fingernails had grown really long. It had been boring, though, and they were glad to leave.

I told her I thought I would really like Algeria, the land was beautiful and the people seemed friendly. She said the tuberculosis rate was very high, the hospitals filthy, and there was nothing worth buying in the shops. However, she said she was happy to be with her husband again.

I realized I hadn't finished the dishes and went back to the kitchen; I broke a glass and cut my hand, the blood dripped onto the tile floor.[8] I ran to the hallway where Kathleen was unpacking and asked for a bandage, a rag, or something. She said she hadn't been in the house for months, couldn't spare a diaper. She turned and walked away. I stuck some tissue on the cut and went into the living room where Tim was reading the Panther newsletter. I told him I was finished in the kitchen and wondered if we could go back to the hotel.

Do not wrong the orphan, nor chide away the beggar, but proclaim the goodness of your Lord.[9]

---

8. In another version Rosemary says she cut her "wrist."

9. Koran, Surah 93 (*Ad-Dhuha*, The Morning Hours), verses 9–11. The translation Rosemary quotes is by N. J. Dawood (London: Penguin Classics, 1956). All her direct quotations from the Koran are from this paperback translation, which leads to a *speculative* inference that it was one she had with her in Algeria. John Schewel confirmed to me that she had a paperback Koran with her during their later travels.

Eldridge wanted us to go to the embassy with him. We followed his car down through the winding, narrow streets at a very fast pace and parked in front of a walled house with a wrought-iron gate. A woman wearing a white shawl was polishing a square of brass on the entrance pillar; in passing, Eldridge introduced her as Zora, the embassy maid. We followed Eldridge through the plainly furnished rooms of the Panther embassy and on to a small room filled by a large conference table. Eldridge motioned to the chairs and took his place at the head of the table, on which was placed a bottle of ginseng liquor, a tape recorder and microphone, and a large catalogue.

DC came in and sat down. He started leafing through the catalogue. I could see it was full of photographs of guns. He made a few check marks on the pages with a pen. Eldridge set up the tape recorder and picked up the microphone.

"This is Eldridge Cleaver of the International Sector of the Black Panther Party. On this day, September 28, 1970, those present are . . ." He handed the microphone to Tim. "Dr. Timothy Leary, formerly of Harvard. Fugitive, exile, and guest of the Black Panther Party, Algiers." He smiled engagingly. Eldridge did not respond nor did DC seem to be amused; he took the microphone from Tim.

"Donald Cox, Field Marshal, International Sector of the Black Panther Party, Algeria." He gave me the microphone and I managed to whisper my name into it. I started to hand it back to DC but Eldridge motioned me to put it in the center of the table. He adjusted the dials and then looked at me, with suspicion, I thought.

"Why didn't you arrive together?" he asked.

"Well, uh, I was rather nervous after the escape and I, uh, needed some time to myself." I stuttered.

"What would you have done other than come here?"

"Well, I thought about Chile but I don't know anyone there and I thought about going back to the states and joining Weather." Tim looked startled at hearing me say that.

"Why did you decide to come to Algeria?" DC asked in a low rumbling voice.

"I wanted to be with my husband; I missed him."

"Why did *you* come to Algeria?" Eldridge asked Tim.

"Because of the tremendous respect we have for you, Eldridge, and all the Panthers, and what you have suffered at the oppressive hands of the police in America. We want to help you, we want to be with you in your struggle, we will do all we can to help you in your efforts to broaden the understanding of . . ."

"All right, all right, now what made you think you'd be welcome here?" Eldridge demanded.

"Bernardine Dohrn of Weather said that you had been approached and that you'd be receptive to our joining you."

"Bernardine!" For the first time there was animation in Eldridge's voice. "She's some witch, she's some kind of witch," he said admiringly. "No one told us you were coming and I'd like to know why." He was suddenly angry, and I felt a flash of fear. Were we going to be suspected rather than accepted? Tim took the microphone and recapitulated his escape and our days with Weather. He said again that we were there to help, to do anything that Eldridge wanted us to do, and his sword was at Eldridge's disposal. It was my turn to look at him with surprise. Eldridge again interrupted him.

"All right, all right, this isn't the time to discuss that, see? I don't know how we're going to handle this, see? It's going to take a lot of money to handle your case and we need a lot of things to keep this embassy going. We need a teletype machine, we need electronic equipment, we want to get the Panther women and children over here."

He picked up a leather bag from the chair next to him. It gaped open—there was a large black metal gun inside. He zipped the case closed and shut off the tape machine.

"DC will be conducting political orientation classes this week; you'll be expected to attend." We were dismissed.

The Asian woman and her three sleepy children were in the underpass again. She looked at me but I had no money to give her. She was thinner and more worn-looking than when I had first seen her. Instead of standing near the stairs where the beggars usually stand, she slumped against the wall, her children tucked around her. It is cold and damp underneath the streets but it is the only place beggars are allowed to be seen, kept away from the crowded streets of downtown Algiers. How did she come to be here, so far away from Korea, Vietnam, Japan, China, Laos; did her husband die, was she abandoned, or was she part of the South Vietnamese mission whose headquarters had been given to the Black Panthers? I never saw her again. I'll never know her fate.

Eldridge and the beautiful young woman came to the hotel. He talked to Tim about renting a villa where we could entertain visitors. We would be the cultural mission; Tim could conduct seminars on the new psychology. Eldridge's mellow voice filled the room, Malika lay on the bed smoking.[10] I watched her, thinking how pretty she was, and wondered what her life was like.

The talk turned to lysergic acid; it seemed that Eldridge wanted some.[11] He said he had taken it several times; it had been all right! Now he had a problem to solve and maybe it would help. Tim gave them his blessing with advice to increase the dosage for greater effect. I gave Malika a hug and some candles and they left.

She sat in the dust of the street. Although the market was crowded there was a space around her that no one entered. She cried soundlessly, her mouth open to the sky, red lipstick smeared, black tears on her face. She pulled at her hair and the bodice of her dress, tearing the flimsy silver-threaded fabric. Her stockings were ripped, one brocade slipper was missing. Some cloth, perhaps meant to cover her, was abandoned on the ground. What was her grief, her crime, that she cried in the market, uncovered, with no one to aid her? Was she a prostitute, a rebellious daughter, an unfaithful wife? Two

---

10. In another version Malika is called "Rangina."
11. LSD is lysergic acid diethylamide.

black-leather-jacketed policemen came and jerked her roughly to her feet. She swayed between them, her head thrown back, soundless screams disappearing with her down the narrow street.

Eldridge and Malika came back to the hotel the next day looking angry and depressed. Malika's hand shook when she lit a cigarette. The phone rang harshly—it was Kathleen, sounding worried. Eldridge went down to the lobby to take the call; we could hear his voice above the sound of the soccer match on the television. I said something that made Malika laugh and when Eldridge came back into the room we were giggling. He wanted to know what was so funny.

"You are, Eldridge," I said out of a real feeling of friendliness, thinking he'd laugh too. He didn't. He said that he'd felt immobilized by the acid, worried that he might not be able to get to his gun in time if the pigs were going to move on him. No pretty paisley patterns appeared to interfere with thoughts of prisons and guards. He'd spent the night looking at Bobby Seale's picture on the wall, thinking about him seized and locked up all this time.[12] Soberly, we thought about it too, and then they left. I was worried that I'd offended Eldridge and wondered if any of his problems had been solved.

We lived quietly at the hotel waiting for mail and newspapers from the States to arrive. The Panthers had lent us the five volumes of Kim Il-sung's biography, but it was difficult to read. We worked on a book about the escape from prison and a chart of levels of consciousness, devising symbols to match, arguing at times, but happy on the whole to be left alone.

---

12. Seale was one of the original "Chicago Eight," indicted for conspiracy and crossing state lines to incite the "riot" at the 1968 Democratic Convention in Chicago. Seale, denied his counsel of choice, defiantly refused to cooperate with the trial held the following year. His case was severed from the others, and Judge Julius Hoffman sentenced him to four years confinement for multiple counts of contempt of court. It is possible that Cleaver felt some personal guilt about Seale's imprisonment. "Since Seale had been in Chicago for only two days during the convention and had been invited to come only at the last minute as a substitute for Eldridge Cleaver, the evidence against him was sparse." Jason Epstein, "The Trial of Bobby Seale," *New York Review,* Special Supplement December 5, 1969, archived at perma.cc/u4rn-28q6.

Our social life was a twice-a-week dinner and taping session with Eldridge's secretary Elaine. Cooking roast lamb and making salad, she would translate Tim's jokes into French for her boyfriend, an Algerian government official, and his questions into English for us. She was gay and friendly; I admired her. We'd sit down to a delicious dinner, drink liters of strong Algerian wine, and try to cope with questions about the Korean War, Hiroshima, and biological warfare. The wine made me sleepy and left Tim less than deft. He had to field his problem of a real lack of interest in the subject.[13] The tapes of the questions and responses were to be made into a book that would, hopefully, establish Tim as the revolution's philosopher.[14]

Although there were stacks of jazz records I hadn't heard in years, I stopped attending the dinners after I committed to tape the tender story of our romance. Tim continued valiantly each week, explaining the importance of the counterculture and the effect that a society of LSD users was having on the American economy and the war. The young Algerian official remained unconvinced and Elaine supremely impartial. Reels of tape, reams of typescript, and liters of wine were consumed by the drug guru and the survivor of a successful revolution, each understanding little of the other's way of life. The Moslem could hold his liquor: chemical warfare indeed.

In the reception room at the embassy, one day late in October, Tim was sitting on the couch cross-legged, his socks and shoes scattered on the floor. One of the Panthers entered the room and scolded him: "Sit right, this ain't a hippie pad." He did look a bit out of place amid the shined boots and almost military air most of the Panthers wore, black leather coats, each carrying a bulging zippered leather bag.

Tim drooped. He languished into frowning concentration over the rare American newspaper found at the embassy. Confronted by DC or Eldridge, he wore a false joviality that I felt grated on the men's ears. His hearing difficulty interrupted their usually soft-voiced exchanges

---

13. Another version says Timothy was less than deft "pretending an interest in war games."
14. The proposed book was never published.

and his look of anticipation at their response made them stiffen their attitude. I suffered agonies of embarrassment and protectiveness at what I imagined to be their offstage comments: *that motherfuckin honkie don't know his . . .* and so on.

Kathleen and Barbara were never at the embassy during our rare appearances there to pick up mail, and they never tried to get in touch. I had equally lurid imaginings when I thought how they might think of us. The promise of "political orientation" hadn't been fulfilled, and other than Eldridge asking if we could send for some Boy Scout manuals on camping and possibly get hold of United States coastal maps, we had not been called on to do anything.

The phone rang and a little while later Eldridge said a group of Youth International Party members were arriving at the airport and he wanted us to go with him to meet them.[15] We drove to the airport happily anticipating this unexpected appearance of, just possibly, some white expatriates with a commitment to join us and the Black Panthers.

The contingent of North Americans passing through customs was a welcome sight, though the only familiar faces were those of Abbie's wife Anita Hoffman and Stew Albert from Berkeley.[16] The others in the party were introduced, and I was surprised to meet Jennifer Dohrn, Bernardine's sister, with the other Yippies. Their colorful clothes and exuberant greetings were reminders of the world we'd left behind.

Stew, Anita, and Jennifer got into our car; the others went in a Panther car, which we were supposed to follow. I was asking Jennifer about Bernardine, Tim was asking Anita about Abbie, Stu was asking us about Eldridge. Somehow we missed a turn and realized we were

---

15. The Youth International Party, called the Yippies, was a semi-ironic radical movement founded on the last day of 1967. It was intended to bring a political consciousness to the hippie ethos. Its flag combined a red star and a marijuana leaf.

16. Abbie Hoffman (1936–1989) and his wife Anita Hoffman (1942–1998) were co-founders of the Yippies. Abbie was a longtime antiwar and civil rights activist and author of many books and was one of the Chicago Seven acquitted after the disturbances at the 1968 Democratic convention. Stewart Albert (1939–2006) was a radical activist and another cofounder of the Yippies. He helped arrange the Learys' reception in Algeria.

following the wrong car into an unfamiliar part of Algiers. There was a car full of angry Algerian men in front of us on a dead-end street. They had gotten out of their car and, shouting, were coming toward us. We all leaned out and shouted back *Amis, Friends, Excuse.* One of the Algerians picked up a paving stone. Tim hastily turned the car around but too late. A rock crashed through the window, scattering splinters of glass over everyone. It was a very subdued group that got to the embassy, where Eldridge was impatiently waiting.

October 27, 1970

Dear Family,

There is very little to remind us of the life we left behind. A new life entirely. We are living in a little fishing village outside of Algiers. The sea is calm today, the sky clear. The weather is something like San Francisco though there isn't any smog and it is warmer. I've just made tea on my camping stove and I'm waiting for the sun to come round the corner of the balcony. Our life here is full of little rituals, a chat with the boy at the desk who is practicing English, a stop at the tobacco shop, lunch at the café across the street. When T's fractured French fails him, he draws pictures on the table cloth for the waiters . . . we shake hands constantly and say bonjour to everyone.

Yesterday the maids leaned over the balcony to wave to me. I invited them for tea, spread a rug here on the terrace. We tried to talk using a French and Arabic dictionary. We laughed a lot. One's face is delicately tattooed in blue. She says she is from the Sahara.

Tim's birthday was an exciting day.[17] The Yippies arrived and we were to have held a press conference but the government freaked at the sight of all those long-haired crazies so we had a party instead. I almost felt like I was back in New York. Our friends said that no one can believe Tim's statement about self-protection.

I wish I could explain clearly to you what we and so many minority groups have faced at the hands of the sadistic jailers in America. But your

---

17. Tim turned fifty on October 22, 1970.

world is so different. I know that despite our differences you love us and your prayers and love have sustained me all these years.

Please write soon, c/o Black Panther Party, Grande Poste, Algiers.

Eldridge came in with the Algerian papers. Translated, the headlines said: Afro-American Psychiatrist and Wife Given Asylum. That got us all laughing. Then Eldridge said the government wouldn't allow the planned press conference to take place. By the afternoon, the government had banned the Yippie/Panther press conference and television and newspaper correspondents were being turned away at the airport, unable to enter Algeria. In New York Bouteflika, the Algerian minister at the United Nations, had planned to speak on South Africa.[18] Instead he'd been bombarded with questions about Algeria's stand on drugs and hippies.

A compromise to our expulsion was hastily arranged. Tim would have to go to Beirut with the Yippie delegation immediately! They would meet with the Palestinians and Jean Genet, who was their guest of the moment.[19] They would hold a press conference in Beirut and declare solidarity with the Palestinian movement. Then he would, *inch'Allah,* return to Algeria.[20] His fare would be paid, but not mine. I would have to stay behind. I didn't want to smile for the cameras or talk to reporters, so I didn't mind. Friends from New York were in town, and I thought I'd drive around with them and see some of the sights. Eldridge had some other plan, he said they had a mess of files that needed reorganizing and I'd be doing a real service if I straightened them out.

Tim went off to Beirut. I went to work at the embassy categorizing atrocities. APARTHEID, BANS, BOMBINGS, BUSING, CASTRATION, CONTEMPT, DEATHS, EDUCATION, ENVIRONMENT, FRAGGING,[21]

---

18. Abdelaziz Bouteflika (born 1937) was minister of foreign affairs in 1970. He became president of Algeria in 1999 and remained so until he was deposed in 2019.
19. Jean Genet (1910–1986) was a French author, playwright, intellectual, and activist. He had been a habitual criminal and frequent prisoner before becoming recognized as a writer.
20. *Inch'Allah* is Arabic for "God willing."
21. Killing of military officers by their own men. The word, introduced among American soldiers in Vietnam, derives from *fragmentation grenade,* the weapon of choice.

GHETTOS, HARLEM, INSECTICIDES, JURIES, KU KLUX KLAN, LEAD POISONING, MADNESS, MURDER. Eldridge enjoyed telling me about the possibilities Tim faced on this trip. He could be "offed," kidnapped, imprisoned, or disappear and never be heard of again. If he did make it back to Algeria, perhaps he wouldn't be let in. "What would you do then?" the owl-eyed rapist speculated.

After a half-day's work in the file room our friends said they'd rather trip out and explore the Old City. They were getting into arguments with the Panthers about the use of drugs, and short of dosing them they could not persuade them that they were leading a useful life. I stayed with the files; I wasn't prepared to argue the merits of drugs rather than guns as a revolutionary tool. I wanted to visit the casbah too, but Eldridge said to stay out of sight.[22]

|||[23]

Wednesday is ladies' day at the *hammam*.[24] The baths are in the basement of a modern apartment building in central Algiers, but one step into the room is a step into another time and space. Children play on the mat-covered floor, women talk and laugh, not veiled and not hidden. Women and children are at ease in the comforting warmth of the hammam. When I stepped past the curtain covering the doorway, they stared at me, the European stranger. I paid a small fee to the attendant, who took my clothes and assured me by gesture that she would guard

---

22. The casbah of a North African town is its ancient citadel, and often by extension, as here, the surrounding Old City laid out before European colonization.
23. My general editorial approach has been to insert into the basic version of each section of the memoir any additional elements found in other versions that add information. As a result the edited version is usually somewhat fuller than the basic version, which was itself in no sense canonical, but just the best-preserved starting point. However, in the case of the set piece that follows, I found that it had already been skillfully edited, and adding elements not in the "original" version did not help. The original version seemed noticeably better. Accordingly I have left it in place. But I have added the Koranic postscript included in some other versions.
24. A public bath, called a *Turkish bath* in other countries.

them. Gathering my towel around me and clutching my toilet articles, I followed her into the next room.

The walls are white tile, wet with steam, the room a series of alcoves, in each a group of women. My guide found a vacant spot next to three young girls and motioned to the water tap near the floor. I removed my towel and squatted beneath the faucet, relishing the warm flow of water on my back. Hot water at the beach hotel was a luxurious rarity, turned on only when the Russian airline crews checked in. It was then in scant supply, as they seemed to take baths all day. Then much laughter, and the sound of slapping wet towels filled the corridor.

I was the only solitary bather. One woman washed another's hair, one scrubbed the back of her companion, an old woman lovingly soaped a little girl. The three young girls near me arranged each other's hair in soapy coiffures. There was a symmetry to the women's bodies, no one was obese or too thin, most had hair hennaed to a rich purple or deep red.[25] I was circumspect in my observations; out of politeness or disinterest no one looked at me.

Perhaps I'd lost my foreignness with my clothes. If only that were true, if I could speak the language, alter the way I looked and moved, forget what I'd been and what I'd become and lose all fear. Could I, veiled, leave the hammam unrecognized, elude the constant watchers, the men who followed everywhere, and disappear into a house of tender gestures? Would I be a beloved aunt, sister, daughter, sheltered from the world? I could be deaf, mute, daft, busy with children and embroidery.

A middle-aged woman with long dark hair and hennaed feet crossed the room and settled at my side. Her face was lined from the sun and unknown worries; she smiled a gold-toothed smile and picked up my bottle of shampoo with an inquiring look. When I nodded, she thrust my head under the warm water, her fingers were strong, massaging and soaping my head. She hummed while she washed, her breasts touched my back, filmy skins met and slid apart. I leaned over, tensions and

---

25. Henna is a vegetable dye used to mark complex but temporary patterns on the body, especially the hands. It is an important part of bridal customs in many cultures from India to Morocco.

tautness eased as she soaped and sang. I was a piece of washing, a rag, a bit of work for her hands. Underneath the water I cried; her hands and labor were love, and I was a child at home again.

> Women shall with justice have rights similar to those exercised against them, although men have a status above women. God is mighty and wise.[26]

IV

Tim returned from Beirut full of funny stories about the Panthers and the camel drivers at the Pyramids. He'd seen the Sphinx, slept in a queen's bed, ridden on a camel and enjoyed himself. I thought he'd gone too far, announcing to the press that he was going to turn Moslem and face Mecca five times a day, but that was his business.

Everyone had stories. The Panthers said that Tim acted irresponsibly; Tim said that he was the only one with enough sense to have a good time. Relations with the embassy were strained after that trip. I wasn't asked back to the filing room, and Eldridge didn't call about finding us a villa where we could entertain. The attitudes of the Yippies toward Eldridge and the Panthers seemed to be composed of liberal anxiety and white guilt, a fawning posture of the activist toward the militant. Their stance toward us was, "Eldridge is insane, but it's your problem." The press releases on their return to the States seemed to reflect their growing disenchantment with armed revolutionary struggle. Our statement of solidarity with the Panthers' liberation army and the need to defend oneself sounded shrill and self-serving.[27]

On our daily walks we explored the village and the rows of shuttered beach houses, hoping to find a place to rent. We talked to the police chief about an empty villa on the beach. It had been the French commandant's house before the war;[28] now it was an abandoned wreck

---

26. Koran, Surah 2 (*Al-Baraqah*, Blessing), verse 228.
27. In another draft Rosemary called it "Tim's statement."
28. Meaning the Algerian War of Independence (1954–1962).

with a gaping hole in the kitchen where a bomb had exploded. We gave up the thought of renovating its marble floor and smashed windows and continued our search farther from the village.

One walk led us toward a modern-looking apartment building that commanded a fine view of the curving coast. The green fields and the village below grew small as we approached the huge white building. The road was dusty and unpaved. No colorful rugs hung from the balconies as they did from most houses. There were no women brushing bright-patterned wool in the morning sun.

As we approached, the building seemed almost deserted; the windows were blank and empty, graffiti was scrawled on the walls. The ground was littered with broken bottles and rusty bits of metal. We stood in the sun looking down at the tiny village; we'd walked a long distance, the breeze was cold. There was a group of children in the courtyard; they shouted when they saw us, two tourists on their hill above the sea. They sang a ragged chant. The wind tore at their words.

More children came into view. They pointed at us; a laughing and leaping barefoot band of babies, there were few that looked older than six. We watched them as they drew closer. Some searched in the rubble. What were they shouting? We stood still as they grew nearer. (What are the words in Arabic for *my daughters, my sons?*) A hundred or so children watched and mimed our self-conscious smiles. What game were they playing? They stopped a little distance away, stones, coat hangers, bottles in hand. A moment of fear: they didn't mean to harm us, surely? The sun flashed on broken glass: a stone fell at our feet. Behind us, a piece of metal slashed the air.

We turned, looking for escape. Then two men with hoes came from the fields; they stopped and picked up rocks. Shouting, they threw stones at the children, who scattered and then regrouped farther away, waiting. We stayed where we were, indecisively, till the men pointed to a path through the fields. They stood confronting the children until we were well on our way. We walked back to the hotel and the sea, cold and frightened, looking forward to a cup of tea in safety. I felt middle-aged, privileged, and threatened. I'd never felt that way before.

* * *

Late one night Kathleen and Eldridge came to see us. I was pleased to see them, thinking it a friendly visit. Eldridge and Tim went into the other room. I asked Kathleen if she wanted some coffee, she said no. I was nervous, as I usually was with her, fearing her dislike. I asked about the children, perhaps she'd like to have a horoscope done for them? She said she would, and I busied myself with a paper and pencil, though I felt like a fool saying *hour of birth, date, and place* like some bureaucratic clerk asking computer questions.[29] Kathleen wore a strained expression, she seemed unwilling to answer; our silence was tense.

Tim was assuring Eldridge about something when they returned. Kathleen suddenly demanded of Tim why he was so committed to drugs, when it could only delay the revolution to have a lot of lame-brained dope addicts around? Eldridge told her not to start in on that shit again and then, abruptly, they left.

I asked Tim what had happened in the next room. He said Eldridge had flashed a gun and wanted to know when to expect the money needed to support the maintaining of political exiles. The price was $10,000 or he would denounce us to the FLN, the Algerian revolutionary party sponsoring liberation groups.[30] I looked in the *Moon Sign Book*.[31] Balance, a virgin, two bulls.[32] It was going to be a difficult time for all of us.

---

29. *Computer questions* is an anachronism for 1970, an indication that this passage in Rosemary's draft was written years later.

30. The FLN, *Front de Libération Nationale* (National Liberation Front), was a socialist party and the main Algerian nationalist movement during the War of Independence and the period of massacres and one-party rule that followed, during which this chapter is set.

31. It is not exactly certain what book this is, but (George) *Llewellyn's Moon Sign Book: The Planetary Daily Guide for All* was in its 65th annual edition in 1970. I therefore *speculate* that Rosemary was consulting its 66th edition, published in 1970 with predictions for 1971. At this writing in 2018, *Llewellyn's Moon Sign Book* is still appearing annually, published in St. Paul, Minnesota.

32. That is, Libra, Virgo, Taurus. Timothy was born under the sign of Libra (October 22); Eldridge was a Virgo (August 31); Rosemary (April 26) and Kathleen (May 13) were both Taurus.

When you enter a house, salute one another in the name of Allah
and let your greetings be devout and kindly. Thus Allah makes clear
to you His revelations so you may grow in wisdom.[33]

Mina, Fatima, and Hadija taught me Arabic while we sat on the
roof folding laundry. Mina would mime the different situations,
greeting a guest, seating a guest; old or young, each had a separate
decorum. They were delighted when I used the expressions correctly,
amused when I confused the greetings. We kissed cheeks in the morning and again when they left in the evening, putting on their veils to
walk to their homes in the next village. They lived with relatives and,
when asked about husbands, each had a tale of woe and neglect. They
said they preferred the independence of work in the government-
owned hotel.

Mina showed me how to arrange the haik, a sheet of material three meters long, white or black depending on whether one is
from the North or South. The black cloth is worn by the women
of a southern desert tribe who offended the mullahs of Allah long
ago.[34] The women I saw on the streets wearing the black haik were
dark-skinned, robust, and exotic looking with their tattooed cheeks.
They seemed less concerned with keeping their faces covered than
their northern sisters. Their jewelry and embroidery flash against the
dark cloth.

But it is a white cloth that Mina is covering me with. On top of
the head, so, across the nose, the left arm is held close to the body and
immobilized by the fabric. The right underarm keeps the fabric across
the breasts. The only movement possible is with the right forearm.
One can point, beg, carry a child or a bundle, but other gestures are
restricted. One hand, that is all the world is allowed to see. I looked in
the mirror. I was invisible.

---

33. Koran, Surah 24 (*An-Nur,* The Light), verse 61. Slightly paraphrased from the
Dawood translation.
34. Another version says "who offended Allah in some way," which is not the same thing.

Behind the veil there is a woman. She is kin to me and I to her. She had nothing to forgive me nor have I to give her recompense. She is my sister.[35]

The manager of the hotel, Mr. Hamid, wanted us to accompany him to his mountain home. I would meet his wife and he would take us boar hunting in the forests of Jakunan. We would also go to the groves of Pan where storks are sacred and the hot springs which the djinns created for Solomon still run.[36]

As the oldest son of the village elder he was responsible for the welfare of his village. He cried when he spoke of the revolution and his father's death during the last days of it. He'd been wounded while protecting his father from a rain of machine-gun fire. Two days later the war was over and the village buried its dead. Now the forest had started to grow again amid the bomb craters.

December 5, 1970

Dear Family,

We've just returned from a trip to the desert, to a ninth century village, Bou Saâda, the City of Happiness. It is an oasis at the edge of the Ouled Naïl desert. We drove into the desert and met shepherds leading their flocks down-river to sell. They showed us the way to a quiet spot and said "go with God." We sat all day watching the wind carve the dunes into fantastic shapes. The sand is so fine, it is like silk or water. It is the purest substance I've ever seen. The desert is all form, there is only the sky and the earth, blue meeting white.

We took some pictures, I'll send them to you. Tim sent one to the judge

---

35. This indented paragraph had been placed at the ends of various drafts but seemed to fit best here.

36. Djinns are powerful but invisible beings, mentioned in the Koran and prominent in Islamic folklore. Many stories link them with King Solomon, who also appears in the Koran. "And there were gathered together unto Solomon his armies of the jinn and humankind, and of the birds, and they were set in battle order." Koran, Surah 27 (*An-Naml,* The Ants), verse 17 (Yusuf Ali translation).

in Santa Ana.[37] *I couldn't persuade him not to, he thought it funny, us here, under a palm tree. Please don't send anything for Xmas, use the money to get something for the house. Packages and mail quite often don't get through to us. Please write soon.*

LOVE

We worked on the book about our escapades, hoping a publisher would accept it and we would be able to pay the Panthers the money they demanded. The hotel was comfortable but expensive, and we had very little money left to last us through the winter. Eldridge's secretary introduced us to an English woman named Eirene who knew of an apartment for rent. The owners were moving to France and wanted to sell their furniture and lease. The rent would be about fifty dollars a month and we'd have to keep their maid who'd been with them for years and had no family. She was called Zora. (All maids are called Zora or Fatima by Europeans). She would help me continue with Arabic lessons. The apartment was in the center of town, it was comfortable.

Apartments were so scarce that, should the flat be empty for a day, another family would move in. A country family, we were told, would immediately put their chickens and sheep on the terrace and we would be out of a home. We could just manage to pay for it all while we prayed for a check from a publisher. We made the arrangements and prepared to leave the hotel the day the former tenants left for France.

Eirene and Louis were an Anglo-French couple who'd lived in Algeria for many years. Eirene was a reporter for the *London Times,* and Louis worked for a French television news service. They were charming, hospitable, and very knowledgeable about Algeria. They'd watched the change from the French regime to independence with admiration. They described to us the day of victory[38] and the pride and generosity of the Algerian people.

---

37. Judge Byron K. McMillan in Orange County, California, where the Laguna Beach arrest and trial had taken place, leading to the imprisonment from which Timothy escaped.
38. March 19, 1962.

They bore a tender amusement for the Panthers and their difficulties during their first few months in Algeria. The Panthers' arrival coincided with an African music festival, which was a week of gaiety such as Algeria had never known. Musicians from all over the world participated and only the Panthers seemed ill at ease, their black leather coats and stoic faces an anomaly amid the festival throngs.

There was a sense of rather stressful pleasure in accepting Eirene and Louis's hospitality, for they were reporters, sophisticated observers of the international political scene. For once, we were cautious about talking freely. When they invited us to a cocktail party given by the representative of an East German news service, we thought it best to check with Eldridge before accepting. We received a grudging OK, but were warned not to discuss the Panthers or their organization. It was a wise warning, for almost every one of the guests seemed to be obsessed by the desire to know "just how many Panthers are there at that embassy?"

When we got to the new apartment Malika was waiting for us with her suitcases beside the door. Then Eldridge arrived to tell us that the FLN wanted us under constant supervision. He thought we'd prefer Malika to one of the Panther men. Well, there was the couch in the living room, and Tim had said he'd do anything Eldridge wanted him to do. Eldridge needed a place where he could visit Malika, or perhaps it was just his way of ensuring that he'd see more of us. Whatever the reason, if Eldridge was going to call in the FLN to solve his housing problems, there didn't seem to be much I could do about it.

I liked Malika; she was intelligent and beautiful. When she wasn't being unhappy about her confusing role as spy-mistress, we would talk about the desert people, the Tuaregs. She said that the women didn't wear veils, nor were they kept in seclusion. They maintained the right to choose their lovers and divorce their husbands. But Malika's "job," as she called it, made communal living difficult. Spying on our rare visitors, listening to our conversations from the bathroom, and checking it out with Eldridge each night made the apartment seem cramped and uncomfortable. She was often tearful and complained that Eldridge would not let her talk to Kathleen about the domestic crisis they faced. It was classic soap opera, and I was an unwilling viewer.

One of our Algerian acquaintances, met through Elaine, was a young reporter for the government-owned French language daily newspapers. He'd lived in Manhattan for a few years and was nostalgic about his time there. Son of a mullah of the old city of Algiers, he described the sinful pleasures of pork dishes in New York's Chinatown and the grass, music, and girls of Greenwich Village. He had a large collection of rock music, and one of his favorite songs was John Lennon's "Imagine," which he would sing as *Imagine there's no Boumedienne . . . and no Allah.*[39]

Houari Boumedienne (1932–1978) rose to power in Algeria through the military wing of the FLN and seized power in a coup in 1966. In 1970 he still ruled as "Chairman of the Revolutionary Council" but became president of Algeria in 1976 and died in office two years later.

He introduced us to his haunts in the city: an officially frowned-upon French restaurant and disco where women wore miniskirts and the innards of the casbah where he'd grown up. He pointed out the bombed buildings and described some of the battles of Algiers and the boarded-up passageways to underground tunnels where arms had been cached during the War of Independence. He said they were still used by men who wanted to smoke a pipe of hashish, which was harshly prohibited. The Revolutionary Council had promised that it was a temporary measure during the war, but reprisals against smokers were enforced after victory, and for those who wanted to continue the age-old custom of a contemplative pipe, it was a risky venture.

One of the shops we looked into during a walk suggested an opening into an unimagined hell: two bare-chested men in leather aprons stiffened with blood stoked an open, smoky fire. In the dim recesses of the shop were row upon row of blackened animal heads reaching to the ceiling, the eye sockets empty, black tongues protruding, hair matted with gore, curled back lips. There were piles of charred bones on the floor.

---

39. Lennon's famous song includes this verse, "Imagine there's no countries / It isn't hard to do / Nothing to kill or die for / And no religion too." One problem with this recollection is that according to Rosemary's time line, the Learys left Algeria on May 3, 1971, but the song was not released until October 9 of that year.

There were gentler scenes in the Old City, small terraces of cafés in the sun of a Mediterranean winter. The turbaned old men sipping mint tea could have been there, unchanged, for centuries, watching the harbor below after prayers in the mosque. The only change in the view was the absence of Turkish or Foreign Legion soldiers and the presence of Russian freighters.

Zora made a great couscous; we decided to invite some of our Panther-approved acquaintances to dinner.[40] I asked Malika if she and Eldridge would join us; she said they would and she'd show me where to shop. The open-air market was crowded and colorful with pyramids of oranges, heaps of raisins and dates, almonds, spices, young lamb, and wild boar.[41] I was happily choosing artichokes when I saw Kathleen's proud profile above the shawled heads. I looked for Malika and hoped we could all have coffee together, but she was walking away quickly.

I greeted Kathleen and, confused, asked her, "How is Malika?" She looked at me disbelievingly. "Barbara, I mean, and the children?" She laughed, disdainfully, and walked away. Malika reappeared looking rather pale, and we moved on to the next aisle where I saw Elaine, Eldridge's secretary. I asked if she could come to dinner that night and was surprised by her abrupt refusal and sudden lack of warmth, she'd always been so friendly. She left without a word of goodbye.

While the crowd moved past I wondered at the sudden shifts of humor. There was a slight tug at my pocket. My shopping money was gone. I caught up with the thief, my hand touched his shoulder; he turned and looked at me. He was about six years old, ragged, frightened. Then he was gone and the crowd closed around me. Robbed, snubbed, and stupid, all in one day. What next?

It is midday, the market is quiet, green shadowed under thatched stalls. I am in the sun looking at golden flowers, red pollen, brown seeds. Is there an herb to make me wise? A shape moves behind the mounds of color;

---

40. Couscous is a staple North African cereal, made from wheat and served as a base for meat and vegetable dishes.

41. If this really was wild boar, it is unclear why it was offered in the market as it is a forbidden food for Moslems. Perhaps it was some other local wild game.

a woman looking at me. Old yellow eyes do not blink; her face is black.
Several heartbeats. I see another's eyes, staring wide and frightened. Her
eyes are brown. She is white. Will she buy my herbs? I blink, the shadows
shift. The yellow eyes close. Is there an herb to make me wise?

V

I was slicing vegetables when the doorbell rang. Four Panthers, looking grim, wanted to see Tim. No handshaking visit. DC followed me into the kitchen and took the carving knife away. Tim was carried into the hallway struggling and kicking. They muffled his cries for help.

Help? Who would help us? We didn't know our neighbors and we were six flights above the street. Their guns were out of their briefcases, turned on us. They checked out the hallway, then put Tim in the elevator and dropped out of sight. DC told me to get a coat and some shoes, we'd use the back stairs. I looked around the apartment. The table was set. We owed Zora two weeks pay; what would she think when she came in the morning? I turned off the stove, locked the door, the Panther took the keys. There was no one on the streets, the shop on the corner with the friendly boy who liked to practice English was closed, the women I nodded to shyly were in their homes cooking dinner; our guests were late.

It was a silent and swift ride through the city. We stopped in front of an apartment near the sea. Upstairs, Bobby Seale's picture looked down on a room full of closed-face men at ease on the mattress-covered floor. What's happening? Was it a trial, a bit of enforced humiliation, or a quick shot to blow us away? I was full of dread; the hatred and the power of that hatred in the closed room were palpable, it hovered like cigarette haze above my head. I didn't know these men, they were recent arrivals. Perhaps they were like the new pledges of the Hell's Angels at Altamont, there to prove their strength.

They have deadly weapons with which to inflict pain on the human body. They know how to bring about horrible deaths. . . . They have bullets and guns with which to tear holes in the flesh, to smash bones, to disable and kill.[42]

We were told, "Sit down over there and be quiet. This is a prison, no bail, no lawyer." Tim demanded to see Eldridge, but no one responded. We sat close together and whispered scared jokes. We were the last passengers on the *Titanic,* talking of Maynard and Flo and Viva's book. I could not look at our jailers and face the contempt I thought was there. A shaggy-haired white man with a television camera walked into the room and started to film us. THE LEARYS WERE LAST SEEN . . . I threw my coat over my head and practiced breathing exercises until the camera stopped whirring. When I emerged, the room had emptied but for two Panthers. Stay away from the windows, ask if you want to use the toilet.

> They have cells and prisons to lock you up in. They pass out sentences. They won't let you go when you want to. You have to stay put until they give the word.[43]

The windows were two flights above a rubble-strewn street. I curled against Tim and tried to go to sleep. The jailers slept on mattresses blocking the doorway. A clock ticked loudly all night. Did I fear them because they'd said they could kill us, or was it the obvious dislike I feared?

> Every soul shall taste death. You shall receive your reward only on the Day of Resurrection. Whoever is spared the fire of Hell and is admitted into Paradise shall surely gain his end; for the life of this world is nothing but a fleeting vanity.[44]

---

42. From Cleaver's *Soul on Ice.*
43. Also from *Soul on Ice.*
44. Koran, Surah 3 (*Al-Imran,* The Family of Imran), verse 185. Slightly paraphrased from the Dawood translation.

The next day we were put into separate cars and sped through the city to an unfamiliar neighborhood, then hustled into a dark, shuttered house and up worn stairs to a damp, empty room. Ten-year-old copies of French illustrated magazines were scattered on the floor. The one grimy window faced an inner courtyard littered with broken bottles and a shed too far to leap to. After a quick glance, the guard went out, locking the door behind him.

It was freezing in the room; my dress had split down the back and my feet were bare in sandals. I looked at the dentist waiting-room magazines. I could hear furniture shoved about and the guards arguing about blankets and choice of rooms. I shouted, asking if there was a pair of socks I could use; some large white athletic socks were handed in. (Thanks, you saved my life.) A sprung mattress was shoved into the room; one blanket followed. The door was locked again. A tape machine played Aretha Franklin; the smell of grass wreathed through the keyhole. Distant prayers from a mosque beat against the window; the record stuck: *La ilaha illa'llah.*[45]

If they come in with guns would I cover Tim or jump through the window? I don't want to die a violent death. Aretha is shouting, "Your mind won't let yourself be free, *Freedom, Freeeedom.*"[46] Sleep, child, sleep. Tim and the guards snored most of the night.

The next day I asked to go to the bathroom, no water in the taps. I told the guards, and after an argument one left to make a phone call. Cars again, another apartment. This one was comfortable, full of furniture, rugs and books; everything was black, white, and red, Eldridge's decorating colors. We were told to stay in the living room; the windows would not be opened. On the floor by the mattress there was a half-smoked joint; I palmed it and smoked it later in the bathroom. I had permission to take a bath, but my head was too full of horror movies to climb naked into the tub.

---

45. The Shahada: There is no god but God.
46. From "Think," by Aretha Franklin and Ted White (1968). "You better think (think) / Think about what you're trying to do to me. / Yeah, think (think, think) / Let your mind go, let yourself be free. / Oh, freedom (freedom), freedom (freedom) . . ."

The sock-lending guard told me there were leftovers in the kitchen for soup, "go and cook, woman." I recognized Malika's spoor: greasy pots, spice, half-rotted meat in the fridge. The guard hung around the kitchen while I made an inspection. He was friendly and I forgot for a moment the game we were playing of prisoner and guard.[47] The leftovers had been left too long, so I made out a list of fantasy foods,[48] ice cream, apples, peanut butter, chocolate cookies. He returned and said the stores were closed; it was a holiday.[49] "Kathleen will send over some food later."

Two foil-wrapped baking tins arrived with the change of guards, former hand-slapping friends. They made notes of our conversation. We all sat down to eat: there was one pan of pigs feet, one pan of ribs. One says he's a Moslem, doesn't eat pork. I fast; Kathleen is a fine cook, but is it our last meal?[50]

Later the guards lay in the doorway to sleep. One still suffers pain and disfigurement from a policeman's bullet; there is no hospital he will trust in Algeria. The other jumped three stories and hijacked a plane to get where he is. They hold their breath to hear our whispered conversation. I read Fanon on women and veils.[51] The French tried to take them off; the revolution put them back on to hide guns, knives, explosives, men. Traffic on the street below slows down; everyone sleeps. I felt alone. I was alone.

The next morning I awoke to find an old friend in the doorway: Michael Zwerin, once a jazz musician, now a reporter for a New York

---

47. In another version Rosemary says she forgot "it was still a prison."

48. Another version has "tasty foods," but *fantasy foods* seems better.

49. *Yennayer,* the New Year according to the Berber calendar, is January 14 (although sometimes it is celebrated on the twelfth or thirteenth). Rosemary gives January 13, 1971, as the date of the "revolutionary bust," and her account in this chapter has a night intervening before the day the guard says is a holiday. So it is well possible that stores were closed on that day, and that the (presumably American) Panther guard would not have known this.

50. Another version reads, "but my soul hurts."

51. Frantz Fanon (1925–1961), a Martinique-born psychiatrist, was a pioneering writer on the psychopathology of colonization. His most famous work was *The Wretched of the Earth* (1961), but it is more likely that Rosemary was reading *A Dying Colonialism*, about Algeria, originally published as *L'An V de la Révolution Algérienne* (Year Five of the Algerian Revolution) in 1959, and translated into English in 1965.

weekly newspaper.[52] He talked to Eldridge and negotiated our conditional release; we could go back to the apartment on Rue Lafayette.

Believers, remember the favor which Allah bestowed upon you when he restrained the hands of those who sought to harm you. Have fear of Allah. In Allah let the faithful put their trust.

The sound of children playing and mothers calling was familiar, reassuring. It was good to be on the street again, standing in the sun, no one herding me into a car to an unknown destination. I wanted a hot bath and a change from the filthy bedraggled party dress, but I wanted to stay outside for a while before facing the apartment, and possibly Malika who watched me buy and cook all that food, knowing all the while the plan to imprison me.[53] And Elaine, whose political advice Eldridge depended on: was she a CIA agent sowing confusion and distrust? Did Kathleen go along with this "discipline" of Eldridge and DC?

There was an odor in the air I couldn't quite place. Flies were thick in the gutters. Blood, there was blood in the street; sluggish and thick near the sewer, it was a slow-moving stream glistening darkly in the sun. There were small, red handprints on the white buildings; fresh sheepskins hung from the balconies. It was the feast of Abraham, the rite of sacrifice in memory of the day Abraham raised his knife to slay Isaac, his firstborn son, on the altar Isaac raised on a mountaintop. Abraham was willing, but before the knife descended, he heard the Lord say he'd proved his faith; he was to sacrifice the fine ram caught in the bushes instead of his son.[54]

---

52. From 1969 to 1971 Michael Zwerin (1930–2010), musician and jazz critic, was the European editor of the *Village Voice*.

53. In another version Rosemary writes here of Malika, "Little sister, indeed, watching me buy and cook all that food, listening to her lovesick tales."

54. *Eid al-Adha*, the Feast of the Sacrifice. In 1971 this feast fell on February 6. The appalling story of Abraham's attempted sacrifice of Isaac is told in the Bible in Genesis 22:1–18. It is really a metaphor for the cultural transition from human to animal sacrifice. The Koranic story (without the ram) is found in Surah 37 (*As-Saffat*, Ranged in a Row), verses 100–13. In another version Rosemary, Bible-trained in

On this day, lambs and rams died. Their throats were slit, blood flowed into the gutter or the ground, or bathroom drains; entrails, steaming and slippery, were drawn from the belly of the beast by the eldest male of each family, Abraham's descendants.[55] Inside the apartment, the ashtrays were full, dirty dishes covered the sink. I could still smell the bloodied air.

Malika kept a closer watch on us: "house arrest" it was called. Eldridge came over to eat her cooking; we'd talk, but it was not a uniting intelligence. I called him a pig and said I didn't like him sitting on my head, meaning my mind, which I instantly regretted for the sadistic, sexual images it conjured. "So I'm a pig, but we need the practice to be able to handle this kind of political necessity in the future, see," the leader of the Intercommunal Sector of the Liberation Army replied. He told Tim to write a video script on why the Berrigan brothers should be "offed." "Death to all those who deserve to die."[56] I hated the way he looked at me when he left, a narrow-eyed speculative stare.

There were men following me when I went to do the shopping on Rue Mohammed V. Two men in belted raincoats and brimmed hats, with sharp but strangely indistinct features, always turned aside when I saw them. They paused to light a cigarette, lingered in front of an uninteresting shop window. I knew I'd seen them before, but now they scared me. Eldridge had said that we could be kidnapped by the Americans, or arrested by the Algerians, or he could "blow us away," and no one would know or care. But they didn't look like Algerians

(cont. from p. 193) girlhood, continues, "instead of the son who lived on to beget Jacob and Esau who later quarreled over some lentil soup." In Genesis 25:29–34, Esau comes to Jacob famished and begs some lentil stew (red pottage), but Jacob insists that Esau exchange his birthright (his inheritance from Isaac) for it first.

55. Arabs claim descent from Ishmael, son of Abraham by his wife's handmaiden Hagar and therefore Isaac's half brother. But many Algerians are not Arabs.

56. It is not clear who or what is being quoted here. Daniel Berrigan (1921–2016) and his brother Philip Berrigan (1923–2002), both Roman Catholic priests, were radical activists for peace and social justice. Timothy must have had a hard time imagining any reason at all for them to be offed.

or Americans: in the dreary twilight of a rainy night they seemed like images from an old war film, Vichy French. "I'm not in your movie," I wanted to shout at them, but I paid the sullen shopkeeper and hurried toward the apartment. When I reached the corner and turned, the two mysterious men were entering the shop I'd just left.

Tim was seeing himself as a captive poet in Stalin's Russia and went to the embassy every day as Eldridge ordered. He said he didn't mind, he could read the newspapers. Eldridge seemed to want him there as audience for his dialogue with Huey Newton, the Supreme Commander in Oakland. They were playing king of the hill by international telephone and it was creating headlines.[57] It was a diversion to hear about it, but I was glad I didn't have to witness it too. I drank coffee with Zora and watched Malika clean her nails with the switchblade she always carried. One day I asked her if she ever felt like killing anyone. "Most Europeans," she replied. She told me about French soldiers who had tortured her father and raped her pregnant mother.

The only person I was mad at was myself for not being able to think of a way out of the mess we were in. The anger I felt for Eldridge and the Panthers could not be turned to useful purpose; there was no revenge to be had. Their position was unassailable, they were "protecting" us from our own stupidities and the American government.[58] I spent a lot of time staring out the window or into the courtyard six stories below. Neither the skies of Africa nor fantasies of smashups below brought any peace: there was no one to rescue me. There was no way out. Death, though solitary, was not a way out of it. Even a "revolutionary suicide" was unthinkable.

Rarely seen alone, and never seen at night, gray-sheeted figures move like ghosts through the streets. They peer at me through their veils,

---

57. Another version has "by ITT satellite" (International Telephone & Telegraph Co.). But in 1970 the principal vehicle for private international satellite calls was Telstar, operated by *American* Telephone & Telegraph Co. (AT&T), not ITT.

58. Another version has "our stupidities, our *folie à deux,*" using a psychiatric term meaning a delusion shared by two people.

blue-lidded daughters of Hecate.[59] Occasionally, there is a glimpse of miniskirts and stockinged legs, but more often it is a plastic slipper and wispy flutters of pantaloons. If not enveloped in their shrouds, a lace-edged triangular handkerchief covers nose and mouth. A country woman scurries along with a fold of her cloak in her teeth. Proper, modern young women wear knee-covering gray or blue raincoats, matching head scarves, and doilies over their faces. I am naked in the streets and envy their invisible uniformity. Winking, blinking eyes and mouth-smacking noises follow me. I wear a scarf, turn up my coat collar, hunch my shoulders, avoid others' faces as I walk, but always there are gestures, beckonings, pointed fingers, and male laughter. Alone in the city I feel like some wounded beast that has wandered into the wrong territory. When Tim is with me, it is possible to relax a bit; he is a shield, a veil I wear to face the world.[60]

Lydia, a friend from California, came to visit us, bringing a whiff of San Francisco. Hoping she could make some sense out of all the madness, she went off to the embassy to do the filing I was to have done. She came home with our censored mail and an article that Kathleen had written and wanted edited. It was a strong statement of her feelings about white women and black men. Full of historical rage, it was lucid, flowing with anger and had rhythm and purpose to it, ticking off white women with black lovers who laid claim to sisterhood. I felt her rage but no guilt for the black lovers in my life; I loved them.

Our California friend tried to rearrange the article to fit her own personal vision, attacking it with a shears. When she gave up trying to put it back together Tim mixed up the sequence some more, then gave up, saying the whole problem was beyond him. The article went back to Kathleen all mangled and I wondered if she'd ever be able to put

---

59. The reference is obscure. Hecate was a Greek goddess, later identified with magical practice; the phrase *daughters of Hecate* can mean witches. But that doesn't match the sense of the passage.

60. As with other such set pieces, this seems complete as presented, and I have not included additional material found in other versions.

it back together, or figure out what had happened to it while it was at my house. I wished she'd asked me to help, but it was unlikely she would as I'd told her I couldn't type very well and wouldn't make a good secretary. I didn't think she'd want to hear any tales about my black lovers if we ever did get together.[61]

I decided to make some toys for the children. I knew they had toy soldiers and guns made from downed American planes,[62] but I'd never seen any cuddly things. I made Kathleen's boy a red velvet heart stuffed with powdered cloves and cotton, put a silk ribbon on it so he could drag it around. I used a flannel belt to make a soft, funny snake with a red felt tongue and crossed button eyes for Barbara's baby. A week after the toys had been sent I called to ask if they had been received. Barbara's voice was flat; she said it was a funny coincidence, Bobby Seale had written warning her to beware of serpents in the babies' crib.

Had it been Our will, We could have raised a prophet in every nation. Do not yield to the unbelievers, but fight them strenuously with this Koran.[63]

Ron, Lydia's husband, arrived with his early psychedelic vibes, and wanted to know why we hadn't turned on with Eldridge, dosed the embassy, had some street sense to begin with, showed some style, got it on with those motherfuckers. I was properly contrite and suggested that they give up following rock bands around and come join our little commune. He said we ought to at least have a party before they went back to the States. Sure, why not party with the pigs, we haven't got anything else to do. I'd get to see Kathleen and Barbara and find out what they thought about our revolutionary arrest.

Lydia and Ron went over to Kathleen's to barbecue steaks and I started a large cheesecake. It was the wrong kind of cheese, demi-liter

---

61. The original version this sentence comes from says, strangely, "my black lover brothers."
62. Presumably brought back from North Vietnam.
63. Koran, Surah 25 (*Al-Fuqran,* The Criterion), verse 51. It is unclear which translation Rosemary is using here.

measurements instead of cups, oven temperature too high. I had to buy some store-bought cake. We arrived late; the cooking was done, the table set. I had nothing to do except feel embarrassed. We were with our jailers and we were all smiling at one another, as if we hadn't been victims of theirs just the week before.[64] Elaine, just back from seeing *Hair* in Paris, was describing a scene with a machine gun. She'd go *taka-taka* across my face and it made me kind of nervous, so I went into the kitchen to do the dishes. Our friends were in there giggling; they swore they hadn't dosed anything, except themselves, and wasn't it a great party?

It was kind of nice at times, actually. DC was sitting with his shoes off playing with his baby. I liked him that night being tender with his child. Eldridge wasn't around so there wasn't any tension in the air. Kathleen sat in a rocker, tired out from the cooking; she looked peaceful. Barbara made a conciliatory statement about our all having to live together.[65] I told them I wanted to help in the nursery with the children and went home with the hope that the "political necessity" was past and we could live in peace.[66]

Tim came home one day and said that Eldridge insisted that I do some work for the Party. When I got to the embassy Eldridge was playing with his video equipment. Kathleen was in the reception room. I went in to say hello and stayed to say she looked wonderful in the blue suit matching her eyes. She was beautiful always, but this day the vulnerability of her startling blue eyes was not hidden behind dark glasses, and there was some friendliness in her attitude.

She told me that she would check on countries where I could go for medical attention: Romania, North Vietnam, and North Korea were possibilities. I was doubtful that there would be a doctor familiar with the experimental surgery I'd had done in the States and that needed completion, but I was grateful for her concern.[67] The second

---

64. Another version says, "as if we hadn't been victims and victors."

65. Another version says, "about the need to live closer together."

66. In another version Rosemary says she went home wishing "I'd been able to break through my self-consciousness and fears when we first got to Algeria."

67. The surgery had been undertaken to correct infertility.

operation was long overdue, and I was in considerable pain at times.

She also said that they had the nursery set up and could use some help. I was pleased that she was being friendly and I'd get to see Barbara and the children. We worked out a schedule, and when she had to answer the phone I went out to the porch where Eldridge and Tim were sitting in rocking chairs. I told them what Kathleen and I had arranged for the week.[68]

"Kathleen is just the receptionist, she hasn't any right to schedule anyone for anything. Tim is going to do manual labor from now on and you'll be in the file room every morning at nine." He stomped inside. Tim handed me *EVO,* one of the underground newspapers.[69] "Look at this." Eldridge had written a letter to our friend Jaakov Kohn, the paper's editor. "Don't worry about the Learys," Eldridge wrote. "*Poppa* is going to take care of them." He went on to denounce Jewish publishers, peace lovers, Yippies, and hippie freaks in general. Tim said, "And here's the latest from the East and Chairman Mao." He pointed to an article in the *International Herald Tribune.* It was dated the day of our "revolutionary bust" by the Panthers.[70] The Chinese were denouncing the use of LSD by Western youth.

Dearest Mother,

We are in a small hotel on the edge of the desert, an oasis between miles of sand. It is unique in that all the house roofs are domed instead of flat. Thousands of white houses looking as though cut from a mold, sand everywhere, dusty camels with firewood, coming from nowhere, going nowhere, men and women veiled in blue. Storms for the past few days. Waves of sand on the horizon, the edges topped with green where the palms have drowned.

I dreamed this afternoon of you and Nana.[71] It was such a pleasant dream I didn't want to wake, kept going back to sleep to be with you

---

68. Another version says, "for work."
69. The *East Village Other.*
70. January 13, 1971.
71. Nana was Matilda Hegel, mother of Rosemary's mother Ruth.

again. It was much more real than this egg-shaped room in the desert.

We've been having a vacation from all the political intrigues. We escaped in a little rented car with blankets, pillows, pots, and pans, heading for the mountains where Pan is said to hide. Actually like any middle-aged couple in search of health cures we were going to visit the thermal springs. We visited one ancient spring, had a lovely bath, skin all silky by candlelight down mountain paths. Found the bloated corpse of a wild boar on the road. Storks are sacred though all other birds are killed by even the little children. The mountain regions were hardest hit by the war, everywhere there are cemeteries and memorials.

We went to the golden coast where the sun rises from the sea. We drove through deep gorges and saw wild baboons.[72] Up to the high plateaus, lunar strange landscape, fierce winds, the site of pillage and waste, once Roman wheatfields. Children gave me a bouquet of sweet yellow flowers, they perfume this room now. Over the mountains and into the desert. We stopped at a bath built by the Turks, all minarets and stained glass. The nomads carry away inner tubes and goat skins full of the healing sulfur water. There are huge tourist installations going up ugly and oil digging rigs.

I miss seeing other women. Strange isolated feeling to be an object of curiosity. One of the maids calls me daughter, she is a lovely lady all tattoos and gold teeth. I miss you very much, going back to sleep, hope to dream of you some more.

LOVE

The I Ching said a flying bird would bring a message.[73] It brought Pierre and Anita from Paris, our psychiatrist friends. They made a formal call at the embassy and met Eldridge, who was very polite. He asked them about the possibility of LSD causing brain damage; he kept hav-

---

72. Actually there are no wild baboons in Algeria. Rosemary must have seen Barbary macaques, as they are the only native monkeys in Algeria.
73. The Judgment of Hexagram 62 reads: "Preponderance of the small. Success. Perseverance furthers. Small things may be done; great things should not be done. The flying bird brings the message: It is not well to strive upward, it is well to remain below. Great good fortune." Wilhelm-Baynes edition, 240.

ing these headaches, see? He was curious about the use of truth serums too. That wasn't their field, but they thought we ought to leave if we could, at least get out of the apartment to a place where there would be Algerians in sight at all times.

We decided to take their advice; Eldridge could have the apartment. I packed a few favorite pots and pans, made a bundle of things for Zora. I was just going out the door when she arrived. She saw that I had packed hurriedly and told me to wait. She returned from the kitchen with a bag of salt. She handed it to me and placed her hand for a moment on top of my head. I don't know what it meant, but it was good and she was wishing me well.

Mr. Hamid of the hotel was happy to see us. He renewed his invitation to his village in the mountains. Hadija brought her grandchildren with bouquets of flowers from her garden each morning. She said I was her child and her daughters were my sisters. She made tea for me when I was ill, claiming that her herbs would cure me and she would see my sons. Mina said she'd take me to the desert when she visited her father.

The sun is a whirling mandala boring a hole in the sky,[74] *a tunnel leading out of the desert across the ocean leading to a waterfall and a hut woven of willow branches. The sound of bells and goats recedes; the cricket repeats its message. "At the ranch, at the ranch, they think of you, they pray for you, trust in God, peace in love."*

The cricket stops, the sun is a huge black spider scurrying across the sky. The voice of the herds: Baa ahaa à la llama ill'Allah.[75] *Cover your face, cover your face, bow your head. Space all around, sand whispering past. The sun is red, the sky is white, the sun is black, the sky is red, the sun is white, the sky is black, the sun is . . .*

"How long have you been staring at the sun, beloved?" Fools duel with the sun. Blind sinners pray: *Lord, have mercy on me.*

---

74. Another version calls it a "whirling swastika."

75. Rosemary intends a sheeply parody of the Shahada here. I have adjusted her words slightly to make this intention clearer.

Tim and I continued our argument about the book we were writing telling of his escape from prison.[76] Or rather, he was writing it; I was hesitantly contributing notes on the difficulties in aiding and abetting him. I was reluctant to publish names and places for fear of endangering the people who had helped us. He, however, as the hero of an adventure tale, was impatient with my fears. We argued about levels of consciousness and drank too much wine at dinner. We walked to the port every evening to watch the fishing boats return in the setting sun, happy to be away from the city and among people who liked us.

Government officials from the president's office called and presented us with our residency cards. They'd been ready for months; why hadn't we claimed them? We were welcome guests, the FLN was not curious about our living habits. The bird brought another message, an invitation from the University of Copenhagen to speak at a conference of writers.[77] They would pay our fare and a lecture fee. We could leave Algeria for a short while.

Hotel Méditerranée

April 27, 1971

Dearest Ones,

Your birthday greetings arrived yesterday, right on time. Dear Nana I will use the money for something pretty and no, I won't give it to the Panthers. Thank you. We are getting very brown. The manager of the hotel compliments me on my bathing costume, a bikini under a hooded robe. He says it is "correct."

We are waiting for our exit visas for Denmark. I feel so unprepared, our clothes are rather shabby. We might have to leave owing the hotel. Fantastic complications, a friend writes "you have been betrayed, whom can you trust," melodramatic letters yet. Really this year has been horrible.

---

76. Later published under the title *Confessions of a Hope Fiend* (New York: Bantam Books, 1973).

77. Rosemary wrote "University of Denmark," but there is no institution with that name, and the conference was almost certainly at the University of Copenhagen.

It is all different now. Seems it's possible to have a house and garden.
T can teach if he wishes. We are quite safe, free, healthy, in the sun. But
that's the rhythm of our life, darkness, light. I long for something a little
less extreme. I feel like some international robot on greased wheels. Well,
two sheets of air-mail stationery cost two dinars in postage. Write me.

LOVE

ADDENDUM

Editor's Note

This note by Rosemary appeared at the end of one of the many variant versions of this chapter in the archive at the New York Public Library.

This section is not yet complete in characterization or characters. Some of the things left out are:

- The student uprising, students beaten and imprisoned.
- The gas installations in the desert. American oilmen with crew cuts wearing burnooses and cowboy boots.
- The lonely disc jockey waiting for jazz musicians.
- The Brazilian soccer players with their sambas on cassettes.
- Egyptian orchestras on TV. Om Kadoun's voice everywhere.[78]
- The Algerian official and his French wife; the story of the CIA man and father of five whose life he'd saved.
- Tim's capitulation to a fake presidential aide.
- The sheikh who refused to dine in the same room with me.

---

78. Umm Kulthum (1904–1975), an Egyptian singer, songwriter, and actress, was for decades, including Rosemary's time in Algeria, one of the most popular entertainers in the Arab world.

- Eldridge confiscating a gram of LSD brought by visitors; my stealing half of it back.
- Eldridge, Kathleen, Barbara, DC, and other black warriors.
- The Brazilian liberation group.
- Ramadan: unsafe in the streets, the fasting waiters serving.[79]
- Cool Hand Luke from *Oui:* how insufferably together we were excluding him, how intrusively klutzy he was, prying, able to leave us behind under a byline.[80]
- The bar and dancing women, kneeling, their movements mimicking the daily chores. Pastel thin fabric dresses, silver spangles, flayed brown feet.
- The beautiful mistress of an official guarded by her mother, walked through the streets like a proud heifer.
- The poor rug seller and his ugly rugs, two years' work and six months' wages.
- Algeria was like a delayed bill, I'm still paying it.

---

79. During the month of Ramadan in the Islamic calendar, May to June in the Western calendar, Moslems are required to fast from sunrise to sunset.

80. *Oui* was a semipornographic magazine with articles in the *Playboy* manner. Originally the French magazine *Lui,* Playboy bought and renamed it, but it was not published under the new name until October 1972, after Rosemary had left Algeria.

TEN

Changes

> *Wealth shields from immediate judgment, takes you out of the subway crowd to enclose you in a chromium-plated automobile, isolates you in huge protective lawns, Pullmans, first-class cabins. Wealth, cher ami, is not quite acquittal, but reprieve, and that's always worth taking.*
>
> ALBERT CAMUS, *THE FALL*

We arrived in Geneva with a few American coins and some useless Algerian money.[1] We sat at the back table of the bar of the airport's International Lounge wondering what to do. The plane for Copenhagen wouldn't leave for six hours. A waiter decided he'd accept our dimes and we ordered lemonade.

"Where's the agent from the plane?"

"Off duty probably and a new one to take his place." I'd grown accustomed to his following us, in the streets, into bars and cafés, though I couldn't distinguish among the many travelers anyone who seemed interested in our actions.

"Perhaps there's a message from Pierre, let's go to the telegraph office." Tim spoke briefly to a girl behind the counter, then waved a slip of paper at me and stepped into a phone booth. I watched the people pass, still looking for the government agent. Which government? I don't know.

---

1. According to Rosemary's time line the date was May 3, 1971.

Our departure from Algeria had been delayed for several days; we'd lacked the necessary exit visas and missed three planes before we'd been allowed to leave without them. Whether we'd be let back in was something we preferred to think about later. We had hoped to slip away quietly to Denmark to attend a conference scheduled for the first week in May. At the airport in Algiers we encountered several Panthers, our first meeting in several months. When I saw them I ducked behind a pillar, thinking that they'd come to shoot us or drag us back to captivity. But they gave us an unusually affectionate greeting and a warm goodbye.

We'd eagerly accepted the opportunity to leave the quiet political safety of Algeria temporarily. We were completely broke, and the only possibility of income was the promised lecture fee. Another reason was my need to have an operation. I was in considerable pain at times and feared there was something seriously wrong. Pierre and his wife, Anita, had said they would find a doctor in Denmark while they waited for our arrival.[2] We were to wait in Geneva for a message from them.

On the plane to Switzerland we speculated that the invitation to speak at the university might not have been arranged by the students after all. The signature on the letter of invitation was illegible, and it had been a stranger's voice on the telephone to confirm the date. Perhaps we were being set up for extradition or another "revolutionary" bust.

Tim was still in the phone booth. A well-dressed middle-aged man approached the counter. I watched him curiously. He radiated a smug sense of well-being and confidence, preening his silver hair, touching the knot of his silk tie. He bulged a blue-eye glance over his shoulder at my travel-worn boots, sniffed, and turned to the girl behind the counter. She motioned toward the booth where Tim was talking animatedly into the phone. He smiled broadly at the man as he did at any casual stranger. The man ignored him and made a quick profiled exit, tasseled

2. Dr. Pierre Ben Sousan is the Parisian psychiatrist from chapter 8. In this chapter Rosemary changed their names to Pablo and Annouchka, and calls Annouchka Pablo's wife (in chapter 8 Anita is Pierre's "friend"). I have changed the names back to avoid confusion.

shoes slick on the marble floor. Who is the rich man? I have seven unusable cents in my pocket.

Tim returned. "I spoke to Pierre; they've just come from Copenhagen and think it's a trap. They don't want us to go on."

"Great, what do we do now?"

"There's a friend of his here looking for me. If we don't meet, there are people in Geneva we can spend the afternoon with, and they'll take the evening plane."

"What if Switzerland won't let us enter?"

"Do you want to stay here? I've watched people going through; they just check the color of your passport. Come on, let's see Geneva."

We went past the casual wave of Immigration, through the Nothing to Declare booth, and into the pale spring sun to hail a taxi. The silver-haired rich man was getting into a chrome-colored Rolls-Royce parked in the taxi stand.[3] Our cab followed the expensive car until it turned right and sped away.

"See that man ahead of us, I almost asked him for spare change. How are we going to pay the fare?"

"Pierre's friends will take care of it. Look at the lake and the fountain. Well, beloved, I said I'd show you Europe one day."

"So you did, look, there's a clock made out of flowers."

No one seemed to be following us. The taxi stopped in front of a large apartment building. The bell was answered by a pleasant-looking man. Tim explained the stupid oversight of neglecting to change money at the airport. Our host assured him cheerfully that it was quite all right and ushered us into a formal sitting room. While he paid the driver, his wife greeted us and offered a drink. Pierre had called and said to expect his friends Nino and Maia, and how did we like Switzerland? They were a hospitable couple who quite charmingly behaved as though there was nothing wrong with our slightly manic joviality and arrival without the price of a taxi ride.

---

3. It seems unlikely that the Rolls-Royce was actually *chrome-colored* rather than just detailed in chrome—such a car would be wildly conspicuous—but all versions of the text have it this way so I have kept it.

As the afternoon wore on and we took in more Scotch, the masks of casual travelers slipped off. We offered random bits of our previous existence to our increasingly bewildered and apprehensive hosts. The relief of being away from the tension in Algeria and finding ourselves in a comfortable flat in Geneva with only a social game to play was exhilarating.[4]

Pierre and Anita arrived in time to spare them from further explanations and helped to dispel the feeling of unreality their Scotch and confusion had caused. Nino and Maia indeed, with a face like Tim's immediately recognizable now that his silver hair had grown in. But Nino and Maia had been in all the code messages to Pablo and Annouchka, who were Pierre and Anita in Paris.

Pierre took us aside. "Did they recognize you?" Nino grinned and shrugged.

"Too bad. He's a banker and can't risk a breath of scandal. I don't think they'll be willing to keep you here."

"But what is wrong with Copenhagen, and why couldn't we go on?"

"The airport was full of police and demonstrators; it didn't look like a welcoming committee. When we arrived they thought we were you two and some dark-suited men escorted us from the plane."

"You should have given the lecture."

"I don't think that would have been wise. You're safe enough here at the moment. Maia could have that operation and the Swiss might allow asylum." Putting his arm around me, he said "My friends, I don't think your lives were worth a damn in Algeria."

It was good to be with Pierre and Anita, they were the only people we knew who took our welfare seriously and suggested alternatives to the uncomfortable situations we'd been in. They'd rescued us in Paris, Algeria, and now Geneva. They left us money, clothes, and more importantly hope.

Anita went off with my medical records in the morning to search for doctors. Our host left for the day. Tim chatted with the Swedish

---

4. Another version has "inebriating."

au pair girl about Watson's discovery of the paired strands of DNA molecules while I countered our hostess's puzzlement about our vacation plans. Pierre returned from a morning walk with the newspapers. He pointed to a small column on the third page.

LSD PROPHET, WIFE DROP FROM SIGHT

May 9, Copenhagen. "Timothy Leary the . . . and fugitive from a California . . . who was scheduled to speak . . . after last being seen in Switzerland. Student sources said they had information that Leary and his wife flew out of Algeria Tuesday. A police spokesman in Zürich . . . but it was not known where they went when they left the plane. Leary, convicted of . . . escaped from prison last September and . . .[5]

"Darling, my friends are charming, kind people, but I do not wish them to be involved with this. We must find you another place to stay. I want you to come to the airport with me to meet a friend. Nino had better stay here."

I went to the airport hoping we wouldn't be mistaken for the drug prophet and his wife. We entered the departure lounge.

"There he is." Pierre pointed with his chin to the same stout, gray-haired man I'd seen before. He was dressed a bit more casually today, an embroidered alligator riding his well-fed breast.[6] He held a large German shepherd dog by a strong chain.

"This is Maia," Pierre said. "She might have need of your protection, Michel. Maia, I'm sure he can help you."[7]

---

5. The ellipses are Rosemary's. The May 9 dateline on this story suggests a May 10 newspaper, meaning the Learys would have been in Geneva for a week by this time. The narrative suggests but does not require a shorter period.

6. The trademark of a Lacoste shirt. It is actually a crocodile, an allusion to the founder René Lacoste's nickname as a professional tennis player.

7. Michel, called *Miguel* by Rosemary in her drafts, is called by other names too (for example, Michel Stranieri—the Italian word for *foreigners*). He is actually Michel Hauchard. I have changed it to Michel throughout. Rosemary calls his wife *Bianca*—this may be a pseudonym too.

I was amused by the coincidence, but though he kept his eyes on me appraisingly, he gave no sign of recognition. I felt uncomfortable and looked away. The dog sniffed at my legs.

"I will be at home this evening; I will expect your call." I nodded, Pierre took my arm. Michel walked away with his dog and expensive luggage.

"He has many contacts in Switzerland, and he owes me many favors," Pierre said as we reentered the apartment.[8] Anita had returned with the names of several doctors. We went to see the first on the list. I liked him and decided that I'd trust him with my problems. We discussed the timing of the operations after his examination. He wasn't interested in astrological theories about the flow of blood according to the moon's phases and wished to know which of the two available clinic dates I would choose. I said I'd call the next day and let him know; I wanted to check out the planets before deciding.

Anita and Pierre left Geneva that afternoon; they had a full schedule with their usual psychiatric patients and could not spare any more time away. I was sorry to see them go; with them I felt secure and light-hearted. Alone with Nino again, I was reminded that we were still on the run.

That evening our hosts showed us the late paper. There was a column on the second page about our mysterious disappearance, and a photograph. They were leaving for the weekend; could they give us a lift somewhere?

Michel's flat was in a tall marble building on the lake at Ouchy outside of Lausanne. We confronted the black speaker box with its row of buttons. A disembodied voice said, "*Oui?*" I answered with "Maia" and the door buzzer sounded approval. We took the elevator to the top floor. A dark-haired young girl answered the door; she had the German shepherd on a tightly held leash.[9] As we entered, Michel crossed the long, richly furnished room to greet us, his hand outstretched.

---

8. One version says, "he owes me his freedom."

9. Another version says, "she held the German shepherd by his collar, pulled him aside so we could enter."

"Maia."

"And this is my husband, Nino." They shook hands tentatively.

Another attractive dark-haired girl entered the room carrying a small lap dog. She ignored Michel's attempt to introduce us and whispered urgently in his ear, her eyes fixed on our faces. Michel asked to be excused for a moment. Nino and I were interrupted in the middle of our silent pantomime about the richness of the apartment and the view of the lake and park below.

"Bianca has just told me who you are. I must tell you, I don't approve of drugs. But you are a friend of Pablo's and you are in need. You are at home here with me. Now what would you like to drink?"

"Champagne," said Nino expansively. Michel spoke rapidly[10] to the girl who'd opened the door, then turned to us.

"The champagne is not chilled. We will have white wine and then I will ask you to join me for dinner at a restaurant nearby. The meat is marvelous. Bianca and my secretary will be with us. I will join you shortly."

We sank into the down-filled cushions of a velvet couch. The secretary placed a silver tray with a bottle of wine and two glasses on the table before us, then silently glided away.

"What do you think is going to happen?" I was worried.

"I don't know, but I like this new movie set. This wine is very good, isn't it? Here's to freedom!" Tim lifted his glass, I touched it with mine. Michel interrupted.

"Maia, Nino, we will leave now."

The Rolls was parked in front of the apartment. Would I mind if the canopy was down and my hair blown about?

"Oh no, I can see the stars." The two dogs got in the back with us.

The maître d' greeted Michel with deference. We were ushered to a table set with flowers. Michel arranged the seating arrangements carefully.

"The meat here is superb." He ordered for us and consulted the chef

---

10. Another version has "quietly."

about the cut of veal for the dog's dinner. Wine was poured, Michel offered a toast.

"To freedom. That is what I believe in. I do not know you, what I have read about you I do not like. But you believe in freedom and in that I must agree with you."

The lavish attentions of Michel, and Bianca's appreciative laughter, restored Nino's spirits to a pre-Algerian high. He exerted himself to be charming and had the rapt attention of our hosts between their instructions to the waiter. When Tim paused for a moment, Michel interjected.

"You know, I like you. I do not agree with you about drugs, for me the sky is blue enough, girls are pretty enough, wine is good enough, I do not need drugs to see these things. But I have been in prison, I know what it is like, there is a sympathy between us because of this. You have read *Papillon*?[11] Then you know of what I speak. Have no fear, you are with me."

I could not speak of my prison experiences too and expect to be part of the same cabal. But it wasn't necessary to join the conversation. I had only to laugh in the right places, be appreciative of the good food and wine, and not be miserable that I was so badly dressed in the restaurant full of fashionably attired people. There is a uniformity to worn riches. Despite the casual jeans and T-shirt that Bianca wore, an armload of gold bracelets, expensive shoes and handbag, a chain of gold and ivory amulets were all signals of wealth and ease.

We finished dinner in a cloud of blue cigar smoke from the Havana cigars Michel offered from a leather case. He counted out a lot of large Swiss bank notes and waved the waiters away.

Back at the apartment, the secretary showed us to a guest bedroom. Michel called from the hall to ask if we needed anything, then

---

11. *Papillon,* by Henri Charrière (1969), recounts the author's imprisonment in, and escape from, the Devil's Island penal settlement in French Guiana. It was published in English in 1970, but the famous film version (with Steve McQueen and Dustin Hoffman) did not appear until 1973, after the events portrayed in this chapter. *Papillon* is French for "butterfly."

wished us goodnight. I dreamed that night of the maids of the hotel at El Djamila.[12]

I checked into the clinic the next day, afraid to wait until the end of the month and the possibility that the operation might be postponed. Also there was the prospect of wearing the same travel-stained dress, our luggage was somewhere in Denmark unclaimed. A fear of social embarrassment and the desire to hide in a comfortable hospital bed changed the careful astrological deliberations for the right time to have the delicate operation.

I woke to the sound of Tim's voice. "It's all right, beloved, you are perfect. We'll have babies." I drifted off again and when I woke the room was full of flowers with a note from Michel. The care and cosseting by the clinic staff was so different from the treatment in American hospitals that I looked forward to the ten-day stay the doctor had ordered.

The time passed quickly. Tim visited every day and entertained me with accounts of his social life. He was meeting a young, rich, international set of people and found the experience enlivening. He encountered some hostility from the husbands of the women who were confiding their drug experiences to him. For rather than play cards or backgammon as they did most evenings, they sat before the fire Tim built in Michel's unused fireplace, describing their experiences and longing to turn their husbands on. I felt very weak and could not look at the scar, which felt like a zipper.

"What about the government, can we stay?"

"Michel has a lawyer he wants me to see. He says all it will take is money."

"Where do we get it?"

"He thinks he can interest some friends to form a corporation to support us while we finish the book on the escape. He wants to take a flat for us in Gstaad, it's one of the best ski resorts in Europe. He goes there every year. We'll have the whole summer high in the mountains."

---

12. In Algeria.

Although the operation had been successful and it seemed the problems of freedom and money had been solved, I was depressed. The little I'd seen of Michel's way of life was disturbing, he seemed almost too rich. He was allegedly a fugitive from some government[13] and had secured residency in Switzerland with a bankroll and contacts. He'd hinted that he was in the armament business and friendly with the heads of several countries. It was a high roller's game, and the contrast with the poverty in Algeria was extreme. I wondered how long we'd be able to stay in the game.

Tim was content and at ease. He expressed a growing admiration for Michel. He'd found a friend, a rich and sympathetic friend who offered protection and support. What was there to object to? He'd sent flowers, he asked about me every day. If I was depressed surely it was due to the painkillers. Perhaps I was jealous. Tim was once again the center of an admiring circle and the close dependence we'd had in Algeria was changing.

The doctor inspected his handiwork and declared himself satisfied. He'd saved my life, the doctors in the States must be barbarians, they'd put me together all wrong. He arranged a series of appointments for continued treatment and released me from the clinic. A limousine and driver were waiting; Michel had arranged for the hour's drive back to Ouchy. Bianca declared herself delighted to see me looking so well, would I care to join them for dinner? An old friend, an ambassador, was expected. I declined and went gratefully to the bed the maid prepared. There was still the specter of the much-used dress to wear.

In the following weeks we were Nino and Maia, but our identities were an open secret. Michel was lavish with his hospitality, and we were exposed to a great number of people. The newspapers were still speculating about our disappearance. Michel hinted that he'd had the stories planted to gain time. Nothing was impossible for him, it seemed—all it took was lots of money. His day was arranged around luncheons and

---

13. Another version specifies "France."

dinners at various restaurants with various mistresses, and international telephone calls.

Nino was thriving on the new attention and with the help of Michel's wardrobe achieved a casual elegance that was only slightly hampered by everything being several sizes too large. He looked as though he'd shrunk and in some ways he had. In Algeria he'd assumed a necessary protective meekness; with Michel he played court jester. We were on call for our places at the table whether I wanted dinner or not. Usually I did, but I was feeling lonely and shabby as the fool's wife.

He'd tommed with the Panthers, it was some Amos and Andy game he had going that made it amusing for him to *yassah* and back out of any confrontation with a shuffle and a grin.[14] Not that an eyeballing duel and display of cock feathers would have been more appropriate. There was no easy dignity to be gained there. Everyone knew what the territorial rights were and where they stood in relation to the pack leader. Everyone except me.

I'd never seen him in this light before, in a situation that called for something other than his usual dominance of the time and space. Yes, with the police perhaps, and the prison guards. But while wearing handcuffs one stands straight, the position of the hands, the mudra, requires an erect posture.[15] One seldom plays the fool in front of police cameras, it is too sobering an experience. Before Michel and his display of wealth we were poor fools. Oh, an international reputation lent some esteem, but we'd damned well better be amusing. Michel would never

---

14. The word *tommed* denotes obsequious conduct arising from, and accepting of, inferior social status based on race. It derives from minstrel show misrepresentations of the title character in Harriet Beecher Stowe's novel *Uncle Tom's Cabin* (1852). Its principal use is by African-Americans characterizing the conduct of other African-Americans, and Rosemary's characterization of Timothy's relationship to the Panthers is of course ironic.
Amos 'n' Andy was a hugely popular American radio show, broadcast from 1928 to 1960, in which white actors played black characters in a dialect and style later widely understood to have been stereotyped and racially insensitive. Black actors were used in a television adaptation. Whether fairly or not, *Amos and Andy* became shorthand for a patronizing or racist presentation of black characters.
15. A mudra is a ritual gesture in Hindu and Buddhist religious and cultural iconography, generally expressed by the hands.

concern himself with a political posture or lack of one. He could afford to tolerate his guest's eccentricities. Eldridge couldn't.

He'd had his racial joke in Algeria, we were the slaves this time, he said. I didn't agree, but there could be no argument. Now a different role but the same prisoners' posture: rump first and sly jokes.

"Whose prisoner would you rather be, Eldridge's or Michel's?"

"Well, Eldridge didn't cost as much, that's for sure." And there was the hope that someday we reach some understanding, if only we had time and love enough and could put off anger.

Michel was a problem, he was boring. But Tim had the solution. "Michel needs an LSD session."

"Remember Eldridge and think again." But LSD was always his solution to the world's ills. Racial conflict? Free TV and LSD. Overpopulation? Tantra and LSD. Women's liberation? More LSD. Ecological disaster? And so on. I couldn't argue, I was still asleep, lost in dreams of children and privacy. Gardens and tranquility and love would follow, if only there were time and space and an end to being . . . wanderers.

Also, if I were practical, I was being "pessimistic." If I suggested the impossibility of what he suggested, I was "resisting" him. I'd learned not to resist. I had no alternative to offer, it was better to go on, just go on loving and trusting that he knew of a better way. I was still the hypnotist's assistant and I couldn't embarrass the hypnotist.

But it was the same old movie, and I was getting tired, it was always his movie and I felt that I'd just slapped on some makeup to cover the black eye and didn't know all my lines. I had a movie running in my head too—he wasn't the hero anymore. I didn't want to play Bonnie, meeting her mother on a slag heap and ending up dead in a car.[16]

We were at dinner with Michel and his friends talking about our life in Algeria. Suddenly one of the men exploded.

"How could you live with Algerians or want to? You say they are

---

16. Rosemary is referring to the doomed bank robber couple Bonnie Parker and Clyde Barrow, ambushed and killed by police in 1934. They were played by Warren Beatty and Faye Dunaway in Arthur Penn's 1967 film.

kind, you like them—but they are *barbarians,* cattle, worse! I know what they are like; you cannot tell me they are civilized . . ." He spluttered into silence. There was an awkward pause; someone changed the conversation.

After dinner, his girlfriend said to me, "Poor Maurice, you must understand, his family lost almost everything in Algeria; he cannot bear to think of it. They were there for ages; his father was one of the largest landowners. But you know, Maia, about the Panthers: in my country we have a large black population, but they are so happy, they prefer a simple life. No, really. I have had the same maid since I was a child and she assures me she would not change places with me. When I was a little girl I would open my wardrobe to the poor children and let them take my dresses. My mother would be so angry, but then she would laugh. I almost forgot, I was at a large dinner with one of my young cousins, he fancies himself a revolutionary, imagine. He said that you and Nino are traitors to the revolution, but I defended you. Ah, I must play cards now; it is so boring. But later we will have a smoke, yes? Maurice mustn't know; he would be furious."

She is young, rich, beautiful, and openhearted, but I don't want to change places with her either.

I took the train twice a week to see the doctor. The treatment was painful and the trip fatiguing and dangerous. The newspapers said Swiss authorities would request our departure as "undesirable visitors" if we were found in Switzerland. I complained of pain after each visit and the doctor's wife suggested I stay near their office until the treatments were completed. She gave me the address of a nearby pension.[17] I went to look at the room but the owner was absent and a tenant showed me to a musty sitting room to wait for her return. I glanced idly through a stack of magazines till one labeled *Algeria* caught my eye. It opened to an article about the Panthers. There was a photograph of Nino and Maia, captioned *disparu.*[18] I tiptoed out of the apartment—Michel's was yet the only safe place.

---

17. A pension is a European hotel that offers full- or half-board, including meals with the room.
18. French for "disappeared."

Florists' flowers filled the hall, waiters were unloading cases of champagne and food in the kitchen. Michel was celebrating his Gemini birthday with a party for a hundred guests, he wouldn't hear of my proposed absence.[19]

"You must be here, I will have some very good news for you."

I hastily altered Tim's spare purple velvet pants, borrowed a T-shirt from Bianca and one of the hundreds of silk scarves from Michel's closet, I left my funky boots under the bed. I tried to convince myself I looked great.

At dinner I was placed next to a man who complained of the difficulties of shipping his vast collection of paintings to his new estate in Portugal. Across from me, a woman fed tidbits to her peckish lapdog. The man on my right seemed pleasant. He was Swiss and asked if I was enjoying Switzerland. I said it seemed a sane and pleasant place and I hoped to see more of it.

Later Michel apologized for his guests.

"They are so boring, but I had to invite them."

"I enjoyed meeting the Swiss, he seemed kind."

"How amusing, Maia. You know, he is from the CIA." Michel's good news was that he'd taken a flat for us in a mountain resort. We could move in immediately. Nino would finish the book, the lawyer would arrange for asylum.

"And then we will travel together, I will take a yacht for the summer. I will take you to Morocco, the king is a good friend."

Villars-sur-Ollon is a sunny village high in the mountains. There are quite a few boarding schools in the vicinity, the students are mostly Americans. In the winter it is a prosperous ski resort, the skiers are mostly Americans too. It is not as expensive as Gstaad or St. Moritz, and the rent was paid by Michel. The apartment was three rooms in a newly built chalet. It was one of many such buildings covering the former Alpine meadows. The furniture was hideous but could be hidden in the basement bomb shelter until the owner, a consul from some

---

19. Gemini dates this party between May 21 and June 20, 1971.

Scandinavian country, reclaimed the flat in December. The rest of the building was empty. We had a fireplace, a marvelous view of the mountains to the south, the stars overhead. Privacy, warmth, clear skies, the whole summer before us.

Tim shopped in the village and was stopped several times by autograph seekers. He laughed about it when he got back, delighted by being recognized. I worried about the proximity of so many Americans. The next two days we walked in the mountains, delighting in the sun and altitude. We planned a trip for the next day, the summer solstice, the one day of fertility the doctor had suggested.[20] We would conceive our child in a flowery meadow, the sun would be witness.

I woke that morning to the sound of the outer door opening, then a man's voice, *Mr. Leary!* The hallway door banged. I put my hand over Tim's mouth, woke him, and whispered, "There's someone here." I listened at the door. Tim was up now, and while he dressed quickly. I went into the living room. Three dark-suited men stood there.

"Mr. Leary." Tim looked around the bedroom door.

"You must come with us." They moved towards him. I got to the phone and hastily dialed Michel. I was relieved to hear his voice.

"Ah, but this is terrible; you must call the lawyer immediately."

He gave me the number, and while the phone rang I watched the ominous-looking men. They walked around the apartment with their hands at their sides; they touched nothing but looked at everything. One squatted before the fireplace seemingly about to open the drawer below the grate. He looked to one of the other men who shook his head no. The lawyer answered the phone.

I explained that there were some men who wanted to take my husband away. He asked to speak to them. The chief took the receiver and spoke briefly in Swiss German, then handed the phone back. I listened anxiously.

"There is a request for extradition. They will take him to prison in

---

20. June 21, 1971.

Lausanne. I will speak to Michel, and then you must call me this afternoon." He hung up.

Tim had finished dressing and was questioning the police about their responsibility, but they remained blandly uncommunicative. I slowly packed some shaving gear, cigarettes, matches, chocolate, a few books, a fresh shirt. I offered coffee, but they wouldn't take it. There was nothing I could do to stop them from taking him to prison. Tim stood uncertain looking and sad beside their calm authority. I would not cry before them.

The chief pointed to the vase of wild meadow flowers picked so happily the day before.

"It is forbidden to pick certain flowers; there are severe fines for such an offense. You must check the chart at the station." They closed the door quietly behind them.[21]

I dressed quickly and ran down the mountain to catch the train to Ouchy. The train was crowded; it was a holiday. Most of the passengers were dressed for walking: knapsack, walking stick, sturdy shoes, knee breeches, and woolen socks. Tourists were distinguished by their tennis shoes and flimsy sweaters, an unaccustomed redness to their faces. Their voices were jarring, American Midwest, self-consciously complacent.

Across from me a blind man sat with his face to the sun, unconscious of the wealth of mountains and lakes rolling past. He smiled continually and traced a gentle finger over the arm of his companion. She indicated his state of blindness. She fussed at his shirt collar, wiped an invisible speck from his neatly pressed suit. Her wedding band was new. He caught her hand and his smile deepened. She shrugged her plump shoulders at me and patted his hand.

Michel slammed the phone down as I entered the apartment.

"Can you imagine, it was one of my guests that denounced you, I will never speak to that person again, never. Yes, I know who it was. I

---

21. In her time line Rosemary dates the "Villars bust" to June 21, 1971.

am furious. They thought it terrible that I should harbor a criminal. They are the criminal." He shouted, his face was red, his eyes bulged. I couldn't quite believe the emotion, there was something about him that was too satisfied. But perhaps it was some bedroom affair he'd just come from. He smelled a bit damp.

We paced the long length of the room, his arm confidentially about me.

"How can I get him out?"

"We must have money, lots of it. It is the only way to free him." I told him I'd had to raise quite a bit of money the last time Tim was imprisoned.

"Good, well, then, you know what you must do. We must have at least a hundred and fifty thousand."

"Francs?"

"No, dollars, but the lawyer will be here tomorrow, he'll explain everything."[22]

" How soon can I see Tim?"

"Ah, that is difficult, the Americans have said that he is a very dangerous man, he is in solitary and not allowed visitors. Even I cannot see him yet. But we will see a friend of mine in Lausanne, he is a very important person. You will cry; you will be distressed. He will give you permission to go to the prison."

"When?"

"Monday. But now you must call all of your friends for money. It is the only way, there will be many people involved, and they will all want something. No one does things for nothing. You understand?"

"May I use this phone or the one in the kitchen?"

"No, no, you must go to the telegraph office, I am expecting very important calls. Go now, we will meet at dinner."

I was dismissed.

I walked to the telegraph office, wondering who to call. It was ironic that Michel wanted the same amount of money that last year

---

22. $150,000 in 1971 would have been equivalent to more than $900,000 in 2018.

the lawyers said would be necessary for bail. But then money had been raised through radio appeals, benefits, ads in the underground newspapers, the anonymous dopers of America. Then I had been free to make a few television appearances and rely on the generosity of friends and sympathizers. We had put out a call for money in Algeria, and no one responded. There was no reason to think I could raise the enormous amount of money Michel was demanding, but could I let him know that? And if I did go begging for money again, would anyone care? Would I be extradited too? Well, I'd call the lawyers in the States, collect. I didn't have the price of a long-distance call.

An Israeli boy and I were the only occupants of the telegraph office. He was there to pick up girls, I was looking for help. We were both unsuccessful, but talking to him kept me from weeping. He said that he was discriminated against in Israel as an Oriental and was a Black Panther. Perhaps it was then that the movie started again, the hidden synchronistic cameras in the background catching my every move. I'd felt them in Algeria at all times but for a brief while had forgotten their existence in Switzerland. Now they were grinding away again. When would I hear, *Mrs. Leary, you are under arrest, come with us*?

At dinner Michel was consoling, confident that Tim would not be returned to America. If necessary he could be removed to a clinic. We would plan an escape; planes, a boat to Morocco. The king is a good friend.[23]

But it would be better if he could stay in Switzerland. Under bond it might be possible; all it would take was money, and the right connections.

After a tearful visit to the official in Lausanne I had a pass to the prison. Michel drove me there. He was an arrogant driver, but the car commanded respect, and pedestrians scurried to get out of his way, then gawked at the rich people in the car. He parked in front of the prison

---

23. Another version substitutes *prince,* which Rosemary changed to *minister.* But especially as this is not dialogue, but Rosemary remembering what had previously been said, *king* is needed to echo Michel's earlier words.

gates. It was a medieval fortress with high walls, huge doors studded with iron. I clutched the package of gourmet food Michel gave me and rang the bell. A small door within the large was opened by a gnarled and wizened little man. I stepped inside the dark fortress. A man in prison garb swept the gravel walk with a twig broom, another man trimmed the closely cut grass; they didn't look up.

The door to the prison opened to a highly polished hall. I gave my slip of paper to an attendant, he studied it for a moment, then led me to a small wooden room. He left, locking the door behind him. A few silent minutes studying the barred windows, then shoes squeaked on the waxed floor, the key turned in the lock. Tim and a guard stood in the doorway. I held him close for a brief moment, the guard touched his arm; we sat across from one another at small table. The guard sat in the corner, his arms crossed, a studied look of boredom on his face.

We held hands and smiled reassuringly into one another's eyes.

"Well, here we are again, beloved, how do we get free this time?"

"I've been thinking about that, I've written a letter and I want you to send it right away."

"What else?"

"Do everything Michel tells you to do; he is the only hope I have."

"He says I have to raise $150,000, and he won't even let me use the telephone." The guard looked at me for a moment, then continued the inspection of his cuticles.

"My life is in his hands; he is the only one who can free me."

I wanted to tell him of my fears—that Michel was an extortionist who thought we had rich friends to ransom us, that I might be extradited, that we were robots unable to control our life, that I was scared. But I couldn't, he was so pale and drawn looking, he couldn't eat or sleep. There wasn't any sunshine or fresh air, his cell was dark and cold. I told him that I'd bring him fresh food and a clean shirt every day, but I could only see him once a week. The guard looked at his watch, I had to leave. Tim held me close, he felt so thin. The guard locked the door behind them. Their footsteps receded, echoing hollowly. The door opened, and the attendant motioned to me to leave the room.

Michel was sitting with his face to the sun, smoking a cigar. I got into the car.

"You know, Maia, there are two things I hate to do, that is to be close to a prison and to wait. Today I have done both for you."

It was true, he was being kind and there was no one else to help. I must be mad thinking of him as I did, mistrusting him. I was only half listening to Michel as I read the letter Tim had written.

"I think you must call Pablo and demand that he give you $50,000 or you will expose him and his involvement. He cannot risk his reputation; he will give us the money."

I heard the sum and Pablo's name but didn't appreciate the threat until much later for I was engrossed in the letter. Tim had written to Hugh Hefner, the publisher of *Playboy* magazine, that he was in a Swiss prison because I wanted to have a baby. It didn't make sense, or perhaps it did. If we hadn't left Algeria . . . if I hadn't needed an operation . . . Michel interrupted my thoughts.

"The lawyer has agreed to come from Bern; we are meeting him for lunch. He charges $1,000 to come here. You must raise some money. I cannot do everything, you know, Maia. I have just met you."

Michel parked in front of a restaurant, then swept us into the private dining room. A large, untidy looking man rose to meet us, looking nervously at his watch.

"Michel, Madame, I am here to do what I can. What a sad business this is. I have agreed to take this case because of my friendship for Michel, it is a difficult case for me to accept. But I have young sons, they have sympathy for your husband. As for myself, I have never handled a drug case, it is not a problem in Switzerland."

The waiter hovered solicitously over our table; Michel was looking at the wine list. I looked at the lawyer.[24]

"It is not a drug case; it has to do with American politics."

---

24. The lawyer was Horace Mastronardi.

"What is the hundred and fifty thousand for?"

"Excuse me, I didn't quite understand." He was looking at Michel, who was testing the wine.

"Is there a way to free him?"

"It might be possible to obtain your husband's conditional freedom by getting a bond. The government might allow this while investigating his claim for asylum. Of course the bond will be returned once the affair is settled."

"And if there is an extradition order for me as well?"

"Oh, that is another problem; we must take things as they come."

"I propose that we open an account in Bern for the bond. A banker, good friend of mine, will handle the details."

I nodded assent, Michel and the lawyer spoke of other matters. I thought about the letter to Hefner. I couldn't send it, it would embarrass Tim. But was I responsible that he was in prison again? No. But why was he arrested on the day we planned to conceive a child? Had the events so fused in his mind that he thought it was my fault? I excused myself from the table and locked myself in a cabinet of the restroom to shed pent-up tears of fear and anger.

In the next week I sent out twenty-five begging letters to acquaintances, copying them on a machine in a large department store while an impatient line of people grew behind me clutching single slips of paper.[25] I waited hours in the telegraph office for calls that never got through and knocked at the prison gates once a day with my packages of cigarettes and chocolates.

Michel was impatient with me; I looked awful, and my spirits were very low. I dreaded going back to Villars each night. I could hear footsteps in the empty apartment overhead and in the morning there was always someone repairing the telephone lines outside the window. I thought I would be locked up soon, and there was no one who'd try to profit by freeing me. I played the four tapes we'd managed to

---

25. On another typed version of this chapter, Rosemary wrote "a hundred" over the original *twenty-five*.

acquire on our tinny language-teaching machine, trying to remember some good old days. Janis Joplin, Jimi Hendrix, Otis Redding, Jim Morrison. It was very late one night when I realized they were all dead.

One evening Bianca and Michel insisted that I join them for dinner. It would be a small gathering, most of the people I knew and those I didn't would not be told my real name. What is my real name?

"You must come; I am helping to persuade them to help Nino."

"You must not be so gloomy, Maia, it affects your appearance." He pinched my cheek, hard. I agreed; anything was better than listening to the footsteps overhead. I would drink lots of wine, and perhaps I could sleep that night. Michel had allowed me to claim our luggage finally, and I was feeling a bit more comfortable in my own familiar things rather than an occasionally borrowed shirt of Bianca's. I'd play at being a tourist to Switzerland, entertained in a luxurious home.

We were eight at the dinner table. I smiled and laughed in the appropriate places. Michel smiled at me approvingly. Brandy would be served in the obligatory bomb shelter converted to a gaming room with a bar and Dresden china plates on the walls. Most of the guests were at the backgammon boards when I returned from the bathroom. One of the unknown guests patted the empty seat next to him.

"Come, you must tell me what you do, who you are, you were so silent and mysterious during dinner." He was attractive in a harsh Teutonic way.

"I am an American woman, and at the moment I do nothing interesting." So much for my social graces, but I asked him about himself and he was happy to tell me. An industrialist, German, he had lived in the States and studied at Harvard. He looked about thirty. The conversation got around to Vietnam and the draft. He had a solution: all draft dodgers should be shot. And he had located the root of the problem.

"It is the fault of the Jewish publishing conspiracy and that terrible man Timothy Leary. You have heard of him."

"Well, uh, the wisest, funniest people I know are Jewish, and I'm married to Timothy Leary."

For one long moment I smiled into his face while he stared at me in total horror, then his training and social sense caught him up.

"But of course you are. And after meeting you . . . I mean you are so charming; he must be too. You'll have some more brandy?"

I phoned for a taxi, then waited for it out in the warm summer night. No one would notice my absence; they were playing backgammon for high stakes.

I wept in the streets and on the trains. At each meeting Michel shook his finger in my face at my inability to raise the money. The confusion I felt about him and the lawyers had grown. An organization of Swiss writers had called to offer help. They had formed a committee of protest at Tim's imprisonment. Their representative was shocked by the lawyer's alleged fees and the size of the bond. And the bribes that had been hinted at were impossible to imagine—no Swiss official would take money for doing his job. I wasn't so sure; I had seen the obsequiousness of a few officials when Michel spoke to them. But then he was a very strong personality.

I hoped Tim would be able to solve my doubts. He did, Michel had been there that morning with a notary. Tim had signed a document giving Michel all rights to any work of his.[26]

"But what about the book?"

"That's what he's interested in. He feels he can get a large advance from a publisher; he said he's already incurred great expenses, paying the lawyers."

"But he hasn't paid the lawyer. Listen, what about me, if you're sent back . . ."

"Michel will take care of you; he promised me."

---

26. And indeed, this arguably extortionate contract with Michel Hauchard not only complicated the publication of *Confessions of a Hope Fiend,* but clouded control of Timothy's intellectual property for many years afterward. For a startling account of the publishing negotiation for *Confessions* under this contract, see Robert Greenfield, *Timothy Leary: A Biography,* New York: Houghton Mifflin Harcourt, 2006, 433–34.

I had been signed over too, it seemed.

Help finally arrived, a check from Allen Ginsberg, a sizable amount from the lawyers' broadcast appeal in San Francisco, a few other donations. Totaled up, I was surprised to find almost $10,000. On my next visit I asked Tim what I should do with it: put it in the bond account, give it to the lawyer? He said to give it to Michel, he would know what to do with it. We argued a bit, but his faith in Michel was so strong. He was fading in the dark prison; he complained of soreness around his heart. He would have to be freed soon.

Michel was packing his valise when I next saw him. I gave him the money. He tossed it into the suitcase and closed the lid.

"What a pity that we could not have Nino out by now. I would take you both with me to Beirut. But now I must be gone for a month, and there is nothing to be done. You must be a good girl. As Mrs. Leary there will always be young men around. Now don't be foolish, don't be depressed. When Nino is free we will have a good time."

The lawyer was going on vacation too, he was so overworked; he must rest. Besides it was August, the government would be gone, but he would visit the prison again and explain it to my husband.

We took a taxi to the fortress prison. Again he told me of his need for rest and what a difficult case it was. I must understand he was not a magician. When he came back, perhaps a doctor's certificate could be arranged. We waited for Tim to be brought from his cell. The lawyer clutched a large package of Swiss chocolate; it was unusual for him to bring a gift. On each square there was a village scene, cool mountains, green land. He mopped his brow with a folded handkerchief. The familiar squeak of shoes, the door opened to Tim and the guard.

"*Maître,* how good of you to come." Tim sat down and picked up the package of chocolates the lawyer placed on the table.

"I hope I will be able to see some of these places someday."

"You will, you will." To our dismay the man was crying into his handkerchief. Tim and I looked at one another uneasily.

"You're free, you're free, you can come with me now, this very moment. I have your release papers with me." He blew his nose, then beamed at us happily.

"But what, the bond, and Michel said and . . ." I stuttered.

He explained that he'd received a letter and a check from Tim's good friend Walter Houston Clark.[27] Clark had mortgaged his house for $20,000; the government accepted it as bond. Tim was free. We would go to the hotel, there was a room reserved for us, a television crew was waiting, so was his wife, his children, his dog. There would be a press conference, the wire services were waiting. Then everyone knew hours before that Tim would be released. Why had he pretended? Oh well, it was a happy surprise.

There was a crowd of reporters and television cameras in front of the hotel. They closed in as we stepped from the cab. Tim was grinning and waving his usual victory sign.

"Dr. Leary, look this way please! Dr. Leary, would you say the Swiss government acted fairly? Dr. Leary, you say that LSD . . . Dr. Leary. . ." The clamor followed us into the hotel. We begged for a few moments alone.

"I don't want to go downtown for the press conference, please do it without me. I've had enough of cameras and crowds to last a lifetime." But I had to be there, in the picture too. So we smiled, kissed, looked delighted, pleased, ecstatic for the cameras. Tim told the reporters, one by one, how much we liked Switzerland, how happy we were, how kind everyone was, how civilized. He held a Swiss franc up to the TV camera, pointing out the crown marked *Libertas*.[28]

"The goddess of Switzerland," he shouted. August 6, full moon in Aquarius, just twelve moons after his last prison break.

---

27. Walter Houston Clark (1902–1994), a distinguished retired professor of divinity, had participated in the Harvard Psilocybin Project.
28. Latin for "liberty." The Swiss franc coins of the period showed a female head with a tiaralike headdress inscribed *Libertas*. It represented the Roman goddess of liberty, whose similar image had appeared on Roman coins.

August 25, 1971
Villars

Dear Family,

I'm so glad you heard the good news on TV. Ronald Reagan must be furious.[29] There's been so little time to write, the phone rings constantly with reporters wanting interviews. Tim's recuperative powers are amazing, I'm still worn from all the worry. The lawyer is confident Tim will get political asylum, I suppose that means me too, they are rather patriarchal here.

Everyone has been so kind. Last night we had dinner with the local Protestant minister. On Sunday we met Albert Hofmann, the man who invented LSD, he was charming. We've been hearing tales of Switzerland's magic and alchemy. Tim goes around saying it's so Celtic, he's being welcomed as the King of the Fairies, Lorin.[30] Bern is a much happier place now that I'm not making lonely trips to the lawyer. Very old, full of alchemical and tarot card statues and astrological clocks. A relative of Herman Hesse invited us to visit the house he once lived in. We cannot leave the canton yet without authorization.

Even if the Swiss should not accept us as political refugees no one believes they will allow extradition. The most important writers and scientists have signed petitions. The original order seems to have been California politics, the Federal Government did not join in. So they were trying to get him back for two planted marijuana roaches. Here one would pay a small fine, the crime must be punishable here by a similar sentence and escaping from prison is not considered a crime. We are very hopeful that it will all work out. As usual, there is little privacy, TV crews lurk in the bushes and long-haired kids beat a path to the door.

I hope Nana is feeling better. Kisses to all.

---

29. Reagan was governor of California at this time.
30. I have not been able to identify Lorin, King of the Fairies.

Oct. 14, 1971
Villars

Dear Mother,

Tim was operated on Monday, he has regained hearing in his left ear, he feels fine. I found out the same day that I cannot have children, another operation is risky and the chances are slim. I've been thinking that I need some time to myself, these years have been so hectic. I need a bit of space between us. The public life we've led has occupied so much time and energy, there has been little time for introspection. Tim has agreed to a brief separation but he doesn't like the idea, I think it will be good for us to be without the shroud of marriage. But perhaps I'll feel differently tomorrow. Write soon.

LOVE

ELEVEN

Adjustment

Editor's Note

Only isolated fragments survive either attributed to this chapter or dating from the period after Rosemary separated from Timothy in October 1971. I have arranged them in roughly chronological order, based on their dates where given or their location. Except where noted, I have provided the titles.

The adverse aspect between the planets Saturn and Neptune is an uncommon and strange position that is likely to bring you into remarkable situations at some time or another during your life. It is a very lofty vibration, to the true nature of which present day humanity cannot hope fully to respond, and much of its influence may pass over your head, so to speak. It is not altogether favorable, and appears to indicate that there is some "kink" as it were in the inner nature that time and circumstances may declare, or which, perhaps, may never come to fruition in this life but remain entirely unsuspected. You should always guard against the subtler forms of selfishness which are likely to beset you. The cultivation of the psychic faculties would not be good for you. There is always some melancholy tendency associated with this position.

ALAN LEO,

THE KEY TO YOUR OWN NATIVITY[1]

PART ONE: EUROPE
Splitting Apart

Seemingly at ease on the bed, propped by pillows, he watched me throw my things into a suitcase. Oh, to be away for a few weeks, a month, a year from that scrutiny, that detachment, would I be missing him?

I faltered, started folding things carefully, made selections, matching lingerie pieces. I was tired suddenly. I wanted to lie down next to him, pull the comforter around us and forget that I'd wanted to go anywhere without him.

Say the right word, Tim.

"Marilyn Monroe," he said looking at me and smiling complacently. That did it. He's writing the script again. So I am to be alone, afraid of growing old, wanting to die. Marilyn to his Miller, well, fuck him, I've got better things to do.[2]

I closed the suitcases. "Take care of yourself."

"Call me in a week." He settled into the pillows.

He looked, I thought, almost sad. He closed his eyes.

"Entropy will get us all in the end."

I said you too in the end.

I Could Be Anyone

He called me back from thousands of miles away. I returned a week too late, he said. Another mistress, a new publisher—a different kind of

---

1. See note on page 9.

2. The actress Marilyn Monroe (1926–1962), one of the most potent sex symbols in Hollywood history, married the playwright Arthur Miller (1915–2005) in 1956. The show business newspaper *Variety* summed up the general view of this alliance with its headline EGGHEAD WEDS HOURGLASS.

drug, a face lift. He was altered, yes, no need to play the game of familial telepathy. He had a fat contract for the book and no need to honor any previous commitments. I could be anyone, drop out as it were, but of course he was stuck to play the same old game.

Letters Home, 1971[3]

November 22, 1971

Dear Family,

Another life change. Tim and I have separated for the good of both of us. He has found another woman to share his life and fortune. We will always be close in our hearts but feel it best to live apart. I feel more peaceful than I can ever remember being. I'm living under a different name and until I'm established I won't give you my address. Do not worry! Everything is really all right. I feel happier every day. I'm with good friends in a comfortable house and I look forward to this new life and new year. I know I'll see you soon.

LOVE

November 22, 1971

Dear Family,

Over the years you've collected many excuses for my tardiness in writing and sending holiday and birthday greetings. I know you know that it is not from a lack of love. Now I have to ask you to forgive me in advance for possibly being neglectful again. I might be out of touch for awhile. But don't worry!

I've experienced another life change. Tim and I have separated. I had to get away and I left shortly before his birthday in October. I feel younger and happier every day.

I'll be living under a different name and until I'm established I won't give you my address but I'll stay in touch with you through the lawyers.

---

3. These letters were marked by Rosemary for inclusion in this chapter.

Our political situation is still uncertain but everyone expects the best results. I'm looking forward to my new life.

I thank you for all the love I've had from you. I know I'll see you soon.[4]

December 22, 1971

Dear Family,

Beautiful two weeks skiing in the high mountains. I've stopped smoking cigarettes. Feel marvelous. Miss you all very much this year but feel we'll be together soon. I'm going to ask the lawyers if they can reopen my appeal. I won't be able to call you for awhile and I'll continue this roundabout way of getting letters to you. Sorry it's so complicated, I just don't trust the California Dept of Corrections to forget me that easily. Please continue to send your letters with an outside covering address to the same place, they will reach me eventually. I'm very happy this Xmas, I have two babies to give presents to, Orion and Sunshine are their names, three and five weeks old. The children of friends from Millbrook days.[5]

About your concerns for the law. I feel fairly free from the pressures imagined or real that accompanies being a fugitive. As it is not known that I've left Tim and Switzerland I don't believe that Gov't agencies will be looking for me. I think I'll be able to move around the country in a little while with the exception of California so perhaps we can meet soon. (Don't talk about this on the phone.)

I hope you have A LOVELY XMAS AND NEW YEAR

---

4. It seemed curious that both these letters bear the same date and cover more or less the same material, but that is how they were marked in the documents from which I have taken them. John Schewel explained that the first letter was sent from Switzerland, via messenger, and the second from Canada. "We were never sure communications would always make it and we never sent letters from where we were. The first letter's date covered the fact that we were traveling to Canada. The second letter was sent when we were in Canada at the house I leased before leaving for Switzerland, knowing we might need it in some emergency. It was deep in the snow mountains above Montreal, a wonderfully comfortable three-story house overlooking a lake."

5. Orion was the child of Dennis Martino (Timothy's daughter Susan's husband's twin brother) and his wife Robin Viertel Martino. I have been unable to identify Sunshine.

January 25, 1972

Dear Sweet Mother Love,

So good to receive letter from you. Why do I call you Ruth rather than mother? Well, I feel older than you sometimes as if you were my child and although I feel your beloved mother love all the time and bless you for it and miss you, I wish I could take care of all your worries. Besides I feel myself as you and recognize within me your strength. Then you are Ruth my sister.

I won't be able to meet you for a while. I have to start traveling again, a small adventure to make some money.[6] I hope to have enough to send for you and Daddy in a few months. Be patient please, we will be together soon. It seems unlikely that I can return to California without facing a prison sentence so I'll have to go on this way until the laws have been repealed. The FBI is yet searching out draft dodgers. I have to assume that it is the same in my case. There is some margin of safety in that I am yet thought to be in Switzerland with Tim. (By the way we yet love one another very much and I trust that he has my best interests at heart. He has promised to share the royalties from the book we wrote in Algeria when Michel sells it so I won't have any financial worries.) This past month and half has been so pleasant. There has been time to sew, to reflect, to watch the babies grow. I'm with beautiful young brothers and sisters, we are a close and loving family and I'm at peace.

Rosemary to the Reader

It would be five years before I saw my family again. During those years I changed my name too many times to count and lived in eight or more countries using three different passports. In most countries I could not stay more than three months. I would leave, cross the border praying that I would be allowed to return and take up the fragments of the life and belongings I had left behind. I always knew where the exits were and kept my clothes and papers beside the bed with a small backpack. If men looked at me I assumed they were government agents. I

---

6. Meaning Afghanistan.

suspected everyone. When I thought about the last year in California I remembered the strange doctor whose surgery on me was deemed "barbaric and experimental" by the Swiss surgeon who corrected his bungling. And the intern who asked me about my drug use while he poked me ineptly for a blood sample. Then there were always the bearded telephone repairmen constantly outside the Berkeley house. I suspected my lawyers who failed to file my appeal, my husband whose escape from prison seemed in retrospect to be, perhaps, too easily managed. I felt that it was no longer possible to distinguish who was on my side, to know who were madmen and who might be saints. Perhaps there were only madmen.[7]

PART TWO: AFGHANISTAN
Arriving in Afghanistan

From the air, Kabul looked like an archaeological discovery, a vast interlocking of worn rectangular walls and flat roofs wedged in a triangular valley. A maze, uninhabited, ancient dust obscuring everything. The few modern buildings were stark and white, the monoliths of rulers surrounded by the ancient mud hovels and courtyards of serfs. Snow.

The Visitor[8]

> *This is the Paradise which the righteous have been promised. There shall flow in it rivers of unpolluted water and rivers of milk forever fresh; rivers of delectable wine*

---

7. One draft heads this fragment with an epigraph: " . . . the spirit of rebellion that sustains me is much more precious than any stupid analysis." In a 1973 letter to her Sicilian friend Bubi (Adolfo Frenzi) this quotation is attributed to "Sante," described as a political prisoner serving a life term in a prison in Sicily.

8. Like the hammam episode in chapter 9, this section (which I am calling "The Visitor" although Rosemary did not title it) is presented without change from what seemed to me the best of the "original" versions. There are many versions in the source materials, but this one appears to have been carefully edited already, and adding additional material from other versions did not make a noticeable improvement.

and rivers of clearest honey. They shall eat therein of every
fruit and receive forgiveness from their Lord.[9]

I am the visitor.

The women are in the pomegranate garden, heads covered by
scarves, pastel veils thrown over a shoulder for emphasis as they talk.
There is a constant flutter and rearrangement of veils and sleeve edges.
Everything is arranged carefully, carpets and pillows, the angle of the
spoon on the guest's tea saucer, sticky candies in a pyramid. Children
stand in a row to watch the guest take the first sip of sweet green tea.
They look at the candies and then at the guest. She must take one, and
then they can be distributed. A young girl removes her scarf to fan the
flies away from the sweets.

Less formal attention is paid to the visitor. They have passed her in
the streets, in the bazaar, and she had drunk tea with them before. They
have conveyed with gestures the number of children born; a child's
death is symbolized by a tilt of the head with eyes closed and hand
pressed to cheek. There is sadness expressed for each infant's death. Eyes
filled with tears, beautiful eyes. Strong, slender, child-bearing creatures,
their movements are quick and graceful, their voices are soft. A crying
child is comforted. Sleeping, it is wrapped to immobilization in a long
embroidered cloth. The children who survive are strong-limbed and
straight-backed; sitting like little deities, they are adorned with rings
and amulets, kohled eyes and rouge.[10]

The daughter of the house greets the visitor. She is a grave young
girl, soon to be married to a man not of her choosing. The festivi-
ties in the garden are in honor of her betrothal. Her right palm

---

9. Koran, Surah 47 (*Muhammad*), verse 15. It is not clear what translation is being
quoted—it is close to the Dawood translation but not close enough to match. The verse
continues (in the Dawood translation) with a line Rosemary does not quote: "Are they
to be compared to those who shall abide in Hell forever, and drink scalding water that
will tear their bowels to pieces?"

10. Kohl is a dark mineral-based cosmetic applied around the eyes of women and sometimes children in the Near East, India, and North Africa. Its use goes back far into
antiquity.

is marked by a patch of red henna: it has become a mark of her father's betrayal.

It is known that the visitor reads palms. She had looked at the hands of a chief and the hands of a servant and told them of their wives and children. She had told the truth. Now hennaed palms are raised for inspection. She chooses the hand of a fragile, silver-haired lady of gentle manners who is the chief feminine elder. Her hand is strongly marked. A good and long life; the visitor mimes the many grandchildren and grace from God. What is there to say to the mother of six whose palm is scored by worry, work, and illness, or to the virgin marked with the difficulties of childbirth? The possibility of two husbands is dismissed with a shrug. She points to the lines of travel. Now, there is real interest, everyone wants to know if they will travel far.

She had entertained them, and now they will respond. Two old and musty women who have sat apart sniffing snuff and spitting are summoned. The tobacco pipe is brought for them and a candle to warm their drums. They start a slow dirge and everyone joins the clapping. A shy young girl is persuaded to dance. She steps to the beat, her eyebrows arch, her fingers point and curl; we are aware of her suppleness and beauty. She flicks a quick glance at the visitor and sits down, blushing, a child again.

The two hags rise to dance, voices harsh and bawdy, gestures plain. The larger embraces the other's breast; the embraced one looks bored and moves the hand to her crotch. They ape and mime, in countless ribald ways, the sexual union of man and woman. They are a success, and the guest doubled over in laughter at the unexpected humor. She had never seen anything as funny as this hugging and grabbing dance by two old women singing lustily all the while.

Two young women rise and take small rugs to a corner of the garden. They kneel, bow their heads, stretch out their hands; their lips move soundlessly. It is the hour of prayer. The guest receives a blessing and leaves, for a time, the garden of palms and pomegranates.

PART THREE: EUROPE AGAIN

June 28, 1972

Dear Jim,

It was good talking to you today. I've tried to clarify my thoughts so as to present the situation clearly.

I would like you to find out what penalties I would have to face should I decide to return to America. I do not want to go to prison nor answer questions before a grand jury or any government official. I wish to live as a quiet, useful, private citizen again. Those are my wishes but I realize that it is not that simple. I am an exile, a fugitive distant from my family, estranged from my husband, apart from my friends, living in a country without residency papers or means of supporting myself. I am yet connected to a man who has no concern for my safety or welfare and who upon reflection seems never to have had. He has subjected me to grave danger and public and private humiliation. Here I cannot work, travel, or in any way live a normal life.

I need clarification of my status here. The extradition order did not include me, does the freedom from extradition that the Swiss have granted him include me as well? Will I be allowed to work and travel? Or do I disappear again, not do anything that would affect his status here or return home with the possibility of a lengthy trial. I have been incarcerated before for protecting him, I don't know if I can bear it again. One must have a great deal of hate or faith to survive in prison. I've no desire to lend myself to causes which are not mine or expose anyone else. The question is how best to protect myself without endangering others. I will always be grateful to you and all the people who have done so much to help me.

Rosemary's Passport[11]

Given the name of a lawyer in Basel, I went to speak with him this afternoon. He was most encouraging and felt the problem was not beyond solu-

---

11. This fragment appears in the archive without context. But Rosemary's time line includes a visit to Basel in July 1972, after her return to Europe from Afghanistan, and lists *passport* as an entry for August 1972. I added the title.

tion. Later in the day he told me I could in fact get my new passport at any time. He had spoken to the secretary of the American embassy, who said they had my renewal awaiting me, and had written several letters to that effect addressed to Messieur Michel Hauchard. Suggesting I go to Bern the next day, he felt it wasn't even necessary for him to accompany me.

A slow rage was building within me for all the hours, days, and weeks of anxiety. The meek timid call to Michel, all a scam: Michel, Mastronardi, and Tim. I nervously picked up my passport from the embassy in Bern, new, green, and clean. Five more years, hooray. I returned to Basel at the lawyer's request to discuss any other problems I might foresee. Residency, work, and money. The lawyer said Tim would have to agree to support, strict Swiss laws. The lawyer felt Tim would split Switzerland rather than pay me anything as Switzerland has strict separation laws. Realizing the fears and uncertainness of this past year and how I've been used, duped, and made a fool of. The tarot says I'm crossed by the Hierophant, ahead is the Aeon.[12] Total and complete separation, I must reexamine everything in the light of self-renewal. I have never been so lonely.

September Equinox 1972[13]
Cefalú

The beach is empty except for waves, gulls. Aphrodite bathed here, they say. No shells on the shore. Smooth, waterworn rocks, glass, strands of

---

12. This line is part of a tarot reading. The Hierophant is trump number five. He is a popelike figure, often called the High Priest, the very term popularly applied to Timothy, who in 1968 even published an autobiographical book under that title. Also he famously, if ironically, said he wanted to be pope (page 81), and Rosemary is finding his repetition of the same talking points to be an increasingly boring orthodoxy. A *crossing card* (so called from its position in the spread of the cards on the table) indicates a force or element blocking the seeker. The Aeon (as trump number twenty is called in Crowley's deck, corresponding to Judgment in the Rider-Waite deck) speaks to resurrection and redemption. It would be a fair analysis of this fragment of a reading that Timothy blocks Rosemary's way, and she must get past him to reach redemption and (metaphor of resurrection) emerge from underground (the Rider-Waite card shows the traditional image of the dead emerging from their underground tombs).

13. A separate fragment in the archive. The title in the source document is "September

seaweed. "You were always stranded till I came along." Stranded, like a seashell? The rocks are warm against my back. I watched the clouds appear and then disperse. Air fresh and sweet, blue water. Hold the star map aloft, disappear into its vastness. Thoughts disintegrate into a moment of radiance, part of all. A child's toy, a rag ball, a sphere.[14]

Before heaven and earth there is something, and it is of this I wish to know. Swallows fly on planes, in dimensions just glimpsed. A fold of the wing, head tucked down, then into another space. The light reflects from the sea. Man as radiant sun; woman, mirror moon, how did this come to be?

These patterns, are they always there? Sidereal planes touching, elliptical lines in the air. "Every two hundred years has a door to Eden."[15] Will it ever open?

"What do you do if you can't love a man, Flo, or he won't love you?[16] Plant flowers and love God, I suppose."

Sun, moon, "irreconcilable opposites?" Half wants to be in, half wishes to be out.

"It is a difficult, deep problem for woman to commune with the cosmos." WISE. "She can only achieve it by universal motherhood or the priestess-prostitute way."[17] FOOLISH. Persisting in wishful dreams of children and gardens. Virgin, wife, mother, hag. What happens when you grow old, Venus, is losing your divinity worse than death?[18] Bound feet, fur underfoot, ivory bracelets, copper-coiled neck, tattooed cheeks,

---

(*cont. from p. 241*) Solstice," but Rosemary must mean equinox, which comes in September and March, rather than solstice (December and June), so I have renamed it. Anyway, Cefalù is in Sicily, and Rosemary's time line does not place her in Sicily before September 1972. Another version of this passage is dated September 24, which was the day after the 1972 fall equinox and would therefore likely have been the day of composition.

14. Another version has "a sphere to hurl at a friend."

15. From William Blake's *Jerusalem,* plate 48, line 37.

16. I *speculate* that this dialogue is addressed in Rosemary's mind to Flo Ferguson, a friend from Millbrook (chapter 2, page 30).

17. These are consecutive lines from *The Diary of Anaïs Nin* (volume 3, 1939–1944), 240.

18. Rosemary adds (perhaps here—the drafts conflict), "Old myths? A mad world that produces sons for slaughter and daughters to be sold." I have not included it as it seems an afterthought.

hennaed palms, a thin gold chain around the neck or about the waist.

Rationalization and structure. The swallows swoop lower to tell me my thoughts are dark. Clouds appear. Wisdom or folly. Imagination based on memory, mothering idea, or superstition savagely denying knowledge. *Sophia,* not sorcery.[19] Armed with wit, militant with intelligence, stigma or subterfuge mar me no more. Pass the cup. "We're all in this beauty together."[20]

I did yoga on the sands, across the water the "island of women," a volcanic dot in a sea of deep blue, where the sky kisses the sea, whispers the song of times passed. Sirens perhaps, Ulysses tied to a mast.[21] "We have left out a thousand things, but hope to have made you fall in love and if you don't want to love me, I will make you, I will make you love me by magic."[22]

I leave for Palermo tomorrow early in the morning. Perhaps a letter, some word for me from afar awaits at the post.

Notes from Exile

Editor's Note

The material in this section comes from a file in the library archive marked 1972–1973 Letters written by Woodruff (transcripts). The elements all seem to have been written in Switzerland or in

---

19. *Sophia* is a Greek word meaning "wisdom." The Gnostics personified sophia as a woman.
20. From Frank Herbert, *Dune Messiah* (1970): "If you need something to worship, then worship life—all life, every last crawling bit of it! We're all in this beauty together!"
21. In book 12 of Homer's *Odyssey,* Odysseus (Ulysses) and his crew pass the Sirens, who entice sailors to their deaths with songs of love. Warned by the sorceress Circe, Odysseus has his sailors stop their ears with wax, so they will not hear the deadly songs, but has himself tied to the mast of his ship so he can hear them safely. He begs his crew to release him, but they refuse, as he had ordered them to do, so Odysseus hears the Sirens' songs of love but survives unharmed.
22. I have been unable to identify this quotation, but John Schewel remembers it as having been taken from an English-language tourist brochure found in Sicily. *We* here means Rosemary and John.

Sicily. They are not part of any chapter draft, but I include them in chapter 11 as they illustrate so vividly Rosemary's state of mind during that period.

Indeed, they appear to have been transcribed by Rosemary with the intention of later use. They are typed one after another on similar paper, with spaces separating what were apparently different elements. There are marginal notes in some places suggesting material to be inserted. Most of them may have been Rosemary's notes to herself rather than actual letters (only the two earliest ones name recipients or are explicitly dated).

I have arranged them in what seems like their chronological order of events, from internal evidence, rather than in the order they may have been written. I added the internal numbers, and the dates in brackets. To preserve the chronological order of this chapter I have separated out the two earliest elements, the letters from 1972 reproduced above.

1 [September–October 1972]

This morning we stopped in Marsala to buy a picnic lunch, which we ate in the ruins of Selinunte.[23] Amidst the echoes of white robed worshippers of Jupiter, the coral red pillars carved ages ago offer shade for the passing flock of sheep. The sea used to splash upon the steps of the temple but now has receded to a shoreline far across the green plain. A young man from the tourist office has promised to show us some houses during the afternoon in Agrigento. *Inch'Allah* we shall have a house.

He never met us in the town square, so we decided to drive to the top of the island some two days away. Mt. Etna, Vulcan's forge, the weathermaker, snow catcher, 11,000 feet above the Mediterranean Sea—there a clarity to the light, the vapors of the beast curving against the lip of the mouth, the black and yellow rock against the blue sky, sul-

---

23. A Greek temple site in Sicily. A reconstructed Temple of Hera is the only surviving structure.

phuric belches staining the white mist with yellows. Two English geologists have warned us that the sulphur fumes are dangerous, and if the wind suddenly shifted we could be suffocated. So we've decided not to spend the night at the top, even though the freezing airs are banished by the occasional depressions in the sand filled with warmth from the fires far within.

We've missed the last jeeps down from the top, having filled our day with the glories of the heights. Walking down, the life energies return in small clots of green fungus and moss containing a beetle or two, a lone ladybug on the black silt, gossamer threads of a spider, all conspiring to knit this piece of the planet back together again. Perched on the edge of a small crater close to the Refugio Albergo, the hotel-like lodge a thousand feet down from the top, we wait for the mist to clear and the stars to appear. With map in hand we make some small progress in reading the stars. If we don't find a house in a few days, perhaps we'll go back to Cefalú. "OM" is the logo for a well-advertised truck here in Sicily.

I've been having a really happy life lately; Sicily is warm, the food is good, scenery beautiful, and I have a three-month passport, which I'll have to renew in November in Bern. This last passport, based on the one that was lost last year in Switzerland, was gotten with the help of Tim's protector Michel; he knew the consul or something. I pray he'll be able to do it again.

On the way down the mountain to visit Taormina we thought to stop at this small village and check with the Bureau of Tourism hoping to find a room, house, just a place to unpack and stay for a while. Traveling months now, it seems to be years though. We found a room full of men playing cards, the most distinguished-looking one asked what we wanted and we babbled about *petite villas, piccola casas tranquil, privat avec jardin, vedura, ala montana.*[24] He led us straightaway to a villa on the mountainside, a small three-room guesthouse used in the

---

24. This is a mashup of French, Italian, and Spanish. It means roughly, little villa, quiet little house, private with a garden, greenery (or maybe vegetable garden), on the mountainside.

summer for rental. Seventy thousand lira per month, we agreed and found a home, for at least a month.[25]

The wine making begins this week, we're less than a mile from the sea and half an hour from the snow on the peak of Etna, living amidst volcanic soil, vineyards, apple and fig trees. So far away from Switzerland, I feel at times I'm a character from a nineteenth-century romantic novel; Sicily has harbored exiles before. I still sleep with my passport hidden under the mattress and purse clutched close. The fear of losing my papers plagues me.

II [November 1972]

So I'm off to Switzerland and won't bring flowers this time, just my typewriter and a classic sense of betrayal.[26] I have no defense against Tim's written account of our uncommon experiences except to right myself.[27] It is a bit sad, for I'd hoped our friendship would last forever.

A short trip in Rome where friends suggested I contact the judge who handled my case in America. I returned to the farmhouse outside of Basel, anxiety and the arrival of a note from Tim try to edge me into chaos again. I've really no one to advise me, for, as I've realized, I'm not represented by a lawyer anywhere, my problems being considered too minor to bother with by Tim or Michel. They are quite real problems to me, however. Michel said the consul in Bern received a letter from Washington concerning the temporary passport issued three months ago and as a result he (Michel) could not secure a further extension for me, but I would be safe in Switzerland as long as Tim was here. As long as Tim was here, is not me. I feel like a complaining woman, all the conversations with Michel and Tim about my situation end in argument and anger. A ray of sunlight passes through the rainy

---

25. Seventy thousand lira in 1973 equals about $638 in 2018. The Italian lira was replaced by the euro in 2002.

26. Rosemary's time line puts her return to Switzerland from Sicily in November 1972.

27. Could she have meant *write myself*? Her typescript, which appears to be a fair copy of an earlier manuscript, actually says in Joycean style "right meself."

gray-filled sky, I received a letter from Barritt today.[28] Weather today, along a winding path brings their summer letter to me in winter.

III [December 1972]

When we arrived in Switzerland last year we were escaping from a dangerous situation and on our way to an uncertain future. We paused here, as friends advised us not to go on to Denmark, where we were expected and where, we were told, we could expect to be extradited. I was desperately in need of medical attention, to complete a long delayed two-part operation. Then came the arrest and the well-publicized events that followed. Though in constant fear of arrest myself, and in ill health, I did everything I could to help free my husband once again.

In October I left our house for a respite from the insistent demands of reporters, interviewers, and curiosity seekers. I knew that our marriage had suffered from what seemed to be the necessity of living in the glare of publicity. I hoped to find the peace and quiet I so desperately needed. Less than a week after my departure my husband announced publicly, by telephone (to John and Yoko Lennon, Max Scherr,[29] Jaakov Kohn, and Allen Ginsberg) that he had married again and was very happy. His new wife appropriated my home, clothes, personal effects, and correspondence.

We met in December, and he told me that he was trapped by circumstance in Switzerland and could never live a completely private life but that I was free to live "underground," start over, be anyone I wanted to be, do my own thing, drop out, and so on. I did do just that and for eight months have lived a reality quite different. I would be quite content were it not for the fact that I am yet a fugitive and my status in Switzerland is quite shaky.

A short time ago, I received a message from my husband that he

---

28. Brian Barritt (1934–2011) was a British author and Aleister Crowley fan who had visited Timothy in Algeria (Robert Greenfield, *Timothy Leary: A Biography,* New York: Houghton Mifflin Harcourt, 2006, 430–31).

29. Max Scherr (1916–1981) was the founder and publisher of the *Berkeley Barb* alternative newspaper.

needed me. I met him, expecting a change, a reconciliation. I found instead a man embittered and unreasonable with a desire to cause more pain and confusion, wanting me again under his control. Wanting me to play the role of his wife and mislead friends who had mortgaged their house for his release; I saw a man who has never had any concern except for his own myth, and I saw with clear eyes the person.

IV [December 1972–January 1973]

It's snowing, the trees bare, all covered. Dellier, the hermit farmer, is lighting the big oven to bake bread. He kneads the dough in a huge trough and slips the loaves into the oven on a long wooden paddle. The stove is big enough to roast an ox and projects into his dining room where it is covered with tile and has a shelf large enough to sit on. Last week he was turning his cider into schnapps and the fumes filled the house. His face red, eyes twinkling, and a broad smile, he offered me warm freshly made brew. It's good stuff, a shot of his apple cider spirits and long underwear could keep me warm in the cold pressing winter day.

It's rather primitive here. You need a bucket to flush the toilet and taking a bath involves a lot of organization. The kitchen is below the one of the two rooms that is "home." I have to keep the small wood-burning stove going all the time as it's the only source of heat, except of course when Dellier makes bread. It's been a little winter so far, but in a month or so the snow begins to pile high. I hope I find someplace else by then.

It's a simple life with few expenses, which is good since money is always low. I like living in the country for all its inconveniences. I'd hate a city apartment, traffic noises and smells, living so close to other people. From the windows here one sees wooded hills and gentle pastureland. The house faces south, sits high on the highest hill overlooking the tiny village.[30] There is a mineral spring to bathe in, but only in summer; it freezes early in winter. I've been here for more than the allowed tourist stay of three months. I like to think that one day I'll

---

30. The village of Wintersingen, near Basel.

come back to a united state of consciousness, California mountains, freedom, and familiarity.

V [January 1973]

Today the long-awaited mail came. Mother's letter with clippings about the Brotherhood, all of it disappointing and bringing impressions of chaos and disorder, prison images. Throwing the I Ching for the first time since Switzerland, got The Army.[31] This afternoon I dreamt that I held an owl, which clawed my arm.

We have to return to Switzerland within the next week, calls to Michel are disappointing, no money, no passport awaiting me, thoughts of returning to America. Have a smoke and discuss the possibilities of India, hard to stay in Sicily with no work, papers, money. Smoked some more, talked ourselves back into working to stay here after we return to Switzerland. Leave for Rome on Tuesday and Switzerland shortly after to try to get papers. If I fail, perhaps I'll change my identity. I'm a little freaked at having an invalid passport in Italy, where they are hysterical about dope and love the photo-journal magazines that thrive on this kind of story.

Perhaps I could write, "How I dropped out with the High Priest and got sentenced for life." After all, he's making money by writing about the mess he's gotten us into. Pretty shoddy, but I'm bored with kicking my own ass. I have to find some way back to this villa and vineyards. Perhaps I should write my probation officer (I don't even remember her name), and having served my sentence come back and earn an honest living. It's all beans to a billy goat. . . .

Our landlord arrived to tell us that we must apply to the ministry in Rome for resident permits and once we have the permit he would be happy to sponsor us. Oh landlord, pity the poor immigrant.[32] I love this place and want so much to stay here and raise a garden and feed the

---

31. Hexagram 7. The Image: "The army needs perseverance and a strong man. Good fortune without blame." Wilhelm-Baynes translation, 32.

32. A 1968 song by Bob Dylan begins, "I pity the poor immigrant / Who wishes he would've stayed home . . ."

pheasants and write and feel serene and legal while I'm doing it. All that helping Tim has done is to hinder me from being able to do that. The absurd reality of being broke and paperless in a foreign country is with me constantly despite the beauties of Etna outside.

I received a call from a TV producer from London, got my telephone number from a friend there. He wants to interview Tim, can't find him, can he come to the farmhouse, yes I suppose. I spent six hours telling him of the past year, about disappointments. Poor fellow, all he wanted was a TV interview. Too bad, he went off in the morning unable to shave or bathe, as to heat the water one has to collect the wood, start a fire under the copper still–like boiler and cautiously pour the heated, often boiling water into the old porcelain bathtub bucket by bucket. Rather difficult; anyway he was anxious to follow a lead his studio had given him regarding Tim's whereabouts, he was off to Bern. He said he would call, but I don't believe him.

I spent this New Year's listening to the radio, four hours of Beatles songs from the sixties to today. A strange fading in and out, I think the broadcast came from Amsterdam or someplace far away. The heat from the large tile stove in the kitchen warms the cold night air. I'm thankful for this two hundred-year-old farmhouse; it's solid and offers safety from the winter outside.

Tim called tonight, said he was in love, all was perfect. I told him I wanted a home and needed money, he had just received money from the sale of [*Confessions of a*] *Hope Fiend*—$250,000; Michel sold the book to Bantam on his trip to New York, told the publisher they didn't need my release as I was very ill in a hospital in Switzerland.[33] Tim said he was in Vienna and that he and his new love were happy, could do anything.[34] He gave me the name of a lawyer there, who'll arrange everything and anything, money, safety, or a divorce. Tim probably freaked

---

33. Didn't *get* her release or didn't *need* it? The word is missing in the original.

34. If Timothy was in Vienna, this must have been during the brief period after he left Switzerland with Joanna Harcourt-Smith. Greenfield (*Timothy Leary*, 444–46) places him still in Switzerland on Christmas Eve 1973 and in Vienna "a few days after New Year's 1973," before leaving for Afghanistan in mid-January 1973.

that I talked with the TV reporter who was on his way to Vienna; he'd like to impress his new love.

VI [January 1973]

All horrible nonsense, makes me too sad. All a scam. The next morning I received a call from the TV producer, he tells me Tim is in Yugoslavia. Thanks me for the time we spent and wishes me well. Well? Oh well. All of this making me a little sad again, I wish I could shake this feeling of not really being anywhere. I long for home. But where is home? The fellow called back, his London office says Tim's in Vienna now and so he's off to get his interview. Tim is probably in Switzerland scamming everyone.

There are periods of complete isolation, no letters, no calls, it's only then I really begin to come out of the past and try to live in the small village by the river, looking across the swift rapids a few hundred yards to Germany. What if Tim has left Switzerland? What will this mean to my status in Switzerland? The lawyer couldn't believe Tim would ever leave; after all, the Swiss government has given him asylum. "Why would he wish to leave? In any case you are safe as long as your husband is here; the Swiss would never ask you to leave." Is that true now?

I called the lawyer in Basel, who said that it's best if I got my residence visa, which means finding a sponsor who'll employ me and guarantee my return ticket to America. The irony of it all. I'm to become an au pair girl for a girlfriend and her husband in Basel. "Now you must study German and become a responsible citizen, it will take a few months to draw up the papers. Your friends will say you have money; that you're here to study our language. Do the police in Villars have you on record?" A dear friend from Lugano talks of marrying me so I can get a Swiss passport. It's all too silly.

Bad news comes in lump sums. Today I received a call from the States, a dear "brother" was arrested at a Grateful Dead New Year's Concert in San Francisco. Oh god, I thought they all were safe in a new land. I must write Carol, I hope she'll answer. Is there anything I can do, brave lady with four children to care for?

Thursday, January 18 [1973], the news came that Tim was arrested in Kabul, Afghanistan, flown handcuffed back to America. God be with him, poor man or poor spirit, or whatever it is that resides inside that familiar frame. Who will see that he gets cigarettes and money every month, not Michel or Dennis, not Brian.[35] I'm thankful to be free and in Switzerland, a last bit of emotionalism and my old life is finished, the paths have led far apart. Too late now. Om Tao, Timothy, Goodbye.

VII [April 1973]

Returning to Sicily and the warmer climate reopens the door to happier thoughts and feelings. Being among the vineyards on the slopes of Etna, sharing wine and stories with the friends met on the last trip. I am not unhappy; there has been time for introspection and reevaluation of some old myths. I find myself as apolitical as ever and I hope a bit wiser. Having a valid four more years on my passport has lessened my anxieties about traveling, and as winter sets in it seems that a move to Italy is the right direction to go.[36] I can't bear the paternal attitude my Swiss friends have taken toward me now that I have appeared to be in direct need of their sponsorship. The German lessons and prospect of being a "good Hausfrau," or selling chocolates in a sweets shop, weigh heavy, as does the ever-present cold damp climate. Oh, perhaps I should admit to myself I look forward to travel and the anonymous adventure it brings. I don't believe I can ever be at home in Europe, so travel seems to be the path.

VIII

I've been thinking about having to be in prison. I don't think I could do it again willingly. The terrible fear in never knowing when you'll get out. Time can be tacked on for minor infractions of the rules.

---

35. Michel Hauchard, Dennis Martino, and Brian Barritt.

36. Rosemary's time line notes *Wintersingen* and *passport* in August 1972, and *Sicily* the next month in September.

Once you are inside prison you are completely within the power of the system.

I spent time in the Poughkeepsie county jail for refusing to testify about Tim, and they let me out only when I agreed to testify. I could have served a thirty-day sentence for every question I refused to answer. There were more than a hundred questions. I've been remembering that time and the desolation and fear I felt when the steel doors were shut against me. I had to struggle with myself not to give way to the claustrophobia. The only saving grace was the matron letting me out of the cell to clean the prison and wait on the prisoners that couldn't be let out.

I must learn to live beyond the sorrow of having been a fool for so long and make a life for myself here where I don't have the prospect of prison. If I were to go back to America, I would be scorned by everyone. All those who yet think Tim a brave and good man and by those who would despise a woman who turned against her husband. I struggle constantly with the thought that he cared for me so little and that I was so careless with my life. I hope soon to have all that behind me.

Part of that problem is living here amidst his friends. Many ready to give up their studies and follow him. Now some of them are disenchanted too. They don't want to have anything to do with him, and at the moment that includes me. It is a bit painful, for I thought of them as friends. I understand the change they have gone through, but it makes my situation all the more awkward, for I have no contact with anyone that has not touched Tim in some way. Switzerland is small in this respect.

Most women don't have notorious husbands or lead such escapist lives. I think there is a basic problem that we all avoid thinking about, that is that marriage for the most part is a ridiculous arrangement for two people to make. I see the fallacy of that argument though, for it could be said that it is my own personal failings that make it ridiculous and I am not enough of a misanthrope to blame men entirely.

I have been in societies where women are traded and their hands marked with henna to show that they are promised for marriage. I do not yet understand how all this came about: the enslavement and self-deprecation that women all over the world yet experience. The complacent desire to look upon the man and husband as a god and supreme arbitrator of our fate, though I have decided so time after time, until an intense desire to realize myself sets me free.

I have thought that it might be simpler to return to Tim to once again be in the center of that maelstrom of activities and energy that he creates around him. Being apart from it I have seen how he consumes people and ideas not for a general good but for his self-glory. There is none left of the original Millbrook group who look to him now. No friend from the past days but only new people surround him, pulled by the lure of "everything is perfect," and if it isn't, why, take some more LSD. It might be easier to inhabit that world than it is to sit here now, alone with my thoughts and self-reproach.

I only hope that I am on my way to a better understanding. I had hoped to have the comfort of believing that Tim was a good man and that we were but incompatible with one another. "You can count on me."[37] I know that I cannot and never could. Ah, but I go on and on, my night thoughts repeated over and over. I know there is only myself and I must look within for all the questions and answers. Let things as they are and see what happens. The blues have ended, pre-menses sadness, I guess.

PART FOUR: AFTER EUROPE
Bimini Fragment

We had run out of places to run to. Bimini was the last stop.[38]

---

37. Quoting Timothy during their first romantic evening at Millbrook in 1965; see page 39.

38. Indeed, Bimini in the Bahamas was the last stop before Rosemary arrived in Florida in 1974.

Coming Home

> *There is larceny to returning covertly to your own country*
> *after you have abandoned it. There is larceny to using a*
> *brand new alias and being a new version of yourself. . . .*
> *There is a sense of occasion about your first day in the park*
> *after six years as your undefined self in exile.*
>
>   JOHN LE CARRÉ, *THE NIGHT MANAGER*[39]

Fugitive Dream[40]

"Did you get the flannel nightie and the books I sent?" Doctor, I dreamed I was in Big Sur in the little stone house watching the dragonflies, and the sound of the waves and the humming birds and the wind on the bamboo all made a sound that I've heard before in the mountains, canyons, deserts of California, Algeria, Switzerland. I followed the sound, and there was no light but a feeling of space, then I fell for a little while and landed hard on the thin, hard mattress, the matron locked the door. No, there are no deserts in Switzerland but mountain roads that almost look as if they'll run to a sandy space eventually. Though they go round and stop in some village where there's hot milk and chocolate powder and pale-complexioned waitresses who think you're another American tourist and so you are. Forever perhaps from one end of Europe to the other and always there are roads that never go back to Big Sur or Joshua Tree, or home, wherever that is.

Thoughts of prison plague me like flies, annoying. I don't know if it's a glimpse into a future state (an island on the life line[41] often means incarceration), memory (the echo of steel doors clanging), or a longing for an end to uncertainty that prompts these fugitive reveries. Brushed away, the dreams persist.

---

39. This is an isolated epigraph, evidently intended to accompany Rosemary's discussion of her return to the United States, which either was never written, or if written does not survive among her papers. I thought it fit best here.
40. The draft is dated February 2, 1983, when Rosemary had already been back in the United States for more than eight years.
41. Of a palm.

I am silent in the steel and concrete corridors, I hear the screech of metal, many voices chanting, cursing, laughing. Yes, there might be laughter. Yet I am silent, watchful, fearful. The women with me in this dream, who are they? Soft-tender women betrayed by love into conspiracies against the order of credit managers and banks, chatting of con men and curls? Or women who from long years of hurt and woes exploded pent-up inarticulate rage and exercised their strength? They pad large and heavy-footed through the corridors of my mind, conscious of their power of retaliation. But why imprison myself here, in the sun with these buzzing thoughts? I am free.

I want to go home, I say to myself now and then. Where is home, the other me asks, then the fantasy begins.

It's late afternoon, I've just finished work at the bakery, bookstore, library, I'm walking, or riding a bicycle home. The sun has almost set behind the mountains, the shadows of the Joshua trees are long and blue on the desert floor. A mile or so from town I turn onto the dirt road that leads to the rocks and coolness. The dog barks, runs to meet me. Inside the small hidden house I kick off my shoes and open the windows, put the kettle on to boil. There's still some sun in the doorway, and after I've picked some mint I'll sit there to read the letter from my lover, who is coming soon.

Or it's a clear bright morning. I've just had a bath at the hot springs and I'm walking along the coast highway. The light is dazzling on the waves, but I think I see a whale and then another. The dog pokes happily in the weeds, scaring a lizard into a sudden flash of green. He runs ahead up the steep trail, and at the top I look for the whales again but they have gone. The path descends past the bamboo grove, and the stone house is visible. The cat is washing herself on the terrace. I lie in the hammock with the sound of the humming birds and distant waves wishing me to sleep.

The farmer killed a sheep today. I didn't watch. Its body is in the cellar, the snow outside the door is red.

So I'll call my mother, ask her to find a lawyer, a psychiatrist, visit the judge. What was the name of the congresswoman who asked what was happening to me? I said shush and hoped she wouldn't ask again, for it's quiet I wanted to be, mousy in fact, hidden and not in the papers again. Or go to the embassy and say I want to go back. Put on a plane, arrested-fingerprinted-searched-photographed-tried-taken to court-grand juries-prison. For years getting sadder, wiser, older. Prison dentistry for my bad teeth, prison counseling for my bad head, prison beds, prison nights. Prison, California State Prison for Women. Junkies, whores, shoplifters, bad-check writers, child neglecters, demonstrators, protesters, sisters all. Doris, Frances, Katherine, Betty Lou, Elizabeth, Conchetta, Louise, Sandy. And the matrons, Mrs. Lewis, Mrs. North, Franklin, Higgins, Herkel, Steward.[43] Wardens, guards, parole boards, lawyers, judges, bondsmen. Who would bail me out? Would I cop to brain-damaged or bent, destroyed by "bad acid"? Go to a state hospital for umpteen years with the family visiting once every other month. "Well, you know, honey it's hard to get up here. Your dad hates to drive on the freeways, and working nights, he needs his sleep on the weekends."

---

43. Rosemary used *Mrss.* as a plural of *Mrs.* As this form is pretty much unknown elsewhere, I am guessing she invented it on the pattern of ms., mss. for manuscript(s). It looked distractingly like a misprint, so I tried to communicate plurality by repeating Mrs. before the second name.

TWELVE

Wandering and Return

Editor's Note

As she mentioned in her preface, Rosemary originally planned this work to cover her whole life up to the time of writing. She wrote about her early life, and about her life with Timothy. But she separated from Timothy in Switzerland in 1971, and lived more than thirty years more until her death in 2002. After the separation she traveled the world with John Schewel, as a fugitive, from Afghanistan to Sicily to Latin America, and after her return to the United States lived underground in Cape Cod and in California until she was able to surface in 1994.

Unfortunately the chapters of her memoir covering those years were either never written or if written do not survive beyond isolated notes and fragments. I searched for them in the materials relating to the memoir in Rosemary's papers in the New York Public Library and concluded with regret that they were not there, and that I might have to publish an unfinished work that left off in the middle. But then I was delighted to find the notes the author Robert Greenfield had made of a long interview with Rosemary in California in 1997. These notes, while not quite an exact transcription of the interview (the recorder failed), were presented in a voice eerily close to Rosemary's own. And (beginning with some material also covered in chapter 10) they covered the whole missing period up to 1997. They were in

Rosemary's archive because Greenfield sent them to her for review and correction (she made only a few revisions, which I have retained).

I decided to publish this document almost verbatim, changing (with Greenfield's approval) only the occasional pronoun, phrase order, proper name, or punctuation mark. I am grateful to Robert Greenfield for allowing this use of his copyrighted material. It functions as the final chapter to complete both the physical book and the narrative it contains. Although written by Greenfield, the words are Rosemary's. I added the title.

So there we were in Switzerland being taken care of by Michel Hauchard in his lovely apartment (overlooking the lake?) where we met his mistress. There were all these beautiful people of both sexes about and he would have these dinner parties for us where everyone at the table was an expatriate. Rich expatriates who would make jokes about how stupid the Swiss were right in front of the Swiss servants. And the women would say things to me like, "Oh, Brazil is so good. In Brazil, we have no problems. I give my servants all my old clothes and they love me for it." Clearly, Hauchard was milking Tim's celebrity for all it was worth at the time and we were all sort of dining out on it as well.

I went to the clinic and had the procedure done and then I had to go back for treatments twice a week.[1] I would leave Tim behind and he would sort of be sitting there holding a salon entertaining the wives and girlfriends of all these rich and powerful men that Hauchard knew in Switzerland. Hauchard himself was an arms dealer. We had no idea what that was about and to tell the truth, I didn't want to know. By that time Tim and I were very much into the right now and what was happening in the moment. This was much better than being in jail. It was better than Algeria or Denmark where they had been waiting at the airport to arrest us in what was a set-up.

---

1. The fertility procedure.

Because of the procedure and the treatments, there was now a window of opportunity for Tim and me to try to have a baby. We had made plans to do this by going tripping up in the mountains on the most opportune day. That morning early, there was a knock on the door: the Swiss police. "You are Dr. Leary? We are here to arrest you." We didn't know exactly why, but Tim went and got his stuff, and as they were taking him away one of them noticed this bowl of wildflowers by the door. "Oh," he said as they were leaving, "and you know it is illegal to pick those in Switzerland."

Now that Tim was in jail, Hauchard sort of swung into high gear. He told me it was going to cost a lot of money to get Tim back out again and that it was my job to start raising funds. Hauchard himself was French but he would walk me through these huge Swiss government buildings, telling me about all the people he knew there and all the good he could do for us. He never came on to me sexually, but we were out quite a lot at night in restaurants and in discotheques, and I remember that he would never let me get up to dance in public. "Because you are with Tim Leary," he told me, "you will always be surrounded by young men."

Of course I began writing letters and making phone calls right away. I remember Allen Ginsberg organizing a letter writing campaign by PEN which had quite an effect on the Swiss.[2] Walter Houston Clark also got in touch and offered to help.

Basically what Allen and the other writers were saying was that Tim was a political prisoner who had been jailed for his beliefs rather than the two roaches or the seven flakes of marijuana in his possession, and that the Swiss had no right to act as agents of the U.S. government by keeping him in jail. I've been told that John Mitchell, the attorney general at the time, actually flew over to Switzerland to try to persuade the Swiss to keep Tim in prison, so there was a lot of pressure being exerted

2. PEN is the international association of writers (the acronym stands for "poets, essayists, and novelists"). It advocates for freedom of expression and for the rights of oppressed and imprisoned authors.

on them from both sides.[3] Through Hauchard, we found a Swiss lawyer for Tim named Horace Mastronardi; he was a wonderful man who worked very hard to get Tim out.

Tim went into jail in May and stayed there until August. Hauchard, who had been in prison himself, knew how to take care of someone who was in jail there, and whenever we went to visit Tim together Hauchard would have pâté and tobacco and chocolate for him. The prison itself was far worse than San Luis Obispo. No minimum security. No handball courts. It was old and cold and dark and dank. A dungeon.

It was there, I think, that Tim went a bit zany. He signed everything over to Hauchard, giving him 90 percent of the book about his escape Tim and I had started writing together in Algeria. He left me nothing at all. I think he trusted completely in Hauchard's getting him out, and he was willing to pay the price he demanded without thinking how I might feel about being left out.

In Algeria, Tim and I had started three books together, one of them being *The He and She of It*.[4] I loved to work on his material and edit it and I wanted to write my own book as well. When *Confessions of a Hope Fiend* came out, I remember thinking that Tim was not only a plagiarist but a "paraphrase-ist." He had stolen my material. He had taken what I had written to him and I was not even being compensated for it. I thought of suing Bantam Books and they said, "If she wants to sue us, tell her to come to New York to file suit." Which of course I couldn't do.[5]

I remember going to visit Tim one day with Mastronardi, the lawyer. Mastronardi handed Tim one of those large Swiss chocolate bars with scenes of Switzerland on it. Tim said, "You know, I wish I could see some of these." Mastronardi burst into tears. "But you can. You can.

---

3. John Mitchell (1913–1988), President Nixon's attorney general, later went to prison himself in the Watergate scandal, for conspiracy, obstruction of justice, and perjury.
4. *The He and She of It* was never published. The title was taken from James Joyce's *Finnegans Wake*: "haven't I told you every telling has a tailing and that's the he and the she of it."
5. *Confessions of a Hope Fiend* was published by Bantam Books in 1973.

You are free." They let Tim out because what he had been imprisoned for in the States would not have gotten him jail time in Switzerland. It would have been punished with a fine.

When Tim came out, we had our usual very romantic time together. Then I began getting annoyed with him. He was doing interviews for German television and people were always calling on the phone and I had the same reaction as before in Paris when I'd thought seriously about going back to join the people in Weather with whom I'd felt so comfortable. When I mentioned that idea to someone, I remember his asking me, "Fine. But can you *type?*" As if that was all a woman could do back then, in terms of the revolution.

In any event, what I wanted to do then was get away and be by myself and get clear. Read and write and determine who I was now that the window of opportunity for us to conceive had closed. In order for it to happen, I would have had to have another procedure. Even if it were successful, the chances were diminished. The death of that possibility for me was very hard to get over. For so long, Tim had told me how perfectly suited I was to be a mother and how beautiful I would look as a mother. Now that was not going to happen and it was like I had to find myself another role to play. I wanted to be quiet and retreat and read and write and Tim was doing interviews and jumping up to answer the phone. We began to discuss separating and it took us a week to hammer out the details of how we would do it. "Marilyn Monroe," he would say to me. "Mick Jagger," I'd answer back. It was this shorthand language we had with one another. His way of telling me how it would be for me without him and me answering him back.

John was someone who had been at Millbrook whom I had always liked.[6] While Tim was in prison, we had begun a relationship and when he showed up in Switzerland, it was like, "Go. John can take care of you now." Our agreement was that I would move to a farmhouse not far away and Tim and I could then see one another whenever we needed to.

---

6. John Schewel.

Three days later, I went to visit Tim and there was Emily, a girl from the village, younger than me and quite attractive. She was wearing my clothes and using the kohl and the perfumes I had brought back with me from Algeria, patting her stomach while she talked about having Tim's child inside her. I understood what was going on right away. After I left, he went down into the village, met Emily, and brought her back to the house.

The four of us—Tim, Emily, John, and I—took an acid trip together. I saw she was now listening for him, as I had once done, sitting beside him so she could tell him what everyone was saying. I remembered a time when, after they were no longer together, Nena came to Millbrook and I was sitting in the exact same place next to Tim where she had once sat. Now I saw I had been replaced as well. It was the concept of replaceable parts, something Tim and I had discussed long before at Millbrook.

During this time, Dennis and Robin Martino came.[7] I had never liked Dennis or his vibes. He was a control freak who had never really been a member of the Brotherhood, or anyone they had ever really trusted. I had even asked Dennis to leave our house on Queens Road in Berkeley.

With Dennis there (and he may have been sent by some government or police agency to destabilize Tim's situation there to make it easier to bring him back to prison), Tim had someone to act as his eyes and ears and bring him back all the gossip about what I was doing with John, a man with whom I would spend the next ten years, hard though it was to be underground with someone who was six feet, six inches tall and stunning.

While we were in Switzerland, Kennedy & Rhine sold the house on Queens Road in Berkeley that Tim had had built for himself and his family in the 50s. I remember falling in love with him all over again when I saw old home movies of him with the kids who were so

---

7. Dennis Martino was the twin brother of David Martino, Susan's husband. Robin was his wife.

young back then, all of them out on the deck of that house . . . while it was being built. Tim really loved that house, but they had his power of attorney, so they sold it to a friend.[8] Tim owed them a good deal of money from the appeal, but I'm sure what they did with the house was something that factored in his thinking later on when it seemed as though all the information he was giving was intended to lead the government to Michael Kennedy.[9]

Together, John and I moved to another canton in Switzerland. Then we left the country altogether and went to Canada where I spent a freezing winter in a farmhouse outside Montreal. Dennis and Robin were there, but only for a while. Dennis went back to Switzerland to be with Tim.

Then I went to Afghanistan where I was to help design and decorate a hotel. David Martino was there and people kept giving him tickets so he could leave.[10] Every six months, he would get as far as Kabul and then come back again. Really, there was nowhere but Kabul to go in that country and that was far as David would get. It was a strange place but it is not so unlikely that Tim thought he could pass through there on his way to some beach in Ceylon where he could be safe and warm in exile. I was in Afghanistan when Tim asked me to meet him in Switzerland. I met him in Lugano and we spent the day together. We tried to reconcile and I remember him asking me to come back to where he was then living to see Susan and I realized I couldn't do it. I just could not get back into that family situation.

---

8. I believe Rosemary was mistaken if she thought that Kennedy & Rhine sold the house under a power of attorney without Timothy's knowledge or against his will. I was the law clerk (and later associate) at that firm who handled the translations of French-language documents and arranged for Swiss notarization and other formalities, since Timothy had to sign all the papers himself, in Switzerland. He might have preferred to keep the house, but the mortgage was unpaid and long past due, and so were the property taxes. Timothy cooperated fully in the details of the sale, which he could have prevented or at least obstructed. DFP

9. Kennedy, a radical activist lawyer, was the person (other than Timothy himself) whom the government most wanted. It seems more likely that was the reason Timothy guided the government toward him, if he did, rather than for revenge over the sale of the house.

10. As noted, David Martino was the husband of Timothy's daughter Susan.

John and I went to Sicily and John left me there to go back to America to try to raise some money. I fell in love with a darling man who had taken us into his house in the countryside surrounded by vineyards.[11] He had servants who took care of him, and he was really quite charming and lovely. It was summer and I was truly madly deeply in love.

I remember seeing the picture of Tim grinning as they took him off the plane after they brought him back to America.[12] It was not the same smile I had known. It was inappropriate. It was a smile of resignation and I could see he had changed. Some people thought it was great that even at that awful moment, Tim could smile. But they did not know him as I did. It was not the same smile and it did not fit. The smile of the ego.

It was while I was in Sicily that I got the eight-page letter from Tim in jail.[13] The letter did not come to me directly but was sent to someone Tim knew would then get the letter to me. It was written by hand without a single cross-out, as though it were meant to be published. In the letter, Tim told me things had changed and the war was over and the Reagan people were not so bad and I should consider talking to them. Along with the letter came the business card of an FBI agent with a phone number on it for me to call. By this time the FBI had spoken to Jaakov Kohn and a woman I had known back then, so I knew they were interested in finding me as well.

Then, and for a long time afterward, I was very angry at Tim and very self-righteous. I never once considered talking about people who had helped Tim to get out. I can remember spewing all this rhetoric about it. But then I was not in jail at the time. Tim was.

Who was the one they wanted Tim to talk to them about? If Michael Kennedy has already said so, then I will as well. I believe it was Michael they wanted. He represented Weather, the Brotherhood, and La Raza.

---

11. This was Adolfo Frenzi, the man she called *Bubi*. Thanks to John Schewel for making the identification.
12. In January 1973.
13. It was seven pages—there is a photocopy in the Blue Binder.

I'm sure Tim did identify with his captors. Not only that but then he went ahead and wrote about [it?] in *Oui* magazine. "Tania" Hearst had identified with her captors. The Stockholm syndrome.[14] But I think too it was West Point.[15] That parallel universe. A whole other world. Which was part of the reason Tim could connect so easily with someone like Gordon Liddy, who was another iconoclast.

They were looking for Patty Hearst in Sicily then, and the wife of one of the actors of the Living Theatre in Priano had just died of a drug overdose. I began to see that the man I was with had a serious problem with alcohol and I could not keep up with him when it came to drinking. It just made me sick. Besides, by that point, John was talking to me about Colombia. Emeralds! Jungles! Adventure! I decided it was time to go, and I left.

We went there together, and the woman who picked us up at the airport was a carbon copy of Michel Hauchard, to a T. She whisked us out of there so fast that my luggage was left behind, and drove us in a big Mercedes to a mansion where I noticed the servants were all eyeing us strangely. She didn't really seem to belong, and in the upstairs bedrooms there were framed photographs of SS men. She was a con woman who had conned a friend of John's about what we could expect to find there.

Again, no one could write to me directly. But my mother sent me a long family letter in which she also told me the bad news that my father had been diagnosed with diabetes. Joanna had called her and told her that she and Tim had $25,000 for me. She also offered her $5,000 for my phone number, which my mother did not have. Although it was

---

14. Patricia Hearst was kidnapped as a teenager in 1974 by American desperadoes who called themselves the Symbionese Liberation Army. Hearst did apparently identify with her captors and adopted the nom de guerre of Tania while she worked with them, including participating in a bank robbery. The tendency of hostages and other captives to identify with their captors has been called the Stockholm syndrome, after the experience of hostages taken in a bank robbery there in 1973.

15. Timothy did his unfortunate first year of college as a cadet at the U.S. Military Academy at West Point, 1940–41. His experience there is related in detail in Robert Greenfield, *Timothy Leary: A Biography,* New York: Houghton Mifflin Harcourt, 2006.

Joanna who made the call, not Tim, I knew Tim was actively trying to give me up to them.[16]

I ended up spending two years in Colombia, finally leaving on a flat-bottomed 140-foot, dope-smuggling boat that got caught in storms in the Caribbean. I remember reading about my divorce from Tim in the *International Herald Tribune* in Martinique after a very slow, scary, and dangerous journey there from Colombia. From there, I went to Bimini and from there, John and I got back into America by being put off on a beach in Fort Lauderdale.[17] In the basement of his mother's condo, he unearthed a yellow-and-black Rolls-Royce in which he drove us back to St. Louis.

Coming back was so strange. Turning on the TV one Sunday morning, I heard Eldridge Cleaver on the radio with that reverend from the Crystal Church in Southern California.[18] He had gotten religion and found Jesus, and he was not a fugitive or in prison.

I spent the next fourteen years in Northeast Harbor on Cape Cod.[19] I had a garage sale there and sold all my sheepskin jackets from Afghanistan (which reeked of patchouli) and my spangled glass-beaded hippie dresses, most of it to a psychiatrist and his family. I made $1,700 and that was when I realized I could sell. I began selling convention

---

16. This was Joanna Harcourt-Smith, a European adventuress who was Timothy's companion at the end of his Swiss exile. She was with him during the ill-fated trip to Afghanistan where he was arrested and returned to prison in the United States, and she worked tirelessly to get him out. Her role in the Leariad is still a subject of controversy. Compare Robert Greenfield, *Timothy Leary: A Biography,* New York: Houghton Mifflin Harcourt, 2006, with Joanna's own memoir *Tripping the Bardo with Timothy Leary: My Psychedelic Love Story* (North Charleston, S.C.: CreateSpace, 2013).

17. Rosemary wrote an itinerary of her Caribbean journey, reproduced in appendix B on page 300. Bimini, in the Bahamas, is just 50 miles from Florida. Rosemary told me she re-entered the United States on water skis.

18. Rev. Robert H. Schuller (1926–2015), whose Crystal Cathedral in Garden Grove, Orange County, an enormous postmodern glass building designed by Philip Johnson, was completed in 1980. The building was later sold to the Roman Catholic archdiocese. Cleaver had become a Christian some years before that, while still in exile.

19. This is puzzling. On Cape Cod Rosemary first lived in Eastham, later moving to Provincetown, then to Truro, and finally back to Provincetown. The three towns are all within about 25 miles of each other. Northeast Harbor is in Maine.

space for a hotel at the tip of the Cape.[20] I was living as Sarah Woodruff. In order to get a driver's license, I had to swear I had not been convicted of a felony in ten years. So I had no license and I did not drive. It was during this time that I learned how to be by myself and how to live without a man, how to cook for myself, and how to be alone. I rode my bike everywhere and many people knew who I was. I knew Tim knew I was out there because at the end of *Flashbacks,* he wrote "and this is for Rosemary wrapped in a black shawl at the edge of the jetty." It was a phrase John Fowles had used to describe Sarah Woodruff, which is the name of the heroine in *The French Lieutenant's Woman.*

Being underground is very schizophrenic. As a fugitive, you are so important to yourself yet must appear anonymous to everyone else. After a year or so, a lawyer found out that the federal government would relent if California was willing to do the same on the state charges. The lawyer approached Jerry Brown, who was then still governor of California.[21] My chances of going to jail for violating the terms of my probation if I surrendered were fifty-fifty. I did not want to trade the life I had for the possibility of going to jail. So I stayed underground for thirteen more years.[22]

The first contact I had with Tim after all those years was when I heard that Susan had died.[23] I called and spoke to Barbara[24] and left a number but Tim did not call back. Her death just opened everything up for me all over again. I remembered the time when we'd come down from Millbrook to my apartment on Ninth Street and Fifth Avenue. I was packing my things to go back up there and live with Tim and he said to Susan, "Who does Rosemary remind you of?" It was Marianne he was talking about. Marianne and also Mary Della Cioppa, the woman with whom he'd been having an affair when Marianne killed

---

20. The Provincetown Inn.

21. Edmund G. Brown Jr., a Democrat (born 1938), governor of California 1975–1983 and again 2011–2019.

22. From around 1981 to 1994.

23. By her own hand.

24. Barbara Chase, Timothy's final wife, his fifth (or sixth if we count Joanna Harcourt-Smith, who used the name Leary).

herself.[25] Together, they'd gone to Mexico and gotten married but the ceremony was not legal. This was the first time I ever saw Susan look at me as someone to be reckoned with. A serious rival. I think in some way Tim blamed me for what happened to Susan, the sense being that I had not been a good enough mother to her.

There was a great physical attraction between us. We made each other laugh. But once the bust happened at Laredo, the life we'd had as a couple was over. Those are still the moments I remember best. The quiet ones. Walking in tandem at Millbrook and having dinner by the fire. I was in his thrall but he did not try to recreate or change me. I just loved being with him, and the way his mind worked.

How I finally surfaced was through Tim. By then I was living in San Francisco. I was being kept aware of what was going on with Tim by Super Joel, who had been the famous radical in Berkeley during the riots in 1969.[26] Through Super Joel, we set up a meeting at the Asian Art Museum in Golden Gate Park. I guess I still did not really trust him not to turn me in. I was still a fugitive and I could not afford to be seen with Tim in a place where we would be recognized.

The day we saw one another again for the first time in Golden Gate Park, it was twenty years to the day since I'd left him in Switzerland.[27] He was sick. He was very much aware that his short-term memory was fading. Barbara was gone and he was desolate.[28] Both of us were so physically altered as to be almost unrecognizable as who we had once been. But as always when we got together after an escape or when he'd gotten out of jail, it was a movie. VistaVision. Technicolor. Wide screen. Tim was so good at creating drama and he so loved to play and he was so brilliant at it. He asked me to marry him that day. I said no. And he said, "Well then, I'll have to cross you off my list."

---

25. On October 22, 1955. Marianne Busch was Timothy's first wife, Mary Della Cioppa his second.
26. Super Joel was Joseph Eric Tournabene, a Berkeley activist. He died in 1993.
27. Taking the date from Rosemary's time line, that would place this reunion on October 12, 1991.
28. Timothy's 1978 marriage to Barbara Chase was finally dissolved in 1992.

After we saw one another in Golden Gate Park, we had one law-yer call another.[29] They discovered that Orange County had no interest in me. The statute of limitations on my probation violations was long since past and no charges had ever been filed against anyone in con-nection with Tim's escape from prison. Really, I was out in the cold as long as anyone. I can remember sitting and reading the newspaper as all these people would come in and I'd wonder how long it would be before it happened to me.

I went and saw him in L.A. after that, but he was no longer attuned to my voice and I had to shout to make myself heard, and my jokes were never funny anymore. I didn't like L.A. and I didn't like the scene at the house and I couldn't see what would be in it for me. By that I mean, what would come from Tim to me.

I remember us being on our honeymoon in Laguna Beach, sitting on a cliff by the ocean with Tim. This awful shark-nosed military plane cruised by, and I had a vision of Vietnam and people dying and napalm. Although it was a bit late in the game, I knew we had to do whatever we could to stop the war. At the November Moratorium in Washington, D.C., they wouldn't let us on stage to talk. Benjamin Spock and Norman Mailer were there but we were too radical.[30] It wasn't until

---

29. I was the lawyer who called another. I called and engaged Robert Hanson; I chose him on the advice of my former law professor Bernard L. Segal, because he was *not* a famous high-profile civil liberties lawyer but a workaday practitioner in Santa Ana, Orange County, who knew his way around the courthouse. Hanson worked out the deal, and Dennis Roberts of Oakland (who had been an associate with me at Kennedy & Rhine) confirmed that the federal authorities were no longer interested in Rosemary. And so Rosemary paid a fine and some costs, out of the money provided by psychedelic pioneer and grande dame Nina Graboi (1918–1999), and was at last able to emerge. The fine and costs came to $1,080, which Rosemary saw at once was a multiple of the Hindu sacred number 108. DFP

30. Dr. Benjamin Spock (1903–1998) was a pediatrician whose book *Baby and Child Care,* first published in 1946, guided millions of American parents in caring for and raising their children. Because he was so widely trusted and not a political person, his public leadership against the war in Vietnam broadened and legitimized mass opposi-tion to the war. Norman Mailer (1923–2007) was a novelist, journalist, and cultural critic. His widely read "nonfiction novel" *Armies of the Night,* about the October 1967 antiwar March on Washington (not the November Moratorium), won a Pulitzer Prize.

Peter, Paul, and Mary brought us out with them to sing that we were permitted to appear.[31]

I did everything I could to help arrange a reconciliation between Tim and his son Jack. I had a relationship with Jack. We could always talk. He once called me the closest thing to a mother he'd ever had, which I found incredibly moving. I think Tim disapproved of how Jack's life had turned out. That he was a loving father and a good husband sort of paled beside the working-class life he'd made for himself. Richard Alpert and I set up a meeting for Jack and Tim. Tim never showed up. He was just so terribly scared. Then we got him to write Jackie that letter. I helped him quite a bit on that, suggesting that he just beg Jack's forgiveness and throw himself at his feet, if need be.

Frank Barron and Richard brought Jack to the house on the day of the Harvard reunion and the moment between them that should have happened never did occur.[32] Think what it must have been like for Jack. All those people, just as at Millbrook, telling Jack how lucky he was to have Tim for a father and how they wished he was their dad. It must have been hard for a child to comprehend. In the house in L.A., there were people there who wanted to be Tim's son. People who wanted to videotape their time together. People Jack did not know, telling him what a great man his father really was, and then let him leave without anyone noticing, offering to call a taxi, or take him to the airport.

Tim could not have stayed at Harvard. He was a young psychologist who had discovered something that was going to change people's consciousness. In terms of gravitating to the rich and famous and going to New York on weekends to turn on the stars, Tim was never an egalitarian. Those were the people he felt comfortable with. Richard Alpert.

---

31. The Moratorium March on Washington took place on November 15, 1969. Pete Seeger led the crowd in many, many choruses of "Give Peace a Chance," by John Lennon, which had been released in July. This might have been what Rosemary was singing. Peter, Paul, and Mary were a folk music trio very popular at the time.

32. The Harvard Psychedelic Reunion took place at Harvard on April 23, 1983. Frank Barron (1922–2002) was a distinguished psychologist who had been Timothy's Berkeley graduate school classmate and worked with him at the Harvard Psychedelic Project.

Peggy Hitchcock, from one of the wealthiest and most interesting families in America yet on a spiritual quest.[33] Tim was an intellectual. He was constantly searching for people who interested him.

Even during the fourteen years I spent underground, he was controlling my existence.[34] I did love him. I am not the widow but along with Jack, Dieadra, Zach, Sara, and Ashley, I am an heir.[35] Along with Donna Scott, and Cindy and Michael Horowitz, I am a trustee.[36] As a committee, we get together to try to administer the estate. Someone once said you should never make someone you love your executor, but I have learned a lot about contracts and rights and permissions by doing this for Tim. Tim left only a life insurance policy, which was divided among the heirs.[37] He also left unpaid taxes dating back many years.

To me, his dying was very moving because it was the way he wanted to go out. Again I could see him as he was at Millbrook the day we were going through an old trunk and he pulled out a straw hat and a cane and started doing an elegant *Shuffle Off to Buffalo*. He was a song-and-dance man, and he knew it.

There was a naïveté about Tim and a boyish innocence that was very American. I remember us running around the desert up at the Brotherhood ranch, naked with flowers behind our ears as we were

33. As noted, Peggy Hitchcock, who had inherited the Millbrook estate along with her brothers Billy and Tommy, was a member of the Mellon family.

34. This is confusing. Rosemary was underground for twenty-four years, not fourteen, from the flight to Algeria in 1970 until she surfaced in 1994.

35. Rosemary and the other "heirs" were actually beneficiaries of the trust set up by Timothy's will to receive his estate. Zachary Chase Leary, the son by her previous husband of his last wife, Barbara Chase, is named in the 1995 trust document as one of Timothy's "now living children." Dieadra Martino, Ashley Martino, and Sara Brown, Timothy's grandchildren, were all children of his late daughter Susan.

36. Trustees of the testamentary trust just mentioned. Donna Scott was a Los Angeles friend of Timothy's. Michael Horowitz was Timothy's archivist and author of the *Annotated Bibliography of Timothy Leary* (see page 8 above); his wife Cindy (Cynthia Palmer) is his sometime collaborator, for example on *Sisters of the Extreme: Women Writing on the Drug Experience* (Rochester, Vt.: Inner Traditions, 2000), in which Rosemary's "Peyote Equinox," reproduced in chapter 6 above, was first published.

37. Because the rest of his estate passed into the trust and was distributed from there. Life insurance proceeds are not part of an estate.

being buzzed by these helicopters, and I thought, "What are we doing here?" Not Tim. He loved it.

Do I think he danced with the devil? No. Because someone in the sixties once told me of their experience with the devil. The devil took them up to a hill overlooking the L.A. basin and said, "You can have all that but you will have to give up love."[38] Tim never did. He may not have been a great parent but he loved his children. We loved one another. Granted, as the great man, he may have found it easier to love on a broader scale than to deal with the day-to-day of "ordinary" love.

The celebrity. What choice did he have? Once it was given to him, he accepted it. He always wanted to be an actor, and he loved to be with stars. Thank God, he had a SAG card.[39] Their payments helped cover the medical costs when he got so ill.

Two years, he gave me *tsuris*. Two years, I gave him tsuris.[40] In Algeria, we were together. What I remember are the quiet moments. The day-to-day. Walking in tandem in Millbrook. Having dinner before the fire. Going to the *tabac* in Algeria each morning for our cigarettes and candy.[41]

Editor's Note

What follows was part of Greenfield's interview notes. Although it came at the end of those notes, presumably because it came at the end of the interview, it does not really belong at the end of this chapter, but in chapter 4. However, I am keeping it here in its original position because it is part of Greenfield's text and not of Rosemary's original memoir.

---

38. This reference to the Temptation of Christ (Luke 4:5–7) is part of the story of Tarquin and Penelope that Rosemary tells in chapter 8 (see page 159 and note 26).
39. Screen Actors Guild.
40. Yiddish for "trouble."
41. A tabac is a small convenience store in France (and former French colonies) licensed under the government monopoly to sell tobacco.

In May 1970, I put on a benefit at the Village Gate in New York City to raise money for Tim's defense fund. Invitations were supposed to be sent out but they ended up in someone's mailbox and never got sent. So it was all through word of mouth, but the turnout was astonishing. Everyone was there. Phil Ochs. Johnny Winter. Wavy Gray and a lot of the Hog Farmers came.[42] Poor Wavy. He was in a full-body cast because he had been kicked in the back by a security guard at a Rolling Stones concert. Alan Douglas, bless his heart, got Jimi Hendrix and his band to fly in direct from Chicago to play for us.[43]

We had all these light-show artists come and the plan was to have a battle of the light shows, which was something we had often done up at Millbrook. A lot of people who were then living in Woodstock came down and one of them spiked the punch with acid. The light show artists ended up underneath the tables, gurgling. So much for the battle of the light shows.

For me, the Village Gate was hallowed ground. It was where I had seen Miles Davis and Charles Mingus play. A dark pillared basement. With all the big givers from the liberal left in the city there, I really thought we were going to raise some money to help get Tim out of jail.

Abbie Hoffman had been given too much acid and he got up on stage and took the microphone and began railing at the crowd. This was just after Kent State and he was very frustrated and angry.[44] Here we were dancing when there was a war going on. We should have been fighting. At one point, Abbie either punched or shoved Allen Ginsberg, who was also on stage at the time. Abbie also put his hand through a very expensive speaker. As he was raging at the crowd, I remember watching his

---

42. The Hog Farm was the name of the commune founded by Wavy Gravy (Hugh Romney) and his wife Jahanara. Wavy Gravy (born 1936), a longtime radical and hippie activist, affects a clown persona. Phil Ochs (1940–1976) was a singer, guitarist, and political songwriter, very active in protest against the Vietnam War. Johnny Winter (1944–2014) was a rock musician, singer, and record producer.

43. Alan Douglas (1931–2014) was a producer of jazz recordings.

44. On May 4, 1970, at Kent State University in Kent, Ohio, college students protesting the war in Vietnam were shot, and some killed, by members of the Ohio National Guard. The incident caused national outrage.

wife Anita behind him on stage. She kept opening and closing the black shawl she had on like this was a passion play. As Abbie spoke or ranted, I watched the exodus begin. People started walking out the door. All the big givers I had hoped were going to contribute to the defense fund left.

After Abbie left, I remember poor Wavy Gravy getting up there on stage in his full body cast trying to get the crowd to do some deep breathing exercises together in order to raise the vibes. Then Johnny Winter played and he was just wonderful. It was like prom music. Texas prom music. He was playing the blues for me and Tim. Then this beautiful woman who was with Jimi at the time got up on stage. I remember her clearing the children away, moving them back because when Jimi plugged in and began playing, there would be this current coming off the stage that was so powerful it would have harmed them all. And that was just what happened. When Jimi and his band started their set at about midnight, all the filmmakers there suddenly woke up and tried to record it. When we looked at what they shot, the film was all whited out and there was no soundtrack, as though he were just too powerful to be recorded. The night ended with Allen Ginsberg Om-ing up on stage. It was a wonderful party but a disaster as a fundraiser. It cost about $8000 to put on and we only raised about $5000, so we lost three thousand dollars on the evening. The music and the politics back then never really mixed. They were like oil and water. But they kept coming together all the same, because of the war.

Rosemary in 1998
Photograph © by Robert Altman
Reproduced with the kind permission
of the artist.

APPENDIX A

Synopses and Chapter Structures

If anything is to be changed, either one must divide one object into two parts, or add another unit to it. This principle lies at the basis of all scientific thought and work.

ALEISTER CROWLEY[1]

Rosemary's memoir as finally structured here is composed of ten chapters—some complete, some not, arranged in chronological order through 1971, followed by another chapter with a few later fragments and, as a twelfth chapter finishing the narrative, a transcribed interview in Rosemary's voice, as spoken rather than written. The written chapters (including the fragmentary eleventh) have the names she gave them about midway through the writing process and kept through the latest drafts Rosemary made. The summaries in the following table are mine.

---

1. From Crowley's *The Book of Thoth* (London: O.T.O., 1944), about the tarot and Crowley's Thoth Tarot deck executed by Frieda Harris. This quotation was written in Rosemary's hand at the head of one of her pages of notes for the memoir's chapter structure.

Current Structure of Rosemary's Memoir

1. THE MAGICIAN'S DAUGHTER	1935–65. Missouri girlhood, early marriage, New York City.
2. ILLUSIONS	1965. Timothy Leary. Millbrook. The Laredo arrest.
3. SCARLET WOMAN	1966. The Millbrook raid. Dutchess County jail. Testimony.
4. CELEBRATIONS	1966–67. Millbrook. On the road with the psychedelic light show and other entertainments. Visit to Brotherhood of Eternal Love.
5. INITIATIONS	1967. More time on the road. Return—trouble at Millbrook. Marriage to Timothy.
6. THE LOVERS	1968. Tahquitz acid trip. "Peyote Equinox."
7. ENCHANTMENTS	1969. Morocco: "The Master Musicians of Joujouka."
8. HOLDING TOGETHER	1969–70. California: preparing for and executing the escape and flight.
9. BEHIND THE VEIL	1970–71. Algeria.
10. CHANGES	1971. Switzerland after Algeria. Rosemary separates from Timothy.
11. ADJUSTMENT	1971–72. Exile in Europe and Afghanistan.
12. WANDERING AND RETURN	1971–97. Interview notes by Robert Greenfield—not written by Rosemary.

This simple structure was a refinement and marked reduction from Rosemary's original conception and reflects a severe abridgement of her ambitious plan for the book. At first she had planned twenty-two chapters, numbered 0–21, each corresponding to one of the trump cards in the tarot deck.

The tarot, like the zodiac and the Chinese Book of Changes (I Ching), which also figure in the chapter lists, are all methods of divination that operate as vehicles for projection, and rely on arranging human personalities, experiences, and unconscious imagery into categories for analysis and understanding of the present moment. All of them were important resources in Rosemary's life and in her memoir.[2] Rosemary wrote to Rosalie Siegel, who was briefly her agent for the book, that she "took as a theme that which I was most interested in at the moment, the tarot. Each chapter has significance (for me) as a card from an ancient occult school."[3] One reader of draft chapters wrote, "I really loved the use of planetary aspects to set the tone of the chapters they introduced."[4]

A chart written in Rosemary's hand on accounting paper, found among similar charts in her papers at the New York Public Library, appears as Document 3 on page 289. It lays out her tarot-based conception for the book. Many of the topics on which she adds marginal glosses relate especially to the experience of women. This focus appears too throughout the surviving text of the memoir, and from indications in the various chapter lists and synopses, Rosemary intended this to be even more prominent a theme. Document 4 (on page 290) is a slightly more legible twenty-one-chapter list, similar to that on the accounting-paper chart—the subjects as noted in Rosemary's hand do not correspond to the eventual text. I reproduce the chapter names here.

---

2. The tarot has twenty-two trumps, with archetypal scenes and images, followed by fifty-six cards in four suits, much like modern playing cards. Rosemary was especially interested in the tarot deck designed by Aleister Crowley and his associate Lady Frieda Harris (1877–1962), who painted them. Crowley's images for the trumps, and even his names for some of them, differ from the more familiar Rider-Waite deck, and his *Book of Thoth,* already mentioned, provides a very thorough analysis.

3. Letter to Rosalie Siegel, April 1, 1974. She continues, "If this is too esoteric (and I would not like it obvious that the book is," before continuing on a second page, which, frustratingly, is not present in the archive. Siegel had agreed to represent the book, but then her husband was taken into the navy in the so-called doctor draft and was sent for two years to Guantanamo Bay, Cuba, which forced Siegel to abandon the project. Rosemary never found another agent to represent her memoir.

4. Letter from Vicki Marshall, March 18, 1994.

0. As Symbol	8. Scarlet Woman	15. Absolute Necessity
1. Initiations	9. Lonely Yoni in Lingam Land	16. Law of the Fortress
2. Behind the Veil		17. Star Tripped
3. Daughter of the Mother	10. Changes	18. Make Up Your Mind
4. Vested Interests	11. Balancing Act	19. Be Not Sad
5. Horoscopes	12. Dying Gods	20. Regeneration
6. Loves	13. Suicide Pacts	21. Universes
7. Who's Driving?	14. Union of Opposites	

Here is a transitional list, taken from a letter from Rosemary to Rosalie Siegel on October 30, 1973. It will be seen that the order of chapters is not chronological. This list has no entry for chapters I, II, or XIII.

III	Daughter of the Mother	first session, others
IV	Vested Interest	kings games, Millbrook
V	Untitled	gurus, ashrams
VI	Lovers	wedding ceremonies
VII	Chrome Horse	Switzerland
VIII	Holding Together	prison breaks
IX	Lonely Yoni in Lingam Land	letters
X	Changes	exiled
XI	Balancing Act	contempt of court
XII	Death of the Mind	religious celebrations
XIV	Union of Opposites	psychedelic marriage, lectures
XV	Absolute Necessity	tribal ways, dealers
XVI	Untitled	barn burnings, deaths, arrests, other disasters
XVII	Star Tripped	LSD and flying saucers

But Rosalie Siegel wrote to Rosemary on April 24, 1974, that,

I remain . . . somewhat baffled by the arrangement of chapters and feel that although the tarot order may be meaningful to you, it may not be so

to your reader (unless of course the arrangement were more obvious—which you say you are against—or your reader familiar with the tarot) who would be less perplexed if there were a chronological order.

And in a letter dated May 28, 1974, to a prospective editor[5] who had also advised her to put her chapters in a chronological order, Rosemary wrote:

A month or so ago I rearranged the book into chronological order and it does seem to be better though I regret the loss of the (secret) tarot card arrangement.

Eventually, once Rosemary abandoned the tarot organization, she reduced the twenty-two-chapter structure to between eleven and fourteen chapters. For each one, Rosemary created a synopsis of what it contained (or was intended to contain). The exact number and coverage varied over the years, depending on whether Rosemary felt able to include closing chapters written in freedom, and whether she still planned to include analysis of the meaning to society of the events and transformations of the sixties. On pages 281–85 and 286–87 are two particularly full examples—they give a good idea of what the book was intended to include when scaled down from its original purpose as a coded esoteric text. A lot of the material mentioned, especially the encounters with notable people, was not included in the eventual manuscript, at least not in the portion that survives.

---

5. Ross Firestone, who had edited Timothy's *Jail Notes* and other books (on jazz and edgy cultural subjects), notably the anthology *Getting Busted: Personal Experiences of Arrest, Trial, and Prison* (New York: Arena Books, 1973). Thanks to Michael Horowitz for this identification.

Undated Synopsis (from the 1980s?)	Synopsis from 1994
I. MAGICIAN'S DAUGHTER. Rhythm and Blues. St. Louis to New York City.	CHAPTER ONE: THE MAGICIAN'S DAUGHTER. Childhood as the daughter of a Midwestern carnival magician. In the early 1950s I move to New York City. Experiences as a model, doing commercials, and playing bit parts on live television. Working for El Al Israel Airlines. Marriage to a jazz musician and then life with a classical composer. Experimentation with the beat culture and peyote. Introduction to mysticism and LSD.
II. ILLUSIONS, Castalia Foundation, Millbrook New York. The Bridge of Laredo. The trap of pity and guilt.	CHAPTER TWO: ILLUSIONS. Meeting Timothy Leary, Richard Alpert, and Ralph Metzner at an art gallery. Residence at the community in Millbrook, known as the Castalia Foundation. Consciousness-expanding activities at Millbrook. Arrested with Leary in Texas, while on the way to Mexico. Leary is thrust into notoriety, and our lives into national focus.
III. DIFFICULTY AT THE BEGINNING.[6] Dutchess County Sheriff's raid by G. Gordon Liddy. Contempt of Court Trial. Religious Beliefs. Jailhouse Women.	CHAPTER THREE: SCARLET WOMAN. Fund-raising seminars at Millbrook to pay escalating legal costs. Spring, 1966, G. Gordon Liddy and his posse pull a surprise midnight raid on Millbrook. Bizarre court proceedings. Religious defense. Trial and imprisonment for contempt. Testimony before the grand jury about mandalas, mantras, and gurus.
IV. YOUTHFUL FOLLY.[7] Millenarian seekers. The League for Spiritual Discovery, Psychedelic Celebrations. The Ashram. Hollywood, Magic Theater for Madmen only.	CHAPTER FOUR: CELEBRATIONS. Starting a new religion, the League for Spiritual Discovery. Hundreds of spiritual seekers make their way to Millbrook. The League goes on the road with light shows and celebrations in major American cities, 1966–1967.

---

6. Named after Hexagram 3 in the I Ching.
7. Named after Hexagram 4 in the I Ching.

Undated Synopsis (from the 1980s?) (cont.)	Synopsis from 1994
V. Waiting.[8] Holy men, hippies, and hypocrites. The League moves to the woods. Isolation and disillusion. Wicked stepmother. Generation gap. Storefront religions. College tours lectures and festivals. Free Spirits, Diggers, and Revolutionary Anarchists. Mystic Arts.	Chapter Five: Initiations. Encounters with Alan Watts, Ken Kesey, Allen Ginsberg, Abbie Hoffman, Richard Alpert, Emmett Grogan, Diane di Prima, Swami Satchitananda, and Carlos Castaneda. LSD overdose leads to a psychotic episode and camping in the woods. Navajo peyote meeting.
VI. Lovers. Conflict, love drugs, and marriage. Indian medicine men. Alan Watts's wedding gift. The Sheriff raids the teepees. The League goes to jail. Navaho Easter, Peyote ceremonies. King killed, Ginsberg accuses Hoover of "bugging" him. The Brotherhood buys a mile-high ranch. The Yippies invite us to the Democratic Convention in Chicago. Love in the parks. Laguna Beach bust. Stop the War.	Chapter Six: The Lovers. Joshua Tree, Hindu and Millbrook marriage to Timothy Leary. The growing popularity of psychedelics and resistance to the war in Vietnam provide the foundation for a new culture. The government imprisons thousands for drugs and civil disobedience. Encounters with spiritual revolutionaries and anarchists: the Brotherhood of Eternal Love, the Yippies, the Diggers, the Mother Fuckers, and other outlaws.
VII. Sweet Chariot. The League meets the Brotherhood of Eternal Love. The women of the ranch, bread, and babies. Militant "Mother Fuckers." Supreme Court Decision overturns Federal contraband laws. Leary for Governor. A brother in Nam. Living theater. Our own Chappaquiddick. Flying Saucers. The Bodhisattva drug overdose death of Farmer John. John and Yoko Lennon in Montreal. Madrid, Tangier, and the musicians of Joujouka. The Washington War Moratorium. Fertility Rites and *Rosemary's Baby*. Guru Jam. Altamont and the Hell's Angels. Another Trial.	Chapter Seven: Enchantments. Life on the Ranch (a mountain commune), with tepees, rattlesnakes, babies, LSD, and more raids. Travels to Hawaii and Morocco. "Bed-In" demonstration in Montreal to protest the Vietnam War with John Lennon and Yoko Ono. Dancing with the Master Musicians of Joujouka. The end of innocence at the Altamont concert. Meetings with Laura Huxley, Hugh Hefner, Otto Preminger, William Burroughs, Gloria Steinem, Paul Bowles, the Moody Blues, and the Grateful Dead.

8. Named after Hexagram 5 in the I Ching.

UNDATED SYNOPSIS (FROM THE 1980s?) (cont.)	SYNOPSIS FROM 1994
VIII. HOLDING TOGETHER. Prison, no bail. Rosemary promises to free Tim Leary. Charles Manson and his women. Jackson courtroom escape. Kesey, Watt, Ferlinghetti, McClure, and Ginsberg give advice. Om Orgy at the Family Dog ballroom, San Francisco. Floating Lotus Opera Company and Mime Troup. Kent State. F!B!I!, High Society and the Hog Farm at New York's best party. Abbie Hoffman freaks out. Press conferences, TV appeals, and other disasters. Esalen family and Big Sur people. Hitchhiking and Berkeley sisters. Probation officers. Jackie goes to prison, Susan tries to die, Rosemary joins the underground. Weather-women. Escape.	CHAPTER EIGHT: HOLDING TOGETHER. Another family Christmas ruined by an arrest in Laguna Beach. President Nixon calls Timothy Leary "the most dangerous man in America." Another courtroom trial. I am sentenced to ten years, but let out on appeal. Leary is imprisoned without bail. September 1970, I break Leary out from prison with the help of the Weather Underground. Flight from America using disguises and false documents. Fugitives in Paris.
IX. FUGITIVE. Paris and freedom. Algeria, the Black Panthers, FLN, and CIA. The women behind the veil.	CHAPTER NINE: BEHIND THE VEIL. Imprisoned by Eldridge Cleaver in the Black Panther "Embassy" in Algeria. Algeria as a refuge for the world's revolutionaries. Parties with the international news and spy community. Notoriety and humiliation. Idylls in the desert. Algerian women. Fellow refugee Kathleen Cleaver.
X. CHANGES. Switzerland. Arms dealers and other con men. Rich people. Another arrest, another betrayal.	CHAPTER TEN: CHANGES. Escape from Algeria to Switzerland. Received by arms dealers, scoundrels, and rich expatriates. The Swiss imprison Leary, after Attorney General John Mitchell visits Switzerland on Nixon's order. After Leary is released, fans and television reporters have us besieged. Pressures of exile help to bring about the end of our marriage.
XI. ADJUSTMENT. Wisdom and Folly. Stateless wanderer. Grape harvester and au pair girl, Sicilian hospitality and Swiss diplomacy. Patty Hearst and Martha Mitchell. Final betrayal. Leary tries to become a Judas goat. Hard times in the New World. A spirit of rebellion.	CHAPTER ELEVEN: ADJUSTMENTS. Refugee travels on a false passport to Canada, Afghanistan, and Sicily. Set up for the FBI by Leary bargaining for his freedom. A fugitive, I go into hiding among drug smugglers in South America. Raising cattle in Colombia. Meetings with fugitive financier Robert Vesco. On the run, out at sea, and out of places to hide.

UNDATED SYNOPSIS (FROM THE 1980s?) (cont.)	SYNOPSIS FROM 1994
	CHAPTER TWELVE: REDEMPTION. Secret return to America on a speedboat, Fall 1976. Life on the edge of America underground. Living in a Cape Cod artists' community and small fishing village. Creating a new identity and learning to live without adventure. "I had to be secretive and hermetic, living the life of a recluse in isolation."[9]
	CHAPTER THIRTEEN: RECONCILIATION. Finally, California and the end of a life of hiding. Reunion with Leary whose right connections lead to a dismissal of the charges against me. After twenty-four years underground, I no longer have to "live with my passport under my pillow, my shoes by the bed planning escape routes."[10] Spending time with Tim in the years before his death, I learned to be in love again with the life that we had shared. Being present at his dying was our last adventure together, and we were again able to speak silently heart to heart. For myself and all who witnessed his death, he upleveled dying into performance art.

9. *New York Times,* March 30, 1994. Citation in original. The article was in a "Chronicle" column, titled "One of Timothy Leary's Former Wives Comes in from the Cold." Robert Greenfield, *Timothy Leary: A Biography,* New York: Houghton Mifflin Harcourt, 2006, 661.
10. *New York Times,* March 30, 1994. Citation in original. The article was in a "Chronicle" column, titled "One of Timothy Leary's Former Wives Comes in from the Cold." Robert Greenfield, *Timothy Leary: A Biography,* New York: Houghton Mifflin Harcourt, 2006, 661.

Undated Synopsis (from the 1980s?) (cont.)	Synopsis from 1994
	Chapter Fourteen: Transformation. Beginning of a new life in the '90s when I find some parallel correspondences to my earlier life in the '60s. "I have the joy of being myself again, of not having a dual personality, of not concealing my past from my friends and people I have met along the way."[11]

Although correspondence exists in the archive documenting Rosemary's assertions that all or parts of most of these chapters had been completed and even sent out, almost nothing survives there of chapter 11, and nothing at all of chapters 12 through 14. Confusingly, several later chapter lists mention work completed using earlier chapter titles and order (see, for example, Document 5 on page 291).

The early chapter lists were Rosemary's working documents for composing her plan for the work, but the later ones, and the detailed synopses, were intended to accompany book proposals and attract the interest of agents, editors, and publishers. The more cumbersome synopses were eventually replaced by a shorter, more vividly telegraphic version, in which Rosemary's ironic voice comes through a lot more clearly.

---

11. *New York Times,* March 30, 1994. Citation in original. The article was in a "Chronicle" column, titled "One of Timothy Leary's Former Wives Comes in from the Cold." Robert Greenfield, *Timothy Leary: A Biography,* New York: Houghton Mifflin Harcourt, 2006, 661.

CHAPTER 1: THE MAGICIAN'S DAUGHTER. Daughter of a Midwestern carnival magician. Adolescence in the fifties—gospel music, rhythm & blues. Teen-aged military wife in the Western desert. New York City—model, bit player on live TV, commercials, Israeli airline. Married a jazz musician; left him for a classical composer. Beatnik—peyote, music, McCarthy-era politics, black clothes.

CHAPTER 2: ILLUSIONS. Introduction to mysticism. LSD. I meet Leary, Alpert, and Metzner at a psychedelic art gallery. Visit to Millbrook—I fall in love. Activities at Millbrook—Gurdjieff weekends, expanding consciousness, awareness. While on the way to Yucatan, Leary and I are arrested in Laredo, Texas. This thrusts Leary, his drug research, and our lives into national focus and notoriety.

CHAPTER 3: SCARLET WOMAN. Weekend seminars at Millbrook to pay legal costs. G. Gordon Liddy and posse make midnight raid on Millbrook. Dramatic court proceedings as I am tried and imprisoned for contempt of court.

CHAPTER 4: CELEBRATIONS. Founding of new religion (League for Spiritual Discovery). Masses of seekers and mad people come to Millbrook. Light shows (on national tour), demonstrations, movies. More LSD.

CHAPTER 5: INITIATIONS. Encounters with Alan Watts, Allen Ginsberg, Ken Kesey, Abbie Hoffman, Emmett Grogan, Diane di Prima, Richard Alpert, Swami Satchitananda, Carlos Castaneda, and others. Profiles in Peyote. An LSD overdose leads to a psychotic episode. A Navajo peyote meeting. My marriage ceremonies.

CHAPTER 6: THE LOVERS. The growing popularity of drug use and resistance to the war in Vietnam almost forged a community. The government imprisons thousands for drugs and civil disobedience. Portraits of spiritual anarchists, millennium seekers, free spirits, revolutionaries, and other outlaws. The Brotherhood of Eternal Love.

CHAPTER 7: ENCHANTMENTS. A mountain commune (The Ranch). Teepees, rattlesnakes, babies, more LSD, more raids. Hawaii, Morocco, Montreal. Altamont. The Washington Moratorium. John and Yoko, Laura Huxley, Hugh Hefner, Otto Preminger, William Burroughs, Gloria Steinem, Paul Bowles. Leary becomes the most dangerous man in the world—does this make me dangerous too? Busted again!

> CHAPTER 8: HOLDING TOGETHER. We are sentenced to prison. Free pending appeal, I keep my promise to free Leary (with the help of Weather Underground). Flight from America—intrigue, false documents, extremely radical politics. Paris.

> CHAPTER 9: BEHIND THE VEIL. Algeria. Life in the Black Panther Embassy. The international news and spy community. Notoriety and humiliation. Idylls in the desert. Imprisoned by Cleaver.

> CHAPTER 10: CHANGE. Another escape (to Switzerland). Received by arms dealers, scoundrels, and rich expatriates. Leary arrested again and I free him again! I free myself. Break with Leary.

> CHAPTER 11: ADJUSTMENTS. Refugee travels on a One World passport.[12] Canada, Afghanistan. Sicily. Leary turns me in to the FBI. Flight! Raising cattle in Colombia. Bandits! Central America. Robert Vesco. At sea. On the run.

> CHAPTER 12: THE RESTORER. Secret return to America on a speedboat. Cape Cod—alone in the woods. Danger and reemergence. California. Free at last.

And this is more or less how the memoir turned out, except for the last two chapters.

This seems like a good place to add a handwritten postscript Rosemary added to a letter to her mother on September 17, 1973.

I've solved a problem with the book which I've had since I started, that is how to say certain things or rather, how to comment on the "story" as written without having to make it part of the text and lose flow for

---

12. Actually a World Passport, issued by Garry Davis's World Service Authority and solemnly stamped with visas by tolerant immigration officials. Garry Davis (1921–2013), an American peace and world federation activist, created the World Passport as a way of implementing Article 13(2) of the Universal Declaration of Human Rights, which provides that "everyone has the right to leave any country, including his own, and to return to his country." World Passports have no legal validity but are sometimes used successfully by refugees and stateless people.

honesty. And the problem of quoting T. with the risk of libel or offense was difficult as my memory might not be accurate or kind. Also, from the beginning I thought that many writers had said for all time some of the things I wished to call attention to but lack the skill to do. So, the last chapter will be NOTES, Reflections, chapter XIX, in the tarot deck, the Moon.[13] For example, chapter one. "The photograph called him THE MAGICIAN" and your letter says, "Daddy says he was the assistant" and that would be a note in XIX. As for T., I can quote him at length from his published works or back up any recalled words with his actual statements. Perhaps I can't convey the idea easily to you. It is my hope that it will make the book amusing.

---

13. Actually the Moon is trump number 18.

INITIATIONS, INCANTATIONS, INVESTIGATIONS

by

The Magicians Daughter

Chapter Number	title		
0	Sexually Neutral Diagram		Blue the Vey
I	Initiations	1	"my fathers hands never beat me
II	Behind the Veil	2	("there is a woman etc", He left me with
III	Daughter of the Mother	3	~~Incantations~~ Three Body Problem
IV	~~Vested Interest~~	4	"Daughter of the Mother / The Emperor Has No Clothes ~~Switzerland~~ ("Reich
V	Horoscopes	5	What I Know about Myself
VI	~~LOVES~~	6	Come Together "Lord, I've had 5 husbands," ORGY
VII	Who's Driving?	7	Don't let your Mojo Go much Switzerland "my mother never told me but I should have known
VIII	Scarlet Women	8	The Stigmata, Strength or Lust "whore, yet a very nun etc."
IX	~~Sins~~	9	~~~~ (letters)
X	~~Set Thee TO A NUNNERY~~ Changes	10	Something More Comfortable Blake
XI	~~Lonely~~	11	Accomodation p-p-p
XII	~~Make Up your Mind~~ Dying God	12	Always wanting to be somewhere Other Than... "Going home etc"
XIII	Suicide Pacts	13	Millbrook Hold Together
XIV	Union of Opposites	14	
XV	Absolute Necessity	15	"Retrogress into opposites", Jung ("Crowley
XVI	~~THE JANE WOMEN~~	16	Unified by Love Not Fear ("media militant
XVII	~~Flying Saucers I~~	17	Sessions ~~Sightings~~ ("every man + every woman etc
XVIII	~~Moon Myths~~ Make UP your MIND	18	("Esther Harding
XIX	Be Not Sad	19	
XX	Children of the AEON		what's a Head?
XXI	Uni Verses	21	

Document 3: Tarot-based chapter outline

MAGICIAN'S DAUGHTER

Rosemary Woodruff

0. As Symbol
1. Initiations
2. ~~Behind The Veil~~
3. ~~Daughter of the Mother~~ Susan, Ruth, Carol
4. Vested Interests — Millbrook
5. Horoscopes - Magus, Pope - Celebration Millbrook Crowley
6. Loves weddings
7. Who's Driving? - Switzerland
8. ~~Scarlet Woman~~ Holding Together
9. Lonely Yoni in Lingam Land - Letters
10. Changes - Letters
11. Balancing Act. - Trial
12. Dying Gods - ~~xxxxxxxxxx~~ (?) Poujade's Celebration
13. Suicide Pacts - NY Millbrook
14. Union of Opposites - Birthday Lectures
15. Absolute Necessity
16. Law of the Fortress
17. Star Tripped
18. Make Up Your Mind
19. Be Not Sad
20. ~~Regeneration~~
21. ~~Universes~~

Document 4: Undated twenty-two-chapter working outline
(These chapter headings were almost all later changed.)

MAGICIANS' DAUGHTER
by
R. Wodruff

completed I	INITIATIONS		*your copy*
completed II	BEHIND THE VEIL		last page included
ch 10 III	WHAT HAPPENS WHEN YOU GROW OLD, VENUS?		needs editing
ch 10 IV	CAESAR HAD YOUR TROUBLES		finished, 1st. 7 pgs.
completed V	HIGH PRIEST		included here
ch 10 VI	COME TOGETHER		needs editing
completed VII	SEVEN TIMES SEVEN		included here
ch 10 VIII	HOLDING TOGETHER		half written
completed IX	LONELY YONI IN LINGAM LAND		included here
ch 30 X	CHANGES		half written
completed XI	BALANCING ACT		your copy
ch 30 XII	MAKE UP YOUR MIND		half written
ch 30 XIII	SUICIDE PACTS		3 pgs. included here
ch 30 XIV	TRANSMUTATIONS		notes, needs arr, typ.

Document 5: Undated progress chart
(Indicating completion of portions of lost chapters)

APPENDIX B

Rosemary's Time Line

There are two different three-page time lines in Rosemary's papers, one covering 1967 to 1973 and one covering 1965 to 1974. They are typed in an abbreviated and telegraphic manner and are heavily marked up, including with diagrams and some attempt to show what chapters the events should go in. Document 6 on page 294 is a sample page.

These time lines were very useful for figuring out what happened when, and also for understanding what Rosemary considered important, both in her personal life and in the wider world. I have attempted a transcription of these pages, combining the entries from both time lines into one table, and indicating uncertainties in footnotes. The only entries in the External Events column are those Rosemary herself included.

Date	Events	External Events
Jan. '65	First session	
Feb. '65		
Mar. '65		
Apr. '65	Millbrook session	
May '65		

Date	Events	External Events
June '65	Gallery opening, Allen,[1] Peggy's engagement party, session with Dick and Nena[2]	
July '65	Visit Millbrook, New York sessions, New Jersey suicide session	
Aug. '65	Move to Millbrook	
Sept. '65	Seminar weekends	
Oct. '65	Road workshops	
Nov. '65	Power failure	
Dec. '65	Laredo	
Jan. '66	Defense fund	
Feb. '66	Trial	
Mar. '66		
Apr. '66	Raid	
May '66	Jail	
June '66	Grand jury	
July '66	Summer school	
Aug. '66	League, ashram	
Sept. '66	Celebrations	
Oct. '66		
Nov. '66		
Dec. '66	Hollywood	

1. It says *Allan,* but I am guessing Allen Ginsberg rather than Alan Watts or Alan Atwood or someone else.
2. Peggy Hitchcock, Dick Alpert, Nena von Schlebrügge.

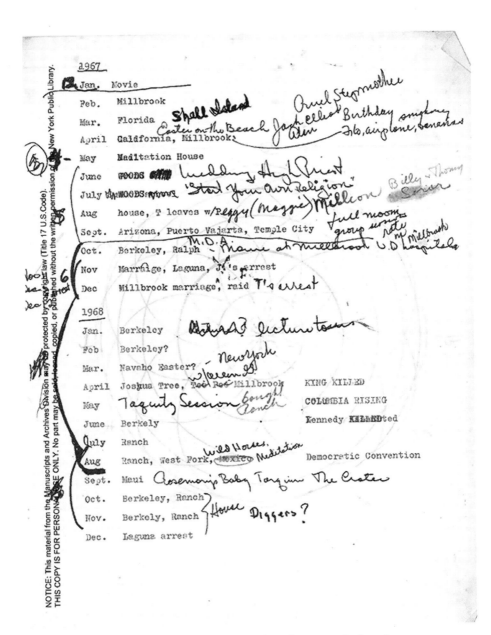

Document 6: A sample page from Rosemary's time lines

DATE	EVENTS		EXTERNAL EVENTS
JAN. '67	Movie.		
Feb. '67	Millbrook.		
Mar. '67	Florida. Shell Island.[3]		
Apr. '67	California. Millbrook. Easter at the Beach. Cruel Stepmother. Jack Elliott. Alan. Birthday.[4] Flo [or Hilo, or something else], airplane, smoking bananas[5]		
May '67	Meditation House		
June '67	Wedding (Bob & Carol), High Priest.		
July '67	Woods. "Start Your Own Religion"[6]		
Aug. '67	House. T leaves with Peggy (Maggie) Million.[7] Tommy, Billy. Soror.[8]		
Sept. '67	Arizona. Puerto Vallarta. Temple City. Berkeley. Full moon. Group [illegible]		
Oct. '67	Berkeley, Ralph. MDA. Maine [or Marie, or something else] at Millbrook. UD hospital.		
Nov. '67	Marriage. Laguna, J's arrest		
Dec. '67	Millbrook marriage, raid, T's arrest		
Jan. '68	Berkeley	lecture tour	
Feb. '68	Berkeley?		

---

3. Shell Island is near Panama City, Florida.
4. Rosemary turned 32 on April 26, 1967.
5. One calendar has *Laguna* in this month. Smoking the scraped lining from banana peels was supposed to provide a legal high. It was legal, anyway.
6. One calendar places "Start Your Own Religion" ambiguously in either April or May. Timothy's booklet of this name (Horowitz A6) was published in 1967.
7. A revealing slip for *Mellon*. Another calendar has *Maggie millionairess*.
8. Tommy and Billy Hitchcock, Peggy's brothers. *Soror* is Latin for "sister," but I may be misreading this word.

Date	Events		External Events
Mar. '68	Navajo Easter?[9] New York with Allen G.[10]		
Apr. '68	Joshua Tree. ~~Teepee~~ Millbrook[11]		King killed
May '68	Tahquitz session. Bought ranch.		Columbia rising[12]
June '68	Berkeley		[Robert] Kennedy killed
July '68	Ranch		Democratic convention
Aug. '68	Ranch, West Fork, wild horses, ~~Mexico~~,[13] meditation		
Sept. '68	Maui. Rosemary's Baby. Tarquin. The Crater.		
Oct. '68	Berkeley, ranch	House.	
Nov. '68	Berkeley, ranch	Diggers?	
Dec. '68	Laguna arrest		
Jan. '69	Berkeley. Free School lectures. Suicide Pact.[14] Union of opposites. Lectures canceled.		
Feb. '69	Buffalo. Drug concert 15		
Mar. '69	Ranch. Tepee.		
Apr. '69	2		
May '69	Supreme Court decision (May 20),[15] Governor.[16]		

9. Easter in 1968 fell on April 7.

10. *With Allen G.* could be on the next line.

11. Strikeout in original.

12. Actually the student uprising at Columbia University took place in April.

13. Strikeout in original.

14. "Suicide Pact" was among the chapter titles Rosemary later discarded. It was clearly a meaningful symbolic phrase for her, but I very much doubt Rosemary ever participated in any *actual* suicide pact.

15. *Leary v. United States,* 395 U.S. 6 (1969). This was the decision overturning the Marihuana Tax conviction. The actual date of decision was May 19.

16. Timothy announced his campaign for governor of California on the same day as the Supreme Court decision.

Date	Events	External Events
June '69	Montreal, John & Yoko; Florida, Seminole Indian Reservation; Bahamas, Abaco Island.[17] Billy.	
July '69	Tepee. Charlie drowns July 17.[18]	Kennedy Chappaquiddick July 18
Aug. '69	John dies.[19] Martha's Vineyard. TV show.	Manson kills Sharon Tate
Sept. '69	Tangier. London.	
Oct. '69	Moratorium October 15 Washington. Movie, operation, pretrial hearing. Holy Man Jan.[20]	Altamont?[21]
Nov. '69	Berkeley. Ranch house burns down. Robbie, Gretchen, Heather. Thanksgiving.	
Dec. '69		
Jan. '70	Trial.	
Feb. '70	Prison (Feb 19/20)	
Mar. '70	Holding Together	
Apr. '70	Om orgy	Courtroom escape[22]
May '70	NY party	Kent State (May 4); Kon Tiki[23]

17. The Abaco Islands are an island group in the Bahamas.

18. Charlie was a young girl—I have been unable to identify her beyond that.

19. John Griggs, founder of the Brotherhood of Eternal Love, died on August 4.

20. Actually Holy Man *Jam,* an event with music and speakers held by the ocean in San Francisco on October 7 to 9, 1969. Timothy is listed first among the performers; Alan Watts and Stephen Gaskin also spoke.

21. The fatal Altamont Free Concert was actually held on December 6.

22. This entry, underscored in the original, probably refers to the fatal attempt by Jonathan Jackson to free prisoners on trial in a Marin County courtroom in San Rafael, California (see chapter 8, note on page 152). This actually happened on August 7, 1970.

23. It is not clear what the entry for *Kon Tiki* refers to. *Kon-Tiki* was the name of a handmade sail-powered raft, sailed by the Norwegian explorer Thor Heyerdahl (1914–2002) from South America to Polynesia in 1947 to show that Polynesia could have been settled from there.

Date	Events	External Events
June '70	Big Sur	
July '70	Big Sur	
Aug. '70		
Sept. '70	Escape (Sept 12)	
Oct. '70	Algeria	Allende elected (Nov 3)[24]
Nov. '70		
Dec. '70		
Jan. '71	Jan 13—Panther bust	Manson guilty
Feb. '71	Hotel	
Mar. '71	Hotel	
Apr. '71	Hotel	
May '71	Geneva (May 3). Ouchy[25]	
June '71	Villars Bust. Prison (June 21)	
July '71		
Aug. '71	August 6 Free	
Sept. '71		
Oct. '71	October 12? Leave	
Nov. '71	Lugano[26]	
Dec. '71	Full moon session.[27] Lugano. Canada	
Jan. '72	Canada	
Feb. '72	Canada	

24. Salvador Allende, left-wing president of Chile later overthrown by the United States.
25. Ouchy is a town near Lausanne in Switzerland.
26. Lugano is a city in the Italian part of Switzerland.
27. The moon was full on December 2 and December 31 in 1971.

Date	Events	External Events
Mar. '72	[Afghanistan][28]	
Apr. '72	Afghanistan	
May '72	Afghanistan message	
June '72	[Afghanistan] Paris. Switzerland[29]	
July '72	Basel. Wintersingen agreements, lawyer[30]	
Aug. '72	Wintersingen, M. passport	
Sept. '72	Venice, Sicily	
Oct. '72	Sicily	
Nov. '72	Wintersingen. Think about America	
Dec. '72	Wintersingen. Letter to *Rolling Stone*[31]	
Jan. '73	Jan. 19. T busted.	
Feb. '73	Wintersingen	
Mar. '73	Easter? Dr. Hip.[32]	
Apr. '73	Gordevio[33]	
May '73		
June '73		

28. One version of the calendar has Afghanistan in April, May, and June, and another has *A.* for March, April, and May. So probably Afghanistan is right for April and May, and right for either March or June but not both. John Schewel remembers the period as March, April, and May.

29. One calendar has Switzerland along with Paris for this month, but not Afghanistan. See note above.

30. Wintersingen is a town near Basel in Switzerland.

31. Rosemary published a note in *Rolling Stone* magazine that said, "Rosemary Leary wills it to be known that for more than a year she has enjoyed a reality separate from Timothy Leary. She is not responsible for his debts karmic or financial. A wife is not property." Quoted in Robert Greenfield, *Timothy Leary: A Biography,* New York: Houghton Mifflin Harcourt, 2006, 434.

32. *Dr. HIPpocrates* was the pen name of the psychiatrist Dr. Eugene Schoenfeld (born 1935), who wrote a health column for alternative newspapers. But Easter in 1973 fell on April 22.

33. Gordevio is a town in the Italian part of Switzerland, near Lugano.

Date	Events	External Events
July '73	Sicily	
Aug. '73	Sicily	
Sept. '73	Sicily	
Oct. '73	Sicily, Riva[34]	
Nov. '73	Riva	
Dec. '73	Sicily	
Jan. '74		
Feb. '74	Siracusa[35]	
Mar. '74		
Apr. '74	Tim's letter[36]	
May '74		
June '74		
July '74	Colombia	
Aug. '74		
Sept. '74		
Oct. '74		
Nov. '74		
Dec. '74		

34. *Riva* is Italian for "shore" or "water's edge." John Schewel advises that the *Riva* meant here is Riva San Vitale, a village in the Swiss canton of Ticino, at the southern end of Lake Lugano very close to the Italian border. It was the home of their friend Franco Beltrametti (1937–1995), a Swiss-Italian writer John calls "the Swiss Allen Ginsberg."
35. In Sicily.
36. This notation standing alone suggests, and John Schewel confirms, that this was the remarkable seven-page letter from Timothy (in Folsom Prison in California) to Rosemary, urging her to cooperate with the FBI. It was sent to her in care of John's parents. Rosemary's strongly negative view of this letter persisted for the rest of her life; a photocopy of it was even included among the drafts in the Blue Binder. I have not included it in the edited memoir as it is not by Rosemary and is really more part of Timothy's story than hers, but large portions are quoted in Robert Greenfield, *Timothy Leary: A Biography,* New York: Houghton Mifflin Harcourt, 2006, 488–90. However, the letter was dated June 1, 1974, two months after Rosemary's time line entry, so the April notation in the time line is likely mistaken.

Rosemary's Caribbean Itinerary

Among Rosemary's papers I found a list of places she went after leaving Colombia. This journey was taken with John Schewel in 1976 and ended with her return to the United States. Although her surviving chapters do not include this journey, I include it for its intrinsic interest.

1. Colombia
   a. Santa Marta by road to Caracas, Venezuela
2. Venezuela
   a. Caracas by private King Air aircraft to Martinique[1]
   b. Costa Rica not ready
   c. Wait for boat to take us from island
3. Martinique
   a. Board *Queen of the Sea* for short trip[2]
4. Hit "Tongue of the Ocean"[3]
   a. Hit storm between Martinique and Guadeloupe islands
   b. Head for St. Barts
5. St. Barts

---

1. King Air is not an airline but a type of aircraft manufactured by Beechcraft.
2. *Queen of the Sea* was a former Coast Guard rescue ship converted into a charter vessel. Its usual use was for scuba trips.
3. Not the well-known Tongue of the Ocean between Andros and New Providence Islands in the Bahamas, but another between Martinique and Saint Barthélemy, an island in the French West Indies (usually called St. Barts).

a. *Queen* leaves, cigarette stays[4]

b. Cigarette leaves St. Barts for St. Thomas

6. Tortola, British Virgin Islands

a. Stay in Tortola a night, go to St. Thomas

7. St. Thomas, U.S. Virgin Islands

a. Meet *Queen* in St. Thomas

b. Leave for Aruba on the *Queen* to meet the plane to Costa Rica

8. Aruba

a. Arrive in Aruba by raft

b. Meet plane for Costa Rica

9. Costa Rica

a. Arrive Lemón

b. Drive to San José (Swiss Chalet)

c. Move to CIA house in valley

d. Leave in plane for Boca del Toro

10. Boca del Toro, Panama

a. Leave Boca by private plane to Panama City

b. Leave Panama City by private plane to Cancún

11. Cancún, Mexico

a. Refuel, take off

b. Land in Nassau, Bahamas[5]

12. Nassau, Bahamas

a. Leave by plane to Bimini

b. Leave by boat for Coconut Grove, Florida, USA

13. Coconut Grove, Florida

a. Leave by car to St. Louis, Missouri

---

4. A cigarette boat is a long, slender speedboat capable of high speeds, often used for smuggling.

5. Here and on the next line Rosemary wrote "Nassau, Grand Bahamas." She is confusing the name of the country (Bahamas) with Grand Bahama Island. Nassau is actually on New Providence Island.

The Rosemary Woodruff Leary Papers

Almost all the material that forms this published memoir either came from, or now rests in, the Rosemary Woodruff Leary Papers in the New York Public Library's Archives and Manuscripts Division. The division is itself one of the most important such storehouses anywhere, and it sits at the heart of one of the greatest research libraries in the world. At last count the division had more than 10,000 separate collections, with almost 1.2 million "described components," themselves composed of boxes containing folders containing actual documents, more than 64,000 linear feet of them, more than twice the height of Mount Everest.[1]

But it is completely free and open to everyone—all you need to work in Rosemary's archive, or in their thousands of other collections, is a New York Public Library card, which you can get (also free) right inside the famous building at Forty-Second Street and Fifth Avenue, the one with the lions in front. Ask for whatever you want—in advance, by email (see their website)—and it will be brought to you by archivists for you to study in a quiet, comfortable, air-conditioned reading room, open six days a week. Select what you want to copy for further study and they will scan it for you at modest cost.

---

1. Statistics from the website of the New York Public Library at archives.nypl.org, accessed June 15, 2020.

Rosemary's archive extends far beyond this memoir and includes, for example, piles of correspondence both to and from her. And her life extends far beyond what has been collected in the archive, although it may be hoped that as time passes more material by and about her will accumulate there. There is more about her in other NYPL collections (notably the Timothy Leary and Michael Horowitz collections), and there is a lot more about her outside library collections, some of which resides within the brains of people still living. As stated in the Editor's Introduction, this is not a biography of Rosemary, and one is needed. I hope someone reading this will undertake the task, and soon, while people who knew her remain to be interviewed.

With the kind permission of the Archives and Manuscripts Division, I reproduce here the descriptive outline of the Rosemary Woodruff Leary Papers at the New York Public Library.

The New York Public Library
Manuscripts and Archives Division

Guide to the
Rosemary Woodruff Leary papers
1935-2006 [bulk 1965-2002]
MssCol 23932

Compiled by Susan M. Kline, 2016.

Summary

Creator: Leary, Rosemary Woodruff

Title: Rosemary Woodruff Leary papers

Date: 1935-2006 [bulk 1965-2002]

Size: 11.15 linear feet (24 boxes, 1 volume); 11.75 mb (48 computer files)

Source: Donated by Kate Woodruff, 2016.

Abstract: Rosemary Woodruff Leary (1935-2002), (also known as "Ro" and Sarah Woodruff), sought to educate people about the psychedelic experience. Woodruff lived for over twenty years as a fugitive for her role in assisting her husband, Dr. Timothy Leary, escape from prison in 1970. This collection documents her relationship with Leary and her twenty years as a fugitive through correspondence, photographs, ephemera, clippings, and drafts of her unpublished memoir, A Magician's Daughter.

Access: Advance notice required.

Conditions Governing Access:
Sound and video materials are unavailable pending digitization.

Preferred citation: Rosemary Woodruff Leary papers, Manuscripts and Archives Division, The New York Public Library.

Processing note: Compiled by Susan M. Kline, 2016.

Creator History
Rosemary Woodruff Leary (1935-2002), (also known as "Ro" and Sarah Woodruff), sought to educate people about the psychedelic experience. Woodruff lived for over twenty years as a fugitive for her role in assisting her husband, Dr. Timothy Leary, escape from prison in 1970.

Woodruff, born in St. Louis in 1935 to a carnival magician, was raised as a Baptist and dropped out of high school. After a brief marriage, she moved to New York City in the 1950s, where she began to experiment with hallucinogenic drugs and married a jazz musician. She held a variety of jobs, working as a model, in television, and as a passenger agent for El Al Airlines.

Woodruff became involved with Timothy Leary after meeting him in 1965 and visiting the Millbrook estate in upstate New York where Leary lived and conducted his experimental research. They married in 1967 and during their marriage they were arrested and charged with several drug offenses. In December 1968 Woodruff was arrested in California; she was released on bail pending appeal but sentenced to six months in the Orange County jail, while Leary was imprisoned and faced significant jail time for a related offense.

The Weather Underground and Woodruff orchestrated Leary's 1970 escape from confinement. The couple fled to Algeria where for a time they lived with Black Panther Eldridge Cleaver at the Black Panther Embassy. The couple soon moved to Switzerland; however, Woodruff and Leary ended their relationship and separated. They ultimately divorced in 1976.

Despite the end of her relationship with Leary, Woodruff remained underground in Sicily, Afghanistan, Canada, and South America. The FBI offered Woodruff amnesty in exchange for the names of others involved with hallucinogenic drugs; however, Woodruff chose not to accept the deal. In 1976, she secretly returned to the United States, settling in Cape Cod before eventually moving back to California. After 24 years underground, living as "Sarah Woodruff," Woodruff turned herself in to California authorities and all charges against her were dropped.

After returning to the United States, Woodruff worked as an innkeeper. She also served as the executrix of Leary's estate. Woodruff died in Aptos, California on February 7, 2002, leaving behind an unpublished memoir, *The Magician's Daughter*.

Scope and Content Note

The majority of the Rosemary Woodruff Leary papers are arranged in a loose chronological order. Files containing correspondence, photographs, writings, clippings, ephemera, notes, and other items from the 1960s and early 1970s document Woodruff's relationship with Timothy Leary, their extralegal affairs, and her life as a fugitive. Woodruff's time with Leary at the Millbrook Estate and in California; Woodruff's time in the Dutchess County Jail (New York); Leary's imprisonment, and Woodruff's life as a fugitive are well represented in these files. Some items are photocopies or reproductions of originals.

Letters exchanged with Leary, Woodruff's family, and John Schewel (who lived with Woodruff abroad), trace her personal relationships and involvement in the counterculture. Other incoming correspondence was written by friends including Judy Givens; associates, such as Ram Dass and Allen Ginsberg; and lawyers Michael Kennedy and Michael E. Tigar.

The collection provides scant insight into Woodruff's life in the United States in the 1980s; however, the 1990s and early 2000s are documented more extensively. These later files primarily contain personal letters and cards. Woodruff steadily corresponded with her good friend and roommate, Eleanor Dalton of Provincetown, Massachusetts, until Woodruff's death in 2002; multi-page letters from Dalton can be found in boxes 3 through 8.

Woodruff worked on her memoir, *The Magician's Daughter*, from the 1970s until the end of her life. The memoir is represented by typed drafts, notes, and other writings. Some files contain letters (originals and typed transcriptions) and other primary source material Woodruff used to chronicle her life story.

Photographs consist of many color and black and white printouts, though there are some original snapshots taken throughout Woodruff's life. Several of the reproductions are of images taken in Afghanistan. A professional portrait of Woodruff in her El Al uniform is available. Both are in box 18.

Memorabilia and items pertaining to other aspects of Woodruff's life include a childhood scrapbook, Woodruff's World Service Authority passport, Dam Rass's United States passport, address books, astrological charts, Leary and Woodruff's marriage license, and a rare copy of the couple's psychedelic adaptation of the *Tao te Ching*, *In Tao We Trust*. Woodruff's calendars from 1973 to 2002 are available. Sometimes she wrote very brief diary-like accounts of her day-to-day activities in these calendars.

Sound and video recordings contain interviews, lectures, and raw footage for the *Ram Dass, Fierce Grace* documentary. Sound and video materials are unavailable pending digitization.

Key Terms

Genre/Physical Characteristic
Clippings (information artifacts)
Correspondence
Notes
Photographs
Printed ephemera
Writings (documents)

Subjects
Drugs -- Religious aspects
Fugitives from justice -- United States -- 20th century
LSD (Drug)
Married people -- Drug use

Geographic Names
Millbrook (N.Y.)

Names
Leary, Timothy, 1920-1996
League for Spiritual Discovery

Container List

b. 1 f. 1-12   **1941, 1960s-1971**
Includes 1941 letter from Leary to his parents outlining why he wants to leave West Point;
Woodruff's letters to her family; photocopies of letters written by Leary to Woodruff while he was
in prison; Leary's time at Millbrook; photocopies of letters from John Lennon and Aldous Huxley;
League for Spiritual Discovery; Holding Together; flyers and materials circulated as part of
Leary's experiments and the 1965-1966 Psychedelic Sessions; Millbrook session notes;
marriage certificate; photographs.

1970s 1998
er.1 (121 Kilobytes (1 computer file))
Transcripts of letters between Leary and Woodruff.

b. 2 f. 1-15   **1970-1989**
Allen Ginsberg letters; letters to Woodruff's family; time in Switzerland and Algeria; John
Schewel; Joanna Harcourt-Smith; divorce. Copies of letters written by Leary to Woodruff.

b. 3 f. 1-6   **1977-2002**

b. 4 f. 1-7   **1991-1997**

b. 5 f. 1-7   **1993-1996**

b. 6 f. 1-6   **1995-1996**

b. 7 f. 1   **1995-1999**
Legal.

b. 7 f. 2-7   **1996-1997**

b. 8 f. 1-8   **1995-2002**
Woodruff's memorial service and death certificate; letters from students who heard Woodruff
speak; ephemera.

b. 20   **Address Books**

b. 9   **Astrology** 1980s

b. 10 f. 1   **Astrology**
Notebook.

b. 10 f. 2   **Birth Certificate, Marriage Certificate**
1955 marriage to Hubert Schwarts. Leary marriage certificate located in box 1. Death certificate
located in box 8.

Calendars
b. 24   **1973, 1977, 1980-1984, 1986-1987, 1989-1991, 1996-2001**
One calendar contains astrological information. Two are *I Ching: Taoist Book of Days* (1977,
1982). Photographs were inserted into the 1977 calendar.

b. 10 f. 3   **2001-2002**

b. 10 f. 4-6   **Clippings** 1963-1990s

b. 10 f. 7-10   **Court Papers** 1970s
Photocopies.

b. 11 f. 1-3   **Court Papers** 1966, 1970s, 1994
Leary's original 1966 indictment papers. 1994 file relates to Woodruff being cleared of charges.

b. 11 f. 4   **Dass, Ram** 1991, 1993

b. 11 f. 5   Frankel Gallery 1996

b. 11 f. 6   "He and She" 1970?
Manuscript.

b. 11 f. 7-8   *In Tao We Trust* 1972

b. 11 f. 9   Interviews by Nina [unidentified] 1970s
Includes interview with Bjorn [unidentified].

b. 11 f. 10-11   Johnson, Joyce 1999-2001

b. 11 f. 12   Kleefeld, Carolyn 1999-2001

b. 11 f. 13   Leary Archives 1995
Letter from Leary's archivist Michael Horowitz to Leary.

b. 11 f. 14-15   Leary's FBI File 1999
Includes legal bill received by Woodruff for FBI file requests.

b. 11 f. 16   Leary's Star Trip
Photocopy and original edited draft.

b. 11 f. 17   Leary's Sutras circa 1960s
Mimeograph copy of 49 sutras based on Book I of the *Tao Te Ching*.

The Magician's Daughter 1970s-2000s
Woodruff's memoir. Files contain drafts, notes, original correspondence (and typed transcripts) and other material from the time period covered in the chapters.

b. 12 f. 1-12   Chapters 1-5, 9

b. 13 f. 1-10   Chapters 5-8
Includes synopsis.

b. 14 f. 1-10   Chapters 9-12
Includes book proposal.

b. 15 f. 1-2   Chapters 1-11 1994

b. 15 f. 3-16   Contracts, Notes, Source Material, Outline, Synopsis, Grant Request
Some transcribed copies of Algiers letters. Photocopies of Leary and Ram Dass letters.

b. 16 f. 1   Film Options and Book Offers 1980-2006

b. 20   Notes on Index Cards
Various Chapters and Synopsis 1994, 1996-1997
er.2 (549.7 Kilobytes (25 computer files))

b. 16 f. 2   Mars, Brigitte circa 1990s
Photos.

b. 16 f. 3   Mars, Rainbeau circa 1996-1997

b. 16 f. 4-6   Millbrook Estate 1990s, undated
Photocopies of 1960s photographs; brochures; accounts of the raid on Millbrook written by Woodruff; photographs taken on a 1990s visit to Millbrook.

b. 16 f. 7   Mind States Conference 2001

b. 16 f. 8   *The Most Dangerous Man* 1998
Correspondence.

b. 16 f. 9-12   **Notes and Notebooks** 1960s-1990s
One notepad contains journal entries by Woodruff on her relationship with Leary (written in the 1960s). Also one dream journal with nine entries (1990-1991). Handwritten draft by Leary "108 Memories of Our Current Incarnation" - written in 1970 while he was in the California State prison at San Luis Obispo.

b. 17 f. 1-4   **Notes and Notebooks** 1960s-1990s
One lists expenses (1960s?); another contains mostly Tarot information.

b. 17 f. 5   **Passports** 1960s-1970s
United States passport belonging to Ram Dass (Richard Alpert) and Woodruff's World Service Authority passport. Both bear visa stamps. Dass's passport is inscribed by Leary. Woodruff's passport, issued in 1972 in Switzerland, documents her travels from October 1975 to November 1976.

b. 17 f. 6   Peyote Story 1980s-1990s

Photographs

b. 19 f. 1-2   1940s-2002

b. 18   **Afghanistan**
Color photocopies.

b. 18   El Al Employee Photo

Scans 2001
er.3 (11.29 Megabytes (2 computer files))
Pre-1960s photo of Woodruff and photo of Woodruff and Leary in the desert.

b. 19 f. 3   *The Politics of PsychoPharmocology by Timothy Leary* 2001
Uncorrected proof.

b. 19 f. 4   Di Prima, Diane 2001

b. 19 f. 5   *Psychedelic Review* 1971

b. 19 f. 6   Resumes 1990s

Resumes 1991-1992, 1996
er.4 (73.92 Kilobytes (20 computer files))

v. 1   Scrapbook 1935-1949
School and religious mementos. Two programs from children's theater productions Woodruff was involved in.

b. 19 f. 7   Scrapbook
Homemade book containing clippings and biographical information about U.S. presidents.

b. 19 f. 8   Timothy Leary Defense Fund

b. 19 f. 9-10   Unidentified Manuscripts circa 1990s
Busted by Shaw [unidentified]; and another by Sherry [unidentified]. Full names of authors are unknown.

b. 19 f. 11-12   Miscellaneous

b. 20   Miscellaneous -- English Arabic Conversational Dictionary
Signed by Woodruff as "Sarah Woodruff."

b. 21   Published Material

7x7 (San Francisco) October 2001; *"AT" Magazine* (Israel) 2000; *High Times* March 1979; *High Times* Supplement Special Timothy Leary Tribute; *Hot Lava Magazine* May 1996; *The LSD Story* by John Cashman; *New Scientist* 2001 June; *People* 1987 February 9; *Psychedelic Island Views* Volume 2, Number 2; *Playboy* September 1966, 1975 September, 1971 July.

b. 22   Published Material

Rolling Stone 1970 October 1, 1996 July 11, 2001 March 1; *LIFE* 1966, March 26, 1972 November 17, 1972 December 8, 1979 December, 1990 July; *Globe* (tabloid) January 19, 1999; *LA Weekly* May 17, 1996; *OC Weekly* 2005 July 8-14; *The American Weekly*, December 16, 1962; *Argonaut* (San Francisco) January 1996.

b. 23   Published Material

LIFE March 25, 1971; Miscellaneous newspapers including the *San Francisco Chronicle*.

Index

David F. Phillips (1944–2020)

CHRISTOPHER PHILLIPS
(written on the evening after his brother's death)

David Phillips, my brother, has left us. He died this morning (March 26, 2020) in San Francisco. He was seventy-five years old.

He had been in the hospital for a confluence of problems (nothing to do with the current Covid-19 virus). After a rough patch last night, the hospital staff made him very comfortable, and it seems to have been a smooth passage. So he is on the Great Adventure, which, with his Buddhist training, is how he thought of it. He always got the most out of his travels—and what journey is more fascinating or important than this one?

It is still hard to believe that he is gone. It's like the landscape of my world has changed or they took a piece of the furniture out of the room or a constellation out of the sky. For me it is about disorientation. How to make sense of it all? Who am I now, and what is where as I go forward? Truly he was my greatest spiritual guide and teacher.

As one of his friends said to me, "David wins, hands down, the *Reader's Digest* prize for 'The World's Most Unforgettable Person.'" If you want to explore, look at his website Radbash.com (the name is explained there). The many tables of contents in the drop-down menus alone are eye-popping. Travelogues galore, essays and poems on everything you can imagine (including the influence of LSD on his view of the world), an autobiography, even a list of imaginary laws he dreamed up. It is like a one-man museum of ideas, knowledge, and wisdom.

When his health really began to falter, he took the attitude, "Better get busy." And he did, knocking off big projects, one after the other. He was especially determined to finish preparing his friend Rosemary Woodruff Leary's memoir for publication. His collections of heraldry books (on which he based his scholarly books and articles, all of which became definitive works on their subjects) and historical atlases are among the finest in America, and he left typically detailed instructions as to their disposal. His personal papers are going to the Yale University Manuscripts and Archives Library.

From earliest days, I think David saw his ideal future as living in a large house filled with books. And that's exactly what he attained in San Francisco, with a view of the Pacific Ocean outside the window.